FOUR
PLAYS
BY CHEKHOV

The Sea Gull
Uncle Vanya
The Three Sisters
The Cherry Orchard

Produced during a long and fruitful association with the Moscow Art Theatre under Stanislavsky, Chekhov's plays mark a high point in the development of the dramatic arts. Unconventional in their use of staging and character, they are symphonies of voices interacting in a complex structure of nuance and emotion that continues to move and intrigue audiences to this day.

ABOUT THE TRANSLATOR:

Alex Szogyi has taught at Yale University, Wesleyan University, and the University of Maine. He is currently an Associate Professor at Hunter College and the City University of New York. Mr. Szogyi has translated many plays from the French, German, and Russian. He is the first person in the United States to translate all of Chekhov's plays into English.

Four Plays by *Chekhov*

Translated
and with a
Preface, Afterwords and Notes

by *ALEX SZOGYI*

WSP
WASHINGTON SQUARE PRESS, INC. • NEW YORK

FOUR PLAYS BY CHEKHOV

A *Washington Square Press* edition

1st printing.......................August, 1968

L

Published by
Washington Square Press, Inc., 630 Fifth Avenue, New York, N.Y.

WASHINGTON SQUARE PRESS editions are distributed in the
U.S. by Simon & Schuster, Inc., 630 Fifth Avenue, New
York, N.Y. 10020 and in Canada by Simon & Schuster
of Canada, Ltd., Richmond Hill, Ontario, Canada.

FOR PHILIP

PREFACE

Anton Chekhov was born January 16, 1860, in Taganrog, a small Russian seaport, and died July 2, 1904, in Badenweiler, a German health resort. In his short life, he gave the world some eight hundred short stories, which have established him as one of the major prose writers of our time, a memoir on the state of prisoners on the island of Sakhalin, which led to significant reforms in Russian prison life, some of the most noble and touching letters ever written, and sixteen plays that have helped to change the course of modern drama.

Half of these plays are delightful and uproarious one-act farces; the seven full-length plays are exceedingly intricate works of art and difficult to label as belonging to any one genre. Chekhov insisted they were comedies. The last four, which appear in this volume, have found their way into the repertories of the major theaters of the world. Each of them is an original masterpiece. Although they are recognized to be among the most difficult plays ever conceived, they are extremely popular with audiences and theater people alike. They are very difficult to perform because they require ensemble acting of the subtlest and finest kind; unless the forces in the play are carefully equilibrated, any one element may take precedence and upset the delicate balance of the work.

The Moscow Art Theater survives and attempts to perform Chekhov in the manner of its founders, Stanislavski and Nemirovich-Danchenko. Athough the Art Theater's sense of detail is impeccable and its representation of "life as it is" (a favorite term Chekhov used) most meticulously worked out, it has favored a triumphant Chekhov who believed fervently in the intellectual and spiritual progress of mankind. We know that Chekhov disapproved of Stanislavski's contention that his plays were stark tragedies—the first productions of Chekhov neglected many of the inherent ironies within the plays. Only this season, a more modern, ironic and mordant construction of *The Three Sisters* has set off the sharpest theatrical controversy Moscow has known for years. The play is now being interpreted as a rather skeptical commentary on the decadence of its time, as a clairvoyant prelude to the mentality that led directly to the Russian Revolution. In Russia, once again, Chekhov's work is at the exciting forefront of intellectual debate. Although there are those who would insist that all classical works in Russia be presented in a spirit of socialist realism, with emphasis on their "progressive aspects," there are now many who are able to see Chekhov as one of the salient forces of ironic modernism, on a par with Brecht and Pirandello.

As for Chekhov outside of Russia, he is perhaps best performed in France. The Pitoëff family in the thirties, the Barraults, Jean-Louis and Madeleine Renaud, have reproduced Chekhov's poetic realism and lyricism with unusual sensitivity. The British tend to opt for bravura performances, which quite often are brilliant but more than usually lack all understanding of Chekhovian humor and tone. Generally, we in America either exaggerate the farcical aspects of his plays or fall into a heavy-handed sentimental nostalgia. In the late forties and early fifties, productions by David Ross at the 4th Street Theater, a tiny house with its audience divided on either side of the stage, caught a period flavor beautifully. Tyrone Guthrie, Eva Le Gallienne, Ellis Rabb, William Ball and Amnon Kabatchnik have all occasionally revealed the rich ironies inherent in Chekhov's texts.

Chekhov's own career was a bizarre mixture of utter failures and belated triumphs, misconstrued successes and comic struggles. His remarkable lucidity never allowed him to believe that he had triumphed in the fickle theatrical milieu. The man who explained that he wrote with an icy heart often proclaimed that medicine was his legitimate wife and literature his mistress. In a letter to A. A. Pleshcheyev (January 15, 1889), he went so far as to say that the narrative prose form was a legitimate wife and the dramatic form "a harsh, noisy, impudent and wearisome mistress!"

His first full-length play, *Platonov*, written in his second year of medical school, was never performed during his lifetime. He had presented it to Yermolova, an actress of the time, and she rejected it. *Ivanov* was first produced in Moscow, November, 1887, as a benefit performance in honor of the actor N. V. Svetlov. (Most of Chekhov's one-act plays were also written for specific comic actors of the time.) *Ivanov* was both booed and praised. The play went through many a revision for the next two years before it was presented at the Alexandrinski Theater in St. Petersburg in January, 1889. There it met with a tumultuous success. But Chekhov, after so much work, claimed to be bored with the play.

His next work, *The Wood Demon,* was given at a private theater in Moscow, December, 1889. It was an utter failure and although, after the advent of its avatar, *Uncle Vanya* (October, 1899), some did prefer the earlier version, the playwright never wished it to be published or performed again. Easily discouraged, Chekhov discarded his mutilated children. There is recent evidence to the fact that Chekhov transformed *The Wood Demon* into *Uncle Vanya* some time in early 1890. This would change the chronology of the four major plays most interestingly. Indeed, *Uncle Vanya* is a simpler, sparer work than the other three and this is perhaps not only because it is an adaptation but because it came at an earlier moment in his theatrical career, when he had not yet mastered the subtle theatrical orchestration of his last three works.

The Sea Gull marks the beginning of Chekhov's world prominence as a playwright of major importance. Yet, its premiere, at the Alexandrinski Theater, was a resounding failure. It was not until Stanislavski and Nemirovich-Danchenko founded the Moscow Art Theater that Chekhov's work found a definitive theatrical home, though Chekhov quarreled strongly with Stanislavski's inability to see the play as anything but tragedy. The circumstances of its performance, on October 17, 1898, have become modern theatrical legend. Chekhov at this time met Olga Knipper, who later became his wife and lifelong interpreter.

Two more equivocal successes were vouchsafed Anton Chekhov during his short theatrical career. On January 31, 1901, the Moscow Art Theater performed *The Three Sisters.* Again Olga Knipper played the central role, that of Masha. The play took a long time to catch on with audiences. Chekhov was unable to be present at the first performance. Already gravely ill with the family illness of tuberculosis, which was finally to claim his life, he was forced to go abroad and to resorts such as Yalta to look after his failing health.

On January 17, 1904, Chekhov's last play, *The Cherry Orchard*, received its first performance. A tumultuous celebration marked the playwright's twenty-fifth anniversary as a writer, but Chekhov did not appear until the third act. Ill health and embarrassment at the honor kept him away. His friends had to force him to come. As soon as he got on stage, he was seized with uncontrollable fits of coughing. Despite his own great success and the occasion, the audience did not appreciate the play, and indeed acclaim was deferred for a long while. Chekhov died six months later. It is said that he planned one other play, about a man journeying by boat toward the North Pole, haunted by memories of a lost love.

Chekhov was often disillusioned by the theater, acutely aware of the flaws of production and interpretation, deprived by it even of the companionship of his wife. But the theater, which played such cruel jokes on him during his lifetime, has since consecrated his glory. While some critics contend that his great strength is manifested in his prose short stories, others feel that his last four plays will constitute his immortality. Today we see that he is one of the major influences on world theater. Chekhov's theatrical career flourishes and will probably continue to do so as long as plays are performed.

A.S.

CONTENTS

The Sea Gull

A Drama in Four Acts

CHARACTERS

ARKADINA, IRINA NIKOLAEVNA,
   Mrs. Treplev, an actress

TREPLEV, KONSTANTIN GAVRILOVICH,
   her son, a young man

SORIN, PYOTR NIKOLAEVICH,
   her brother

ZARECHNAYA, NINA MIKHAILOVNA,
   a young girl, daughter of a rich landowner

SHAMRAYEV, ILYA AFANASYEVICH,
   a retired lieutenant, manager of Sorin's estate

ANDREYEVNA, PAULINA,
   his wife

MASHA,
   his daughter

TRIGORIN, BORIS ALEXEYEVICH,
   a writer

DORN, YEVGENY SERGEYEVICH,
   a doctor

MEDVEDENKO, SEMYON SEMYONOVICH,
   a schoolteacher

YAKOV,
   a workman
   A chef
   A housemaid

*The action takes place on Sorin's estate.
Between the third and fourth acts, there is an
interval of two years.*

ACT
ONE

The scene is a section of the park on Sorin's property. The view of the lake that dominates the scene is partially blocked by a platform erected specially for amateur theatricals. On either side of the platform there are bushes and a suggestion of greenery. A few chairs and a little table. The sun has just set. There is a hint of fall in the air. It is twilight. On the stage, behind the curtain, we hear coughing sounds and hammer blows. It is YAKOV *and the other workmen.*

MASHA and MEDVEDENKO *enter on the left, returning from a walk.*

MEDVEDENKO: Why do you always wear black?

MASHA: Because I'm in mourning. For my life. I'm miserable.

MEDVEDENKO: But why? *(He meditates.)* I can't understand you. You're healthy; your father's not rich, but he's well off. My life is much harder than yours. I get paid only twenty-three rubles a month, not a ruble more, and there are pension deductions from that, too, but I don't wear black because of that. . . .

(They sit down.)

MASHA: It has nothing to do with money. Even poor people can be happy.

MEDVEDENKO: Perhaps in theory but not in practice. Look at me, for instance. I have to support a mother, two sisters

3

and a little brother—all on my twenty-three rubles. You know we have to eat. We need tea and sugar . . . and tobacco. . . . You can't get away from that.

MASHA (*looking at the stage behind her*): The play will begin soon.

MEDVEDENKO: Yes. Nina will be acting in Konstantine's own play. They're in love and today their souls are joined together in a mutual desire to create . . . artistically. That's not true of us. My soul and your soul . . . they never meet. I love you; I can't stay away from you; every day I walk four miles[1] here and four miles back and you're always indifferent to me. I understand. I have nothing and with all those mouths to feed . . . why marry a man who hasn't even enough to eat?

MASHA: That has nothing to do with it. (*She takes some snuff.*) I'm touched by your love, but I can't reciprocate, that's all there is to it. (*Offers him the snuffbox.*) Help yourself.

MEDVEDENKO: I'd rather not.

(*Pause.*)

MASHA: It's stifling! Tonight there'll be a storm. Oh, Semyon, all you do is philosophize or talk about money. In your mind, there's nothing worse than poverty. To my mind, it's a thousand times easier to be poor and go hungry than to . . . though you wouldn't understand that, would you?

(SORIN *and* KONSTANTINE *enter from the right.*)

SORIN (*leaning on his walking stick*): I'll never get used to the country, my boy. It's obviously not my style. Last night I went to bed at ten and I woke up this morning at nine after a long sleep feeling as if I'd been hit over the head with a sledgehammer, you know what I mean? (*He laughs.*) After lunch I dozed off again and now I'm a complete wreck, as if I'd had a terrible nightmare, you know.

KONSTANTINE: You're absolutely right, Uncle, you really ought to live in the city. (*Seeing* MASHA *and* MEDVEDENKO) You mustn't be here now; we'll call you when everything's ready. Please go, not yet.

SORIN: Masha, will you please ask your father to let the dog off the chain. My sister couldn't sleep a wink last night again.

MASHA: Tell him yourself. I'm not going to. Please don't ask me to. *(To* MEDVEDENKO*)* Let's go.

MEDVEDENKO: You'll let us know in plenty of time, won't you?

(MASHA and MEDVEDENKO go out.)

SORIN: Well, then, the dog will be howling all night again. That's the way it is; in the country I never get my own way. I used to be able to get away for a few weeks and come here for a rest, you know what I mean; but they plagued me with one detail after another so that I couldn't bear another minute of it; I just wanted to flee. *(He laughs.)* I really couldn't wait to get away, you know what I mean. Now that I'm retired, I've got no place else. After all, like it or not, here I must stay.

YAKOV: We're going for a swim, sir.

KONSTANTINE: Go ahead, but be back in ten minutes. *(He looks at his watch.)* We'll start soon.

YAKOV: Very well, sir. *(He goes.)*

KONSTANTINE *(taking the platform in at a glance)*: Now, there's a stage. There's a curtain, wings, some more wings . . . and behind that, space. No scenery at all. The backdrop is the lake and the horizon. We go up at eighty-thirty on the dot, when the moon rises.

SORIN: Splendid.

KONSTANTINE: If Nina is late, then of course everything will be ruined. It's time she was here. But her mother and stepfather never let her out of their sight; it's as hard for her to get out as to escape from prison. *(Straightening his uncle's tie)* Uncle Sorin, look at your hair and beard—all messed up. You need a haircut or something. . . .

SORIN *(combing his hair)*: It's the tragedy of my life. I've looked like a drunkard ever since I was two, you know. Women have never found me attractive. *(Sits down.)* Why is my sister in such a bad mood?

KONSTANTINE: Why? She's bored. *(Sits down beside him.)* She's jealous. She's already dead set against me, the performance and my play because it's not she who's going to act in it, but Nina. She hasn't even read my play but already she hates it.

SORIN *(laughing)*: You're imagining things, really. . . .

KONSTANTINE: Yes, she's annoyed because even on this little stage Nina will have a success and she won't. (*Looks at his watch.*) My mother is a psychological freak. She's without any doubt talented, intelligent, capable of sobbing over a novel; she can reel off all of Nekrasov's[2] poetry by heart; she nurses the sick like an angel; but just try praising Duse[3] to her—ho ho. You dare praise nobody else but her, write about her, rave about her, go into ecstasies over her marvelous performance in *La Dame aux Camélias*[4] or *The Fumes of Life.*[5] But she has no such consolation in the country, so she's bored and bad tempered; we're all her enemies, all guilty; not only that, she's also superstitious, afraid of three candles or the number thirteen. She's stingy. She's got seventy thousand in the bank at Odessa—I know that for a fact. Just ask her for a loan, and she'll burst into tears.

SORIN: It's all your imagination that your mother doesn't like your play and you're upset, you know. Don't worry; your mother adores you.

KONSTANTINE (*tearing petals off a flower*): She loves me, she loves me not, she loves me, she loves me not, she loves me, she loves me not. (*Laughing*) You see, my mother doesn't love me, of course not. What she wants is to live, love and wear suggestive dresses; and I'm already twenty-five years old and a perpetual reminder that she's no longer young. When I'm not here, she's only thirty-two years old, and when I am, she's forty-three . . . and for that she hates me. She knows, too, that I don't care for the theater. But she loves it; she thinks she's benefiting mankind, out of love for her sacred art, but in my opinion, her precious modern theater is conventional and routine. When the curtain goes up on an artificially lit room with three walls, these great geniuses, these priests of that sacred art, portray for us people eating, drinking, making love, moving about and wearing their clothes; and when they try to find significance in these banalities, comfortable little morals, healthy, wholesome homilies, when a thousand times over I am treated to the same thing over and over again, over and over again, ad nauseam, then I run and run as far away as possible, as Maupassant[6] did from the Eiffel Tower and all its crushing vulgarity.

SORIN: But what would we do without the theater?

KONSTANTINE: We need new means of expression, new forms, and if we can't have them, it's better not to have anything. (*Looks at his watch.*) I love my mother, I love her very much, but she leads a stupid life, always fussing over that novelist, her name forever bandied about in the newspapers. . . . It makes me tired. Sometimes a voice inside me—call it the egotism of an ordinary mortal—tells me I'm sorry my mother is a famous actress, and it seems to me then that if she were just an ordinary woman, then I'd be much happier. Uncle, what could be more ridiculous and idiotic than my situation? Especially among my mother's guests, all celebrities, artists and writers—and among them all I was the only . . . nobody. They put up with me only because I was her son. Who am I? What am I? I left the university after three years because of extenuating circumstances, as they say; I haven't any talent, I'm flat broke; my passport will tell you that I'm a bourgeois from Kiev,[7] just an ordinary citizen. My father was just an ordinary citizen; though he was a famous actor, he was still just a bourgeois from Kiev. So that when her artistic friends happened to notice me in her salon, it seemed to me they noticed how insignificant I was—I guessed what they were thinking. It was humiliating.

SORIN: By the way, what sort of man is this writer? There's no making him out; he never says anything.

KONSTANTINE: He's an intelligent man, good natured, and—how shall I put it?—he's moody. He's really a very decent person. He's not quite forty but he's already famous and he's had everything in life. As for his writings, what can I say? They're charming, they don't lack talent . . . but, after Tolstoï[8] or Zola,[9] you wouldn't want to read Trigorin.

SORIN: And I'm very fond of writers myself, you know. There was a time when there were two things I wanted passionately: to get married and to be a writer. But I never succeeded in either one or the other. Yes, it must be pleasant even just to be a minor writer, you know what I mean?

KONSTANTINE (*listening intently*): I hear footsteps. I can't live without her. Even the sound of her footsteps is lovely. I'm so happy. (*Going quickly to Nina as she enters*) My angel, my dream.

NINA (*running in, full of emotion*): I'm not late . . . I hope I'm not late.

KONSTANTINE (*kissing her hands*): No, no, no.

NINA: All day I was so nervous, I felt so awful. I was afraid father wouldn't let me come. He just went out with my stepmother. The sky is red, the moon is rising and I spurred my horse on as fast as I could. (*She laughs.*) I'm so very glad . . . (*Warmly shakes* SORIN'S *hand.*)

SORIN: Tsk, tsk, tsk! One would think these little eyes had been crying. I don't like that.

NINA: Yes. You see, I'm so out of breath. I must leave in a half hour. Let's hurry. I really must go soon. I really must. I can't stay. I just can't. Don't ask me to. My father doesn't know I'm here.

KONSTANTINE: It's time to begin anyway. I must go get everybody.

SORIN: I'll go get them. In a minute. (*Goes off to the right, singing.*) "To France, two grenadiers . . ." [10] Once I was singing just like that and the Attorney General said, "You have a powerful voice, my good man." Then he thought a moment and added, "Powerful but unpleasant." (*Exits laughing.*)

NINA: My father and his wife won't let me come here; they say you're too bohemian. They're afraid I might become an actress. I'm drawn to this lake like a sea gull . . . my heart is full of you. (*She looks around.*)

KONSTANTINE: We're alone.

NINA: I think there's somebody over there.

KONSTANTINE: Nobody's there.

(*They kiss.*)

NINA: What kind of tree is that?

KONSTANTINE: It's an elm.

NINA: Why is it so dark?

KONSTANTINE: It's already evening and everything's getting dark. Please don't leave early.

NINA: I must.

KONSTANTINE: What if I follow you home, Nina? I'll stay in the garden all night and look up at your window.

NINA: You mustn't. The caretaker might see you. The dog doesn't know you yet. He'd bark.

KONSTANTINE: I love you.

NINA: Shhh.

KONSTANTINE *(hearing footsteps)*: Who's there? Is it Yakov?

YAKOV *(behind the stage)*: Yes, sir.

KONSTANTINE: Places. It's time to begin. The moon is rising, isn't it?

YAKOV: Yes, sir.

KONSTANTINE: Is the alcohol ready? And the sulfur? When the red eyes appear, we must smell the sulfur.[11] *(To Nina)* Go now, everything's ready for you. Are you nervous?

NINA: Yes, very. I'm not at all afraid of your mother but your . . . Trigorin—to play before him makes me so frightened and ashamed. A famous writer. . . . Is he young?

KONSTANTINE: Yes.

NINA: He writes such wonderful stories.

KONSTANTINE *(coldly)*: I don't know. I haven't read them.

NINA: It's hard to act in your play. There are no living characters in it.

KONSTANTINE: Living characters! One must express life not as it is, and not as it ought to be, but as it happens in dreams.

NINA: In your plays there's hardly any action, only one long speech. I think love ought to be an indispensable part of a play.

(Both disappear behind the platform. Enter PAULINA and DORN.)

PAULINA: It's getting damp out. Go back and put on your galoshes.

DORN: I'm hot.

PAULINA: You don't take care of yourself. Stubborn. You're a doctor and you know perfectly well that damp air is bad for you but all you want is to make me suffer. You sat out on the terrace all last evening on purpose.

DORN *(hums)*: "Don't ever say I wasted my youth . . ."[12]

PAULINA: You were so absorbed in your conversation with Irina, you didn't even notice the cold. Admit it, you're attracted to her.

DORN: I'm fifty-five years old.

PAULINA: Fifty-five isn't old for men. You've very well preserved. And women are still attracted to you.

DORN: Well, what do you want from me?

PAULINA: Before an actress you're all prepared to go down on your knees . . . all of you!

DORN (*hums*): "Again I stand before you . . ." [13] If artists are loved by the public and treated differently from, say, businessmen, that's only natural. That's what we call the yearning for an ideal.

PAULINA: Women have always fallen in love with you and hung on your neck. Is that also yearning for an ideal?

DORN (*shrugs his shoulders*): Why not? There's a very good reason for the attitude that women have always had toward me. They loved me most of all because I was a first-rate doctor. Ten or fifteen years ago, you remember, I was the only good obstetrician around. Then, too, I've always been an honorable man.

PAULINA (*clasping his hand*): My . . . darling!

DORN: Watch it. They're coming.

(*Enter* MME ARKADINA, *on* SORIN'S *arm*, TRIGORIN, SHAMRAYEV, MEDVEDENKO *and* MASHA.)

SHAMRAYEV: She played in 1873, in Poltava, [14] at the fair; she was marvelous! Admirable! Marvelous! And would you know, my dear, what happened to the actor Chadine, Paul Semyonovich Chadine? He was incomparable in the role of Rasplyuyev, [15] better than Sadovsky [16] was, I swear it, my dear lady. Whatever became of him? Where is he now?

ARKADINA: You always ask me about things that happened before the flood. How should I know? (*She is seated.*)

SHAMRAYEV: Pasha Chadine! There's none like him now. The theater is not what it was, Irina. In those days there was greatness; now we have nothing but mediocrity.

DORN: There are few great talents these days, that's true, but the average actor is far more accomplished.

SHAMRAYEV: I can't agree with you there. However, that's a matter of taste. De gustibus, you know. *De gustibus*, [17] whether you like it or not.

(KONSTANTINE *comes out from behind the stage.*)

ARKADINA (*to her son*): My dear son, isn't it time to begin?

KONSTANTINE: In a moment.

ARKADINA (*reciting from* Hamlet [18]): Thou turn'st mine eyes into my very soul,/And there I see such black and grained spots/As will not leave their tinct."

KONSTANTINE (*reciting from* Hamlet): "Nay, but to live/In the rank sweat of an enseamed bed,/Stewed in corruption, honeying and making love/Over the nasty sty!" Ladies and gentlemen, we're ready! Your attention, please! (*Behind the stage a horn sounds. Pause. Three traditional taps with a stick and he recites in a loud voice.*) O you who hover nightly mysteriously over this lake, noble old shadows, hypnotize us, take us in our dreams two hundred thousand years hence into future time.

SORIN: In two hundred thousand years there won't be any future.

KONSTANTINE: Then let it be that future that we see.

ARKADINA: Well, let it happen. We're already asleep.

(*The curtain rises; a sudden view of the lake. The moon is on the horizon, reflected on the water.* NINA, *all in white, is seated on a huge rock.*)

NINA: Mankind and the animals, lions, eagles and partridges,[19] horned deer, geese, spiders, silent fish inhabiting the sea, starfish and those creatures invisible to the naked eye—in short, in a word, all living things, all living things, all living things, having run their sad course, are extinct. Eons have passed since a living soul has stirred on the earth's surface. And this poor moon shines its light in vain. In the meadows the cranes no longer waken with a cry and the May beetles' murmur is silent in the limes. It is cold, cold, cold! Empty, empty, empty! Terrible, terrible, terrible! (*Pause*) The bodies of the living creatures have crumbled to dust and as eternal matter metamorphosed into rocks, into water, into clouds, their souls arc now as one. That peaceful universal soul is me. I . . . I am the soul of Alexander the Great, Caesar, Shakespeare, Napoleon, and of the lowest of the low. In me the consciousness of man and the animal instinct mingle, and I remember everything, everything, everything, and every life I live anew in me.

(*The will-o'-the-wisps*[20] *appear.*)

ARKADINA (*in a stage whisper*): This is rather decadent.[21]

KONSTANTINE (*pleading and reproaching*): Mother!

NINA: I am all alone. Once in a hundred years I open my lips to speak, and my voice intones dolefully in the void, but no one listens. And you, pale will-o'-the-wisps, you hear me not. . . . Before daybreak the moldy marsh produces you, and you wisp about until dawn, but without thought, without will, without the throb of life. For fear that life may flare up in you, the father of eternal matter, the devil, keeps the rocks, the rivers and your momentary atomic composition in continual flux, and you are ceaselessly changing. In the entire universe, there is but one immovable, immutable soul. (*Pause*) Like a prisoner cast into a bottomless, fathomless well, I know not where I am nor what awaits me. One thing only has been held secret from me, that in the cruel, stubborn struggle with the devil, the source of material force, I triumph; and when all has befallen, matter and spirit will merge, purged in perfect harmony, and the kingdom of the Cosmic Will will come. But that will come only little by little, after long, long thousands of years when the moon and the shining bright Sirius and the earth have crumbled to dust. And until then, horror, horror. . . . (*Pause. Two red spots²² appear upon the backdrop of the lake.*) Behold my redoubtable adversary, the devil. I see his dreaded, blood-red eyes.

ARKADINA: Oh, I smell sulfur; is that supposed to happen?

KONSTANTINE: Yes.

ARKADINA (*laughing*): Oh, it's a stage effect.

KONSTANTINE: Mother!

NINA: But without mankind he is bored. . . .

PAULINA (*to* DORN): You've taken your hat off. Put it on, you'll catch cold.

ARKADINA: The doctor has taken his off to the devil, the father of eternal matter.

KONSTANTINE (*flaring up, in a loud voice*): The play is over. Stop it! Curtain!

ARKADINA: Why are you so angry?

KONSTANTINE: That's enough. Curtain! Pull the curtain! (*Stamping his foot*) Curtain!

(*The curtain falls.*)

I'm sorry. I don't know why, but I had forgotten that only

a chosen few may write plays and act in them. I was trespassing on sacred ground ... my ... I ... *(He wants to say something more, but makes a hopeless gesture and then goes out on the left.)*

ARKADINA: What's the matter with him?

SORIN: Irina, my dear, you've wounded a young man's pride.

ARKADINA: What did I say?

SORIN: You've hurt his feelings.

ARKADINA: But he gave us advance notice that it was a joke; that's the way I took it, of course—as a joke.

SORIN: All the same ...

ARKADINA: And now it appears he's produced a masterpiece. Imagine that! Nothing less! Apparently he organized this spectacle and clouded us with sulfur not as a joke but as a demonstration of how plays should be written and how they're to be acted. It's quite tedious. These continual attacks at my expense, these digs would infuriate anybody, say what you will. He's a capricious, touchy child.

SORIN: He wanted to give you pleasure.

ARKADINA: Really? I notice he didn't choose some pleasant subject but he crammed this decadent raving down our throats. I don't mind listening as long as I'm not asked to take it seriously, but that's not at all what he did. Here we see pretensions to new artistic forms, new eras in art. But if you want my opinion, it's not Konstantine's new forms we've seen, not at all, it's just his nasty temper.

TRIGORIN: A man must write about what he likes and in his own style.

ARKADINA: Well, let him write what he likes and in his own style, but he can damned well leave me out of it.

DORN: My Lord,[23] you're angry.

ARKADINA: I'm not your Lord, I'm a woman *(lights a cigarette)*, and I'm not angry. It's a pity that a young man should waste his time in such a boring way. I didn't mean to hurt his feelings.

MEDVEDENKO: There's no reason to separate spirit from matter, since it is quite possible that spirit itself is a copulation of atomic matter.[24] *(With excitement, to TRIGORIN)* I wish someone would write a play about how we poor schoolteachers live. Why couldn't they play it? It's a very hard life. Very hard.

ARKADINA: How true! But we won't talk about plays any

more, or about atoms. It's such a splendid evening! Listen
. . . music . . . *(She listens.)* How charming!

PAULINA: It's coming from the other side of the lake.

(Pause.)

ARKADINA *(to* TRIGORIN*)*: Sit here by me. You know, ten or
fifteen years ago we could hear music coming from across
the lake almost every night. Then there were six country
estates on the shore of the lake. I remember the sound of
laughter, noise, gunfire and romance . . . lovemaking. And
the *jeune premier*[25] and the idol of all those six households
was at that time . . . may I present . . . *(Nods toward* DORN.*)*
Dr. Eugene Dorn. He's fascinating still, but in those days
he was irresistible. . . . My conscience is beginning to bother
me. My poor little boy. I hurt his feelings! I'm upset about
it. *(Calls.)* Konstantine! Son! Konstantine!

MASHA: I'll go look for him.

ARKADINA: Would you, darling?

MASHA *(calling)*: Yoo-hoo, Konstantine. Yoo-hoo. *(She goes
out.)*

NINA *(coming out from behind the stage)*: If the play's not
going on, I might as well come out. Good evening! *(Embraces* ARKADINA *and* PAULINA.*)*

SORIN: Bravo! Bravo!

ARKADINA: Brava! Brava! We loved you. With such a pretty
face and such a charming voice, it's sinful to bury yourself
in the country. You're very talented, really you are. Do you
realize that? You really must go on the stage.

NINA: Oh, that's my dream! *(Sighing)* But it will never be.

ARKADINA: How do you know? Let me introduce Boris
Trigorin.

NINA *(embarrassed)*: Oh, I'm so happy. I've read everything
you've . . .

ARKADINA *(sitting her down next to her)*: Don't be shy, darling.
He's famous, but he's a simple soul. You see, he's quite
disconcerted himself.

DORN: I suppose now we can have the curtain raised. This
way it looks sinister.

SHAMRAYEV: Yakov, raise the curtain.

(The curtain is raised.)

NINA *(to* TRIGORIN): It's a strange play, isn't it?

TRIGORIN: I didn't understand it at all but I enjoyed it. You acted with great sincerity and the scenery was charming. *(Pause)* There must be a lot of fish in that lake.

NINA: Yes.

TRIGORIN: I love fishing. There's nothing so enjoyable as sitting on the bank of a river toward evening watching the cork bobbing up and down in the water.

NINA: I should think the joy of creation would be greater than any other pleasure.

ARKADINA *(laughing)*: Don't say such things. When people say nice things to him, he simply crumples up.

SHAMRAYEV: I remember one evening in Moscow at the opera, the celebrated Silva was singing; how delighted we were when he sang low C. Well, the bass from our church choir happened to be sitting in the gallery. All at once we heard, "Bravo, Silva," a whole octave lower . . . like this: "Bravo, Silva." The audience was spellbound.

(Pause.)

DORN: The angel of silence.[26]

NINA: I must go. Good night.

ARKADINA: Where to? Why so early? We won't let you go.

NINA: My father's waiting for me.

ARKADINA: How silly, really. *(Kisses her.)* Well, what can we do? We're sorry to see you go.

NINA: If you only knew how hard it is for me to go!

ARKADINA: Someone should take you home, my dear.

NINA *(frightened)*: Oh, no, no!

SORIN *(imploring her)*: You must stay!

NINA: I really can't, Mr. Sorin.

SORIN: Stay for just an hour more, you know. Come now, really . . .

NINA *(hesitating, tears in her eyes)*: I can't! *(She shakes hands and hurries out.)*

ARKADINA: She's an unfortunate girl, really. They say the mother willed the husband every penny and now the girl has nothing, because her father's already left everything to the second wife. It's scandalous!

DORN: Yes, her father's something of a bastard. You've got to give him that much credit.

SORIN (*rubbing his cold hands*): It's getting damp. My legs ache. Let's go in.

ARKADINA: Poor darling, he's got tree stumps for legs. You can hardly walk on them. My poor lamb . . . (*Takes his arm.*)

SHAMRAYEV (*offers his arm to his wife*): Madame . . .

SORIN: That damn dog is howling again. (*To* SHAMRAYEV) Please, Ilya, tell them to let him off the chain.

SHAMRAYEV: If we do that, Mr. Sorin, what about thieves? All our millet is stored there. (*To* MEDVEDENKO) Yes, a whole octave lower. "Bravo, Silva." And he wasn't a professional singer . . . just a member of the choir.

MEDVEDENKO: How much do they pay choir members?

(*They all go out except* DORN.)

DORN (*alone*): I don't know . . . I may be crazy but it's not a bad play. It's rather exciting. There's something to it. When that girl talked about solitude and afterward when the devil's eyes appeared, my hands were trembling. It has spirit, it's original. (*Enter* KONSTANTINE.) There he is. I must congratulate him.

KONSTANTINE: Everybody's gone.

DORN: I'm here.

KONSTANTINE: Masha's been chasing me all over the park. She's insufferable.

DORN: Konstantine, I liked your play very much. It's unusual and I don't, of course, know the ending, but it made a strong impression on me! You're talented. Don't give up. (KONSTANTINE *squeezes his hand and embraces him impulsively.*) What's wrong? How nervous you are. Tears in your eyes . . . What did I want to say? What you wrote was abstract. It's a play of ideas. And that's only right. A work of art should express a serious thought. You can't produce good things without serious thoughts behind them. You're so pale!

KONSTANTINE: So that's what you mean—I should keep on trying?

DORN: Yes. But write only about what is important and enduring. I'll tell you something. I have lived a very full life, I've tasted it to the full and I'm content. But if I had ever known what it must feel like to create—to be an artist—

I would have denied my physical needs and soared toward the elevation of my spirit.

KONSTANTINE: Excuse me, where's Nina?

DORN: And another thing. In a work of art there ought to be a clearly defined idea. You must know why you are writing, for if you indulge yourself in aimless descriptions without a definite goal, you will lose your way and your talent will destroy you.

KONSTANTINE *(impatiently)*: Where is Nina?

DORN: She's gone home.

KONSTANTINE *(in despair)*: What am I going to do? I've got to see her. I must see her. I'm going . . .

(He goes out. MASHA enters.)

DORN: How can I help you? How?

MASHA: It hurts. No one knows how much I hurt! *(She leans her head against the doctor's chest, softly.)* I love . . . Konstantine.

DORN: How nervous they all are, how terribly nervous; so much love. Is it the magic of the lake? *(Tenderly)* What can I do for you, my child? What? What?

CURTAIN

ACT TWO

A croquet field. Upstage, at right, the house and a huge veranda. At left, one can see the lake and, reflected in it, the bright sun. Flower beds. It is noon and very hot. Near the croquet field, in the shade of a lime tree, ARKADINA, DORN and MASHA are seated. DORN has an open book on his knees.

ARKADINA *(to MASHA)*: Stand up, with me. *(They both stand.)* Side by side. You're twenty-two years old and I'm almost twice that. Eugene, which one of us looks younger?

DORN: You, of course.

ARKADINA: There . . . and why is that? Because I work, I'm alive, I'm always busy, and you, you're always sitting in the same spot. You're not living. . . . My guiding rule is: never look ahead to the future. I never think about old age or death; after all, we can't escape the inevitable.

MASHA: And I feel as if I had been born long, long ago; I drag this life along behind me like an old, old train and sometimes I have no inclination to live any more. Of course, that's all so ridiculous. I've got to shake myself free; I must pull myself together.

DORN *(humming quietly)*: "Tell her, my flowers, tell her . . ." [27]

ARKADINA: Not only that, I'm as fastidious as an Englishman. I never let myself go, darling. I'm never casually dressed, and my coiffure is always *comme il faut.* [28] Do I allow myself out of the house even as far as the garden in only a dressing gown and with my hair untidy? Never. The reason I've kept my looks is that I've never neglected myself. I've never let myself go as some women do. *(She walks around, hands on her hips.)* Look at me. I'm as light as a feather; ready to play the part of a girl of fifteen any day.

DORN: Well, I'll go on with my reading nevertheless. . . . *(Takes up his book.)* We were at the corn merchants and the rats.

ARKADINA: And the rats. Go ahead. You read. *(She sits down.)* Oh, give it here. I'll read. It's my turn. *(She takes the book and looks for the place.)* And the rats. Here we are. *(She reads.)* "And, of course, for society people to indulge novelists and lure them into their company is just as dangerous as corn merchants raising rats in their granaries. And yet they are idolized. And so when a woman has chosen the writer she desires to captivate, she besieges him with compliments, courtesies, and little favors. . . ." Well, that may be true for the French, but that's not the way here; we have no such machinations. Here, a woman, before she sets out to captivate a writer, is herself usually head over heels in love with him from the very first. For example, take me and Trigorin . . .

(Enter SORIN, leaning on his stick, and NINA after him. MEDVEDENKO pushes the empty wheelchair.)

SORIN *(in a caressing tone, as if he were speaking to a child)*: Yes? We're jumping with joy? Aren't we the happy ones today? *(To his sister)* We're a bundle of joy. Our father and stepmother have gone off and now we're free for three whole days.

NINA *(sits down beside ARKADINA and embraces her)*: I'm so happy. Now I belong to you.

SORIN *(sitting in his chair)*: Doesn't she look lovely today?

ARKADINA: So elegant . . . so lovely . . . she's the clever one. *(She kisses NINA.)* But we mustn't praise her too much, knock on wood. Where is Boris?

NINA: He's in the bathhouse, fishing.

ARKADINA: It's a wonder he doesn't get bored with it. *(She is ready to continue reading.)*

NINA: What's that you're reading?

ARKADINA: Maupassant's "Sur l'eau," [29] darling.

[MEDVEDENKO [30]: I've never read it.

DORN: You only read what you don't understand.

MEDVEDENKO: I read any book I can find.

DORN: You read Gibbon and Spencer,[31] but you have as much knowledge as a night watchman. For all you know, the heart may be made of gristle and the earth held up by whales.

MEDVEDENKO: The earth is round.

DORN: Why do you hesitate when you say it?

MEDVEDENKO (*hurt*): When you have nothing to eat, it makes no difference whether the earth is round or square. Leave me alone, please.]

ARKADINA (*reads a few lines to herself*): The next part is neither interesting nor true to life. (*She closes the book.*) I'm worried. Tell me what's the matter with my son. It's so annoying. He's always so morose. He spends days at a time by the lake. I hardly ever see him any more.

MASHA: He's not happy. (*To* NINA, *timidly*) Nina, recite something from his play, please.

NINA (*shrugging her shoulders*): Do you really want me to? It's so uninteresting!

MASHA: When he reads something himself, his eyes shine and his face gets so pale. He has a beautiful, sad voice, and he looks like a poet.

(*One can hear* SORIN *snoring.*)

DORN: Pleasant dreams.

ARKADINA (*to* SORIN): Peter dear.

SORIN: Eh?

ARKADINA: Are you asleep?

SORIN: No, not really.

(*Pause.*)

ARKADINA: You don't take care of yourself, dear. And I don't like that at all.

SORIN: I'd like to do something about my health but the doctor won't help me.

DORN: You're sixty! What's the use?

SORIN: Even at sixty a man wants to live.

DORN (*annoyed*): Oh, take some valerian drops.[32]

ARKADINA: I think it would do him a world of good to go somewhere for a cure.

DORN: Well, it might and it might not.

ARKADINA: I don't understand.

DORN: Nothing to understand. It's quite plain.

(Pause.)

MEDVEDENKO: Sorin should give up smoking.

SORIN: That has nothing to do with it.

DORN: No, he's right. Alcohol and tobacco destroy the personality. After a cigar or a drink you're not Uncle Peter any more, you're somebody else; your personality is erased and you look upon yourself as another person. . . . *(Pointing)* He!

SORIN *(laughing)*: It's all very well for you to talk. You've lived your life, but what of me? I've been a civil servant for twenty-eight years, but I haven't lived yet, never tried to do anything much, you know what I mean, so it's natural that I should wish to live. You've had your fill and you don't give a damn, so you can afford to be philosophical, but I want to live and that's why I drink sherry at dinner and smoke cigars. That's why, you know.

DORN: It's all very well to take life seriously, but to go in for cures at sixty years of age, and begrudge the fact that you didn't live it up enough in your youth, that, if you don't mind my saying so, is ridiculous.

MASHA *(gets up)*: It must be lunchtime. My foot's gone to sleep. *(She goes out.)*

DORN: She's going to have a few before lunch.

SORIN: The poor girl doesn't enjoy her life.

DORN: Nonsense, Peter.

SORIN: The words of a self-satisfied individual.

ARKADINA: Oh, what could be more boring than this darling country boredom! Hot, still, nobody ever doing anything, everybody philosophizing! It's good to be here with you, my friends, marvelous to listen to you, but how much better to be sitting in a hotel room studying my part! Ever so much better!

NINA *(rapturously)*: Yes, it must be wonderful. . . .

SORIN: Of course the city is better. One sits in one's study, the servants prevent anyone from entering unannounced, there is a telephone . . . there are cabs to be had in the streets . . . and the rest of it.

DORN (*hums, as before, hearts and flowers*): "Tell her, my flowers, tell her . . ."

(*Enter* SHAMRAYEV, *followed by* PAULINA.)

SHAMRAYEV: Here you are. Good morning! (*He kisses* ARKA-DINA's *hand, and then* NINA's.) You're looking very fit this morning. (*To* ARKADINA) My wife tells me that you intend to go to town together today. Is that so?

ARKADINA: Yes, we intend to. Very probably.

SHAMRAYEV: Hmm, that's very nice. But how do you intend to get there? They're bringing the hay in today and all of the workmen are occupied. Which horses did you intend to take, if I may be permitted to ask the question.

ARKADINA: Which horses? How should I know which horses?

SORIN: We have a team of horses, don't we?

SHAMRAYEV (*flaring*): A team of horses! And where will I get collars for them? Where will I get the collars? It's astonishing! It's absolutely beyond my comprehension! My dear lady! I admire your talent, I am prepared to lay down my life for you, but I cannot provide you with horses.

ARKADINA: But I must go to town. This is absurd!

SHAMRAYEV: My dear lady, you do not know what it means to run a farm.

ARKADINA (*flaring*): The same old story! In that case, I shall return to Moscow at once today. Will you give the order to rent some horses in town, or shall I walk to the station on foot!

SHAMRAYEV: In that case, I quit! You can get yourself an-other steward! (*He goes out.*)

ARKADINA: Every summer it's like this. Every summer here they insult me! I'll never set foot in this place again! (*She goes out left toward the bathing area on the lake. A mo-ment later she can be seen entering the house.* TRIGORIN *is right in back of her with his fishing equipment.*)

SORIN (*angrily*): What insolence! He's out of his mind! I'm sick of it, you know. Harness the horses immediately!

NINA (*to* PAULINA): To refuse Mme Treplev, a famous actress! Really, any desire of hers, her slightest whim is more important than your whole farm. It's simply incon-ceivable!

PAULINA (*in despair*): What can I do? Put yourself in my position, what can I do?

SORIN (*to* NINA): Let's go find sister. We'll all beg her not to go, won't we? (*Looking in the direction* SHAMRAYEV *has gone*) Insufferable man! Dictator!

NINA (*prevents his getting up*): Calm down, my dear. We'll push your chair inside. (NINA *and* MEDVEDENKO *push his chair along.*) It's just awful!

SORIN: Yes, it is, it's just awful. But he won't quit; I'll talk to him.

(*They go out.* DORN *and* PAULINA *remain alone.*)

DORN: People are so tiresome. Actually they ought to get rid of your husband, but of course it will all end with poor old Peter and Irina begging his pardon. You'll see!

PAULINA: He sent the team of horses into the fields. Every day we have these scenes. If you only knew how it all upsets me. It's making me ill; look, my hands are trembling. I can't bear him. He's vulgar. (*Imploring*) Eugene, my darling, my beloved, take me away with you. Our time is running out, we're not young any more; if only for the rest of our lives, at least, we could stop hiding the truth, stop pretending. . . .

(*Pause.*)

DORN: I'm fifty-five years old. It's too late to change.

PAULINA: I know you're avoiding me. There are other women in your life. But you can't hold on to all of us. I understand. I'm sorry, you're bored with me.

(NINA *appears near the house; she is picking flowers.*)

DORN: No, don't say that.

PAULINA: I can't help being jealous. Of course you're an obstetrician, I know you can't avoid seeing other women. I understand. . . .

DORN (*to* NINA, *who approaches*): How are things going inside?

NINA: Madame Treplev is crying and Sorin is having an asthma attack.

DORN *(rising)*: I'd better go and give them both some valerian drops.

NINA *(giving him the flowers)*: For you.

DORN: *Merci bien. (He goes toward the house.)*

PAULINA *(going with him)*: What pretty little flowers! *(Nearing the house, in a whisper)* Give them to me! Give me those flowers! *(She grabs the flowers, tears them to shreds and throws them aside; they both go into the house.)*

NINA *(alone)*: It's so strange to see a great actress crying for such a silly reason! And isn't it strange that a great writer, a celebrity, his pictures in all the papers, his books translated into foreign languages, spends the whole day fishing, so excited over catching two little fish. I thought famous people were proud, arrogant, above it all, that they used their fame and the glamour of their names to revenge themselves on society for holding rank and riches so high. But here they are crying or fishing, playing cards, laughing or losing their tempers, like everybody else. . . .

(KONSTANTINE enters, carrying a gun and a dead sea gull.)

KONSTANTINE: Are you alone?

NINA: Yes. *(KONSTANTINE lays the sea gull at her feet.)* What are you doing?

KONSTANTINE: I was cruel today. I killed this sea gull. I lay it at your feet.

NINA: What's the matter with you? *(Picks up the sea gull and looks at it.)*

KONSTANTINE: Soon I'll do the same for myself.

NINA: I don't understand you any more.

KONSTANTINE: Yes, I think you stopped understanding me when I stopped understanding you. You've changed toward me. You're indifferent. You're not comfortable with me any more.

NINA: You've been so irritable lately. You don't make sense. You talk in symbols. I suppose this sea gull is meant to be symbolic, too. I'm sorry, I don't understand. *(She places the sea gull on the bench.)* I'm too simple to understand you.

KONSTANTINE: It began the other evening when my play failed so stupidly. Women never forgive failure. I've burned it all up, every last scrap. If you only knew how unhappy

I am! I can't bear your coldness to me. It's awful. As if I had awakened to find the lake all dried up and sunk into the earth. You say that you're too simple to understand me. Oh, but what is there to understand? The play wasn't a success; you hate my work. You already consider me mediocre, insignificant, like so many others. . . . *(Stomping with his feet)* How well I understand it all. It's as if I had a nail stuck through my brain. Damn *it* and my pride. It sucks my life away like a snake. . . . *(Seeing* TRIGORIN, *who enters reading a book)* Here comes the man with the real talent, trippingly, like Hamlet reading on a book. *(Mimicking)* "Words, words, words." The sun merely touches you and you melt in its rays. I won't stand in your way. *(He goes off quickly.)*

TRIGORIN *(making notes in a book)*: Takes snuff and drinks vodka . . . and always wears black. The schoolteacher is in love with her. . . .

NINA: Good morning.

TRIGORIN: Good morning. It seems that we are leaving today, unexpectedly. I doubt if we'll meet again. Pity. I don't often meet young ladies, young and attractive. I seem to have forgotten what it is like to be eighteen or nineteen, and that's why the young ladies in my stories are usually artificial. I'd like to know what it is to be you for just one hour, to find out how you think and what sort of creature you are.

NINA: I'd like to change places with you, too.

TRIGORIN: Whatever for?

NINA: To know what it feels like to be a famous, talented writer. What does it feel like to be famous? How does it make you feel?

TRIGORIN: How? I don't think it makes me feel any way at all. I've never thought about it. *(Reflecting)* It's either one or the other: either you exaggerate my fame or else my fame is not real to me.

NINA: But you read about yourself in the newspapers?

TRIGORIN: When they praise me, that's fine. And when they criticize me, it takes me a few days to recover.

NINA: What a marvelous world! If you only knew how I envy you! Our destinies are so different! Some people have all they can do to drag themselves through their boring, insignificant lives. They're all alike, all miserable! While others, like you, you're one in a million, are lucky enough to have a fascinating, passionate, meaningful life. . . . You're happy.

TRIGORIN (*shrugging his shoulders*): Hmm . . . You talk about fame and happiness, of a passionate, meaningful life, but these are all nice words, if you don't mind my saying so, just words, which, like candied fruit, if you will excuse me, I do not eat.

NINA: Your life is beautiful!

TRIGORIN: What is so especially beautiful about it? (*Looks at his watch.*) I must get back to my work, my writing. Pardon me, I haven't the time. . . . (*He laughs.*) You've stepped on my pet corn, as they say, and it's irritating me. I'm getting annoyed. Let's talk. We'll talk about my passionate, beautiful life. . . . Well, then, where shall we begin? (*After a moment's reflection*) You know some men have violent obsessions; for instance, a man may think night and day of nothing but the moon. Well, I have just such a moon. Day and night, one constant thought overpowers me: I should be writing, I should be writing, I should be writing. . . . I've scarcely finished one story when for some reason I have to write another, then a third, and after the third a fourth. . . . I write incessantly, compulsively and I cannot stop. I'd like to know what is beautiful and meaningful about that? It's an absurd life! Here I am with you, I'm excited and moved; however, I cannot forget for a moment that my unfinished work is waiting for me. You see that cloud, it looks like a grand piano. It strikes me that I must put that into a story somewhere, that a cloud sailed by and it looked like a grand piano. A whiff of heliotrope.[33] Quickly I make a note of that. A sickly smell, the color for a lady in mourning; remember that for the next description of a summer evening. I catch our every sentence, every word, and quickly lock them up in my literary storeroom; it might be useful someday. As soon as I finish my work, I'm off to the theater or to fish; if only I could rest and forget myself. But no, there is a new subject for a story rolling around in my head like a cannonball and I'm drawn back to my writing desk . . . and I must write and write and write. And it's always like that, just like that. I have no rest and I feel that I am consuming my own life; for this honey that I am spreading so thin, I am scattering the pollen from my best flowers, tearing up the flowers and trampling their roots. Don't you think I'm a little mad? Do my friends and acquaintances treat me as if I were sane? "What are you writing at now?" "What shall we have next?" It's always the same, over and over again. And it seems to me that my friends' praise and admiration are kindnesses to deceive a sick man. I am sometimes afraid that they are on the verge of sneaking up behind me, grabbing me and committing me, like Poprishchin,[34] to an insane asylum. And in those early years, the best years of my youth, when I was beginning, my writing was sheer torture. A minor writer, especially when he is not successful, seems to himself to be clumsy, awkward, superfluous; he is attracted like a magnet to people connected with literature and art; nobody understands or recognizes him; he is afraid to look anyone straight in the eye, like an inveterate gambler who hasn't any money. I never saw my readers without imagining that they were hostile and unfriendly. I was afraid of the public, it terrified me, and when my first play was produced, it seemed to me that all the dark-haired people in the audience were against me and the light-haired were totally indifferent. Oh, how awful! It was torture!

NINA: But surely the inspiration and the joy of creation itself make up for it all?

TRIGORIN: Yes. When I'm writing, it is enjoyable and even when I'm reading my proofs it is, but . . . as soon as it appears in print, I hate it. It seems to me it is not what it was meant to be, and that it was a mistake to have written it at all. I am annoyed and disgusted. . . . *(Laughing)* The public reads it and says, "Yes, charming, talented . . . It's charming, but not quite Tolstoi." "It's a fine piece of work but Turgenev's *Fathers and Sons*[35] is much better." And it will be the same till I die: charming and talented, talented and charming—and nothing more; and when I die, they'll be saying at my grave, "Here lies Trigorin. He was a good writer. But Turgenev was better."

NINA: Don't! I refuse to understand you. You're simply spoiled by success.

TRIGORIN: What success? I've never been satisfied with myself; I don't like myself as a writer. The worst of it is that I'm in a sort of trance and I often do not understand what I write. I love this lake, these trees, this sky, I feel nature, it inspires a passion in me, an irresistible urge to write. But I'm not a descriptive writer, I have an obligation to humanity. I love my country, my people, I feel that if I am a writer, I must speak of the people, their sufferings and their future, of science and the rights of man, et cetera, and I write about everything, I am rushed, I dash about, I'm stalked, people become angry with me, I feel like a trapped animal, I see that life and science are steadily advancing while I fall backward, like a poor peasant who has missed his train, and the result is that I am only able to write descriptions—and all the rest that I write rings false, false, false to the marrow of my bones.

NINA: You've worked too hard and you no longer take the time to realize your worth. You may be dissatisfied with yourself but the world considers you a great writer. If I were such a writer as you, I would devote my entire life to the people, but I would realize that the only happiness for them was to hitch their wagon to my star.

TRIGORIN: To my star? What do you think? Am I a god or something? [36]

(They both smile.)

NINA: For the happiness of being a writer or an actress, I would endure being disliked, sacrifice the love of those nearest me, bear poverty, disappointment; I would live in a garret and eat stale bread; I would risk disillusionment and take cognizance of my inadequacies. But in return I would demand fame—true, glorious fame. *(Covers her face with her hands.)* I'm dizzy ... ahhh. ...

VOICE OF ARKADINA *(from the house)*: Boris!

TRIGORIN: They're calling me. It's time to pack. But I don't want to leave. *(He looks at the lake.)* What a paradise! How lovely it is.

NINA: Do you see the house and the garden on the other side of the lake?

TRIGORIN: Yes.

NINA: That used to belong to my mother. I was born there. I have lived all my life beside this lake. And I know every little islet on it.

TRIGORIN: It's very nice here. *(He sees the sea gull.)* What's that?

NINA: A sea gull. Konstantine shot it.

TRIGORIN: It's a beautiful bird. You know, I really don't want to go. Try and persuade Irina to stay. *(Makes a note in his book.)*

NINA: What are you writing?

TRIGORIN: Oh, I'm only making a note . . . a subject flashed through my mind. *(Putting the notebook away)* A subject for a short story: On the shores of a lake, a young girl lives all her young life, just like you, she loves the lake like a sea gull, and is free and happy as a sea gull. But by chance a man comes, sees her and, having nothing better to do, destroys her like that sea gull here.

   (Pause.)

ARKADINA: Boris, are you there? Where are you?

TRIGORIN: I'm coming. *(Goes, then looks back to* NINA; *under* ARKADINA's *window)* What is it?

ARKADINA: We are staying.

*(*TRIGORIN *goes into the house.)*

NINA *(coming forward to the footlights; she dreams a moment)*: A dream!

CURTAIN

ACT THREE

The dining room in SORIN's *house. There are doors at the left and the right. A sideboard, a cupboard for medicines. There is a table in the middle of the room. Valises and hatboxes; preparations for departure.*

TRIGORIN *is having lunch.* MASHA *stands next to the table.*

MASHA: I'm telling this to you as a writer. It's yours. Use it if you wish. I know this for a fact. If he had hurt himself seriously, I wouldn't have gone on living another minute. But I'm braver now. I've come to my senses and I've made up my mind: to tear this love out of my heart, tear it out by the roots.

TRIGORIN: How?

MASHA: I'm going to get married: to Medvedenko.

TRIGORIN: The schoolteacher?

MASHA: Yes.

TRIGORIN: What for?

MASHA: To love hopelessly . . . to keep waiting endlessly. When I marry, there'll be no time for love; all my new troubles will drown out the old ones. Anyway, it will be a change, you know. Let's have another.

TRIGORIN: Haven't we had enough?

MASHA: Oh, so what? *(Fills two glasses.)* Don't look at me like that. Women drink more than you think. The minority drink openly as I do, but the majority drink secretly. Yes, they do. And it's always vodka or cognac. *(They clink glasses.)* Good luck! You're a nice man. I'm sorry you're leaving. *(They drink.)*

TRIGORIN: I don't really want to go.

MASHA: Well, ask her to stay.

TRIGORIN: She won't do that. Her son is not behaving very tactfully. First he shoots himself, and now they say he's going to challenge me to a duel. And what for? He sulks, he mutters, he advocates new art forms . . . but there's room enough for all, the new and the old. Why be pushy?

MASHA: Well, perhaps he's jealous. But that's none of my business. *(Pause.* YAKOV *crosses from left to right stage with a suitcase.* NINA *enters and stops near the window.)* My schoolteacher is not very clever but he's good natured and he's poor and he's violently in love with me. I'm sorry for him and for his old mother. Well, let me wish you good luck. Don't think badly of me. *(Warmly shaking his hand)* Thanks so much for listening. Send me some of your little books, and please don't forget to inscribe them. But don't say: "To my dear friend," but simply: "To Marya, who doesn't know where she belongs or why she's alive." So long. *(She goes out.)*

NINA *(holding out her hand to* TRIGORIN, *fist clenched)*: Odd or even?

TRIGORIN: Even.

NINA *(sighing)*: Wrong. I only had one pea in my hand. I wanted to see whether I would become an actress or not. I wish somebody would give me some advice.

TRIGORIN: It's impossible to give advice about that.

(Pause.)

NINA: You're leaving, and . . . we'll never see each other again. Please take this little locket as a remembrance. I've had your initials engraved on it, and on the other side, the name of your book *Days and Nights*.

TRIGORIN: What a sweet thing to do! *(Kisses the locket.)* What a lovely present.

NINA: Think of me sometimes.

TRIGORIN: I will. I shall think of you as you were on that sunny day—do you remember?—a week ago, when you were wearing that light dress. We were talking, and there was a white sea gull on the bench. . . .

NINA *(pensively)*: Yes, a sea gull. *(Pause)* We can't talk any more, someone's coming. I must see you again a moment before you go, please.

(She goes out at the left. At the same moment, enter ARKADINA, SORIN *in a uniform with decorations, and then* YAKOV, *occupied with luggage.)*

ARKADINA: Listen, old thing, stay here. With your rheumatism, you have no business going anywhere. *(To* TRIGORIN*)* Who was it that just left? Nina?

TRIGORIN: Yes.

ARKADINA: Are we intruding? *(Sits down.)* I think everything's packed. I'm exhausted.

TRIGORIN *(reading the inscription printed on the medallion)*: *Days and Nights,* page 121, lines 11 and 12.

YAKOV *(clearing the table)*: Should the fishing rods be packed, too?

TRIGORIN: Yes, I'll still need them. You can give the books to whomever you like.

YAKOV: Very well, sir.

TRIGORIN *(to himself)*: Page 121, lines 11 and 12. What's in those lines? *(To* ARKADINA*)* Are there any copies of my book in the house?

ARKADINA: In my brother's study. In the corner bookcase.

TRIGORIN: Page 121. *(He exits.)*

ARKADINA: Really, Peter dear, you'd be better off at home.

SORIN: You're going away. Without you it will be so gloomy here.

ARKADINA: And what is there in the city, you tell me.

SORIN: Nothing, but still . . . *(He laughs.)* The laying of a cornerstone, and all that sort of thing . . . I feel like getting away from this miserable life, even for an hour or two, or I'll start getting as stale as an old cigarette holder hidden away in a corner. I've ordered the horses for one o'clock, so we'll be off at the same time.

ARKADINA *(after a pause)*: Oh, stay here, don't be so bored, and don't catch cold. Look after my son. Take care of him. Set a good example for him. *(Pause)* Here I am leaving and I'll never know why Konstantine shot himself. I'm sure it was jealousy, and the sooner I get Trigorin out of here, the better.

SORIN: Yes and no. But there were other reasons. It's perfectly clear: a clever young man, living in the country, in the backwoods, with no money, position or future, has nothing to do. He is ashamed and afraid of his idleness. I love him, and he's very much attached to me, yet all in all, you know, it seems to him that he's not wanted in the house, that he's a parasite, a sponge. It's quite clear it's his pride.

ARKADINA: Why must I have such a cross to bear? *(Pondering)* He might join the Service, perhaps. . . .

SORIN *(whistling)*: It would seem to be a good idea, if you . . . gave him a little money. In the first place, he needs some clothes, you know. Take a look at him: for three years he's been wearing that same old suit; he runs around without an overcoat. It wouldn't do him any harm to enjoy himself a little. He might go abroad, you know; that wouldn't cost very much.

ARKADINA: Well, I think I might perhaps manage a new suit, but as for going abroad . . . no, just at the moment I can't even afford the suit. *(Emphatically)* No money. I haven't any money! *(SORIN laughs.)* No!

SORIN *(whistling)*: Very well. Darling sister, don't be angry. I believe you . . . you're a generous, noble woman.

ARKADINA *(through her tears)*: I haven't any money!

SORIN: If I had any money, of course, I'd give him some myself, but I have nothing, not a kopeck. *(He laughs.)* My steward takes all my pension money and he spends it on the farm, on livestock and beekeeping, and all my money goes for nothing. The bees die, the cattle die and I can't even get one of the workmen to drive me to town.

ARKADINA: Yes, of course I have some money, but you see I am an actress; my wardrobe is enough to ruin me.

SORIN: You're a good, dear thing. I respect you . . . yes . . . but . . . something's the matter with me. . . . *(He staggers.)* My head is swimming. . . . *(He leans on the table.)* I feel sick, you know. . . .

ARKADINA *(alarmed)*: Peter dear! *(Trying to support him)* Peter, my darling! *(Calling out)* Help me! Help! *(Enter* KONSTANTINE, *with a bandage around his head, and* MEDVEDENKO.*)* He feels sick.

SORIN: It's nothing, nothing. . . . *(He smiles and drinks some water.)* I feel better already, you know. . . .

KONSTANTINE *(to his mother)*: Don't be upset, Mother, it's not serious. He's had these attacks often recently. *(To his uncle)* You must lie down, Uncle Peter.

SORIN: A little bit, yes. All the same, I'm going to town. I'll lie down and I'll go to town . . . that's it. *(Goes out, leaning on his stick.)*

MEDVEDENKO *(giving him his arm)*: Here's a riddle: in the morning on four legs, at noon on two, in the evening on three . . .

SORIN *(laughs)*: Exactly! And at night on the back. Thank you, I can manage alone. . . .

MEDVEDENKO: Oh, come now, stop fussing. . . .

(He and Sorin go out.)

ARKADINA: How he frightened me!

KONSTANTINE: It's not good for him to live in the country. He gets depressed. Now, Mama, if you only had a sudden burst of generosity and lent him fifteen hundred or two thousand rubles, then he could live in town for a whole year.

ARKADINA: I haven't any money. I'm an actress, not a banker.

(Pause.)

KONSTANTINE: Mama, Mama, change my bandage for me, you do it so well.

ARKADINA *(takes iodine and a box of bandages out of the cupboard)*: And the doctor is late.

KONSTANTINE: He promised to be here at ten, and it's noon already.

ARKADINA: Sit down. *(She takes the bandage off his head.)* You look just like you were wearing a turban. Yesterday somebody saw you at the gate and asked what nationality you were. But you're almost all healed. It's just a little scratch now. *(Kisses him on the head.)* While I'm away, you won't do any more bang-bang?

KONSTANTINE: No, Mother. It was a moment of despair. I couldn't control myself. It won't happen again. *(Kisses her hands.)* You have such light hands. I remember long, long ago, when you were still working in the state repertory theaters. . . . I was a little boy. There was a fight where we lived; one of the tenants, a washerwoman, was seriously hurt. Do you remember? She was picked up unconscious.

You looked after her, took medicine to her, washed her children in the tub; don't you remember?

ARKADINA: No. *(She dresses the wound.)*

KONSTANTINE: Two ballet dancers were living in the same house we did. They used to come and have coffee with you. . . .

ARKADINA: That I remember.

KONSTANTINE: They were very religious. *(Pause)* These last few days, I've loved you as tenderly and as completely as when I was that little boy. Except for you, I have nobody left now. Only why, why do you let yourself be influenced by that man?

ARKADINA: You don't understand him, Konstantine. He has a noble nature. . . .

KONSTANTINE: Yet, when he heard I meant to duel him, his nobility didn't prevent his cowardice. He's running away . . . shamelessly.

ARKADINA: Don't be silly! I myself asked him to come away. [You may not approve our intimacy, but be reasonable. You're an intelligent boy; please respect my freedom. I respect your freedom but I also want my freedom . . . to think as I like about him.] [37]

KONSTANTINE: Noble nature! Both of us are almost quarreling, and right now he is who knows where, in the drawing room or the garden, laughing at us . . . impressing Nina, trying once and for all to convince her that he's a genius.

ARKADINA: You delight in saying unpleasant things to me. I respect that man and must ask you not to say nasty things about him in my presence.

KONSTANTINE: And I don't respect him. You want me to take him for a genius, too, but I'm sorry, I can't lie. His books make me sick.

ARKADINA: That's envy. People with pretensions to talent have nothing better to do than to disparage people with real talent. That's a fine consolation. . . .

KONSTANTINE *(ironically)*: Real talent! I have more talent than both of you put together, as far as that goes. *(Tears the bandage off his head.)* You second-rate hacks have grabbed first place in the limelight and you see no value in anything but the trash you perpetrate. Everything else you stifle and suppress. I don't believe in you two! I don't believe in you or in him!

ARKADINA: Decadent!

KONSTANTINE: Go back to your darling theater and play there in your trashy little plays!

ARKADINA: I've never acted in such plays! Leave me alone! You couldn't even write silly vaudeville. . . . Bourgeois! Parasite!

KONSTANTINE: Miser!

ARKADINA: Beggar!

(KONSTANTINE *sits down and weeps quietly.*)

ARKADINA: Nonentity! Don't cry! You mustn't cry! *(She weeps.)* You mustn't . . . *(Kisses him.)* My darling child, please forgive me! Forgive your wicked mother. Forgive miserable me.

KONSTANTINE *(embraces her)*: If I only knew! I have lost everything! She doesn't love me. Now I can't write. All my hopes are gone!

ARKADINA: Don't despair! Everything will be all right. He'll be leaving. She'll love you again. *(Dries his tears.)* That's enough now. We've made peace.

KONSTANTINE *(kissing her hands)*: Yes, Mother.

ARKADINA *(tenderly)*: Make it up with him, too. You don't want to fight a duel with him, do you? You don't, do you?

KONSTANTINE: All right. Only, Mama, don't let me see him any more. It's too painful for me. I can't stand it any more. *(Enter* TRIGORIN.*)* Here he comes. I'm going. . . . *(Puts dressings away in cupboard quickly.)* The doctor will have to do my bandages, then. [*(As he goes)* Now he drinks beer, and makes love to elderly women.] [38]

TRIGORIN *(looking through a book)*: Page 121, lines 11 and 12 . . . Here we are. *(He reads.)* "If you ever need my life, then come and take it."

(KONSTANTINE *picks the bandage up from the floor and goes out.*)

ARKADINA *(looking at her watch)*: The horses will be here soon.

TRIGORIN *(to himself)*: "If you ever need my life, then come and take it."

ARKADINA: I hope you're all packed?

TRIGORIN *(impatiently)*: Yes, yes . . . *(Deep in thought)* This sincere appeal from a pure young girl touches me very deeply . . . but why should it fill me with pity? "If you ever need my life, then come and take it." *(To* ARKADINA*)* Let's stay for one more day! (ARKADINA *shakes her head no.)* Let's stay!

ARKADINA: Darling, I know what keeps you here. But have some self-control. You're a little drunk. Sober up.

TRIGORIN: Be sensible yourself, be reasonable, intelligent. . . . *(He presses her hand.)* You are capable of sacrifice; be my friend, set me free.

ARKADINA *(completely undone)*: Are you so infatuated?

TRIGORIN: I'm drawn to her! Perhaps this is just exactly what I need.

ARKADINA: The love of a little girl from the country? Oh, how little you know yourself!

TRIGORIN: There are times when one lives as if in a trance. That is how I am talking to you now, as if I were floating, and dreaming about her. . . . I am filled with delicious dreams. . . . Set me free. . . .

ARKADINA *(trembling)*: No, no . . . I'm only a woman. You can't talk to me like that. Don't torture me, Boris . . . it frightens me.

TRIGORIN: If you wanted to, you could be an extraordinary woman. Love—youthful, delightful, poetic—transports us to a world of dreams. On earth it alone can give us happiness! I have not yet experienced such a love. In my youth there wasn't time, I was always hanging around some editor's office, struggling against poverty. Now it's here, this love, it has come at last, it draws me. . . . What sense is there in running away from it?

ARKADINA *(in a rage)*: You've gone mad!

TRIGORIN: Then let me. . . .

ARKADINA: Everybody in this house is conspiring today to make me unhappy!

TRIGORIN *(clutching at his head)*: She doesn't understand! She doesn't want to understand!

ARKADINA: Is it possible that I am already so old and ugly that you dare speak to me of other women? *(She puts her arms around him and embraces him.)* Oh, you are mad! My wonderful one, my angel, you, the last chapter of my life! *(She kneels before him.)* My joy, my pride, my de-

light. *(She embraces his knees with her arms.)* If you were
to leave me if only for an hour, I would die. I would go
out of my mind. My wonderful, my magnificent one, my
master.

TRIGORIN: Somebody will see you. *(He helps her to get up.)*

ARKADINA: I don't care. I'm not ashamed of my love for
you. *(She kisses his hands.)* My treasure, my reckless boy.
You want to be mad, but I won't let you do it. *(She laughs.)*
You're mine . . . mine. This forehead is mine, these eyes
are mine, and this silky hair is mine, too. You're all mine.
You have so much talent, intelligence; you're the greatest
of all living writers, you are the only hope of Russia. You
have so much sincerity, simplicity, freshness, healthy humor. In one stroke you go to the heart of the matter, a
character or a scene, you describe what people are really
like, you capture a landscape, your characters palpitate
with life. One cannot read you without becoming ecstatic.
. . . Do you think I'm flattering you? Look me in the eyes,
look—do I look like a liar? You see? Only I can appreciate
you; only I tell you the truth, my darling, my precious
darling. . . . You'll come with me? Won't you? You won't
leave me?

TRIGORIN: I have no will of my own . . . I never had any.
I'm soft, lazy, always giving in. Is it possible that women
could love a man like that? Take me, lead me around, but
don't ever let me out of your sight. . . .

ARKADINA *(to herself)*: Now he's mine! *(Nonchalantly, as if
nothing had transpired)* You can stay if you like. I'll go
and you may join me later, in a week. There's no reason
for you to hurry.

TRIGORIN: No; since everything's decided, let's go together.

(Pause. TRIGORIN *notes something in his notebook.)*

ARKADINA: What are you scribbling?

TRIGORIN: I heard a lovely expression this morning: "a forest of young girls." It might be of use. Well, then, off we
go. It's all beginning again—the trains, the stations, the
dining cars, the veal cutlets, the conversations. . . .

*(*SHAMRAYEV *enters.)*

SHAMRAYEV: I have the pleasure to announce that the carriage awaits you. It's time to leave for the station, dear lady. The train arrives at five minutes past two. If you remember, Mme Treplev, please find out about the actor Suzdaltsev, whether he's alive? Is he well? We used to have a drink together now and then. He was incomparable in *The Mail Robbery*.[39] I remember, at that time, the tragedian Izmailov was at Elisavetograd; he was a remarkable person, too. . . . No need to rush, dear lady, we still have five minutes. Once, in a melodrama, he played the role of the conspirator, and when they caught him, he was supposed to say, "We have fallen into a trap," and you know what Izmailov said? "We have tallen into a frap." (*He laughs wholeheartedly.*) Tallen into a frap! A frap!

(*While he speaks,* YAKOV *busies himself with the baggage, the maid brings* ARKADINA *her coat, hat, umbrella and gloves; everybody helps* ARKADINA *to get dressed; the chief cook appears at the door on the left. Enter* PAULINA, *and then* SORIN *and* MEDVEDENKO.)

PAULINA (*carrying a little basket*): Here are some plums for the trip. They are sweet. I hope you like them.

ARKADINA: You are so kind to us, Paulina.

PAULINA: *Adieu,* my dear! If things haven't been satisfactory, please forgive it! (*She cries.*)

ARKADINA (*embracing her*): Everything was perfect, perfect, really perfect. Don't cry, come, come, come now. . . .

PAULINA: Time marches on.

ARKADINA: Yes, so it does!

SORIN (*with overcoat, hat and cane, entering from the door at left and crossing the stage*): It's time, sister dear, come, come, or we'll be late. I'm going to the carriage. (*He goes out.*)

MEDVEDENKO: I'm walking to the station. I'll see you off. On the double . . . (*He goes out.*)

ARKADINA: Good-bye, my friends. If we are still alive and in good health, we shall see each other again next summer. (*The maid,* YAKOV *and the cook kiss her hand.*) Don't forget me. (*She gives the cook a ruble.*) Here's a ruble for the three of you.

COOK: Thank you so much, madame. *Bon voyage,* madame. Thank you so much.

YAKOV: God keep you.

SHAMRAYEV: Write to us sometimes! Good-bye, Trigorin.

ARKADINA: Where is Konstantine? Tell him I'm leaving. We must say good-bye. Now, don't think too badly of us. *(To* YAKOV*)* I have given the cook a ruble. It's for the three of you.

(Everyone goes out at the right. The stage is empty. Backstage we hear the noises of departure. The maid returns to get the basket of plums on the table and then goes out.)

TRIGORIN *(returning)*: I forgot my walking stick. I think it's down there on the veranda. *(Enter* NINA.*)* Is that you? We're leaving now.

NINA: I knew we'd meet again. *(Agitatedly)* Boris Trigorin, I've made up my mind. The die is cast. I'm going to be an actress. I'm leaving here tomorrow. I'm leaving my father, leaving everything. *I'm* leaving, too, to begin a new life. I'm going to Moscow, too. We'll see each other there.

TRIGORIN *(a cautious glance around)*: Go to the Slavyansky Bazar. . . .[40] Let me know as soon as you get there. . . . Molchanovka, the Groholski House. . . .[41] I must go now. . . .

NINA: Wait just one more minute. . . .

TRIGORIN *(in a low voice)*: You are so beautiful. . . . How wonderful to think we will see each other again so soon. *(She places her head on his chest.)* I'll see these eyes again, this lovely, tender smile . . . these gentle features . . . this angelic face. My darling . . . *(A long kiss. He exits.)*

CURTAIN

Between the third and fourth acts, two years pass.

ACT
FOUR

One of the drawing rooms in the SORIN *household, which* KONSTANTINE *has remodeled into a study. On the left and at the right, doors lead to other rooms. We face a French window leading to the terrace. Besides the usual drawing room furniture, a study is installed in the corner of the room and near the door, at the left. A large Turkish divan, a bookshelf, and books lining the window seat, some chairs.*

It is evening. The room is lit by a single lamp with a large shade. Semidarkness. Sound of trees rustling and the winter wind howling in the chimney. The night watchman taps.

Enter MEDVEDENKO *and* MASHA.

MASHA *(calling)*: Konstantine! Konstantine! *(She looks around.)* Nobody! Nobody's here. The old man keeps asking, "Where is Konstantine?" He can't live without him.

MEDVEDENKO: He's afraid to be alone. *(He listens intently.)* Such awful weather we've been having these last two days!

MASHA *(turns the light up)*: There are waves on the lake. They're huge.

MEDVEDENKO: It's so dark in the garden. We ought to have them tear down that stage. It's as bare and awful as a skeleton and the curtain is flapping in the wind. Last night, when I passed in front of it, I thought I heard someone crying.

41

MASHA: So . . .

(Pause.)

MEDVEDENKO: Come on, Masha, let's go home.
MASHA *(shakes her head no)*: I'm going to stay here tonight.
MEDVEDENKO *(begging)*: Come, Masha. The baby must be starved.
MASHA: Don't get upset. Your mother will feed him.

(Pause.)

MEDVEDENKO: Poor little thing. He's been without his mother for three nights.
MASHA: Don't be tiresome, Semyon. In the old days, at least, you liked to philosophize. Now you only harp on one thing: the baby, let's go home, the baby, let's go home.
MEDVEDENKO: Come, Masha.
MASHA: Go yourself.
MEDVEDENKO: Your father won't lend me a horse.
MASHA: Oh, yes he will. Just ask him.
MEDVEDENKO: All right, I will. You'll be home tomorrow?
MASHA *(taking snuff)*: Yes, tomorrow . . . Stop nagging!

(Enter KONSTANTINE and PAULINA: KONSTANTINE brings in pillows and a quilt; PAULINA, some sheets; they put them on the divan; then KONSTANTINE goes to his desk and sits down.)

MASHA: What's this for, Mama?
PAULINA: Uncle Peter wants to sleep in Konstantine's room.
MASHA: I'll do it.

(MASHA makes the bed.)

PAULINA *(sighing)*: When they're old, they're like children. . . . *(She approaches the desk, leans her elbow on it and reads the manuscript. Pause.)*
MEDVEDENKO: Well, I'm off, then, I'm going. Bye, Masha. *(He kisses his wife.)* Bye-bye, Mother. *(He makes as if to kiss his mother-in-law.)*

PAULINA *(annoyed)*: Well, go if you're going, and God be with you!

MEDVEDENKO: Good-bye, Konstantine.

(KONSTANTINE extends his hand without a word. MED-VEDENKO leaves.)

PAULINA *(examining the manuscript)*: Nobody ever imagined, Konstantine, that you'd ever become a real writer. And now, just think, the magazines are even paying you. *(She pats his head.)* Even your looks have improved. Sweet Konstantine, be nice to my little Masha!

MASHA *(making the bed)*: Leave him alone, Mother.

PAULINA *(to KONSTANTINE)*: She's such a dear! *(Pause)* All a woman needs is a tender look, Konstantine. *I* can tell you that.

(KONSTANTINE gets up and goes out without a word.)

MASHA: You see, he's upset. You shouldn't have bothered him.

PAULINA: But, Masha, my dear, I worry so about you. . . .

MASHA: I don't need your pity. Forget it.

PAULINA: But my heart bleeds for you. I see everything, you know. I understand everything.

MASHA: Don't talk nonsense. Unhappy love exists only in novels. The thing to do is not to let oneself go, not to keep waiting, waiting for something. When love worms its way into our hearts, it must be torn out. They promised my husband a transfer to a new district. We'll move, and I'll forget everything. I'll tear it out of my heart by the roots.

(From another room, the sound of a melancholy waltz.)

PAULINA: Konstantine's playing. He must be unhappy.

MASHA *(waltzes about silently)*: The most important thing for me, Mama, is not to see him. If only they transfer Semyon, I'll forget him. In less than a month's time. It's nothing to get upset about.

(The door opens. DORN and MEDVEDENKO push SORIN's chair in.)

MEDVEDENKO: Now there are six mouths to feed at home. And flour is up to seventy kopecks a pound.[42]

DORN: It's a vicious circle.

MEDVEDENKO: It's all very well for you to laugh. You've got money, more than you know what to do with.

DORN: Money? Me? After thirty years of practice, a hard life, in which my time was never my own, day or night, I put just two thousand rubles aside, and that I just disposed of on my trip abroad. I have nothing.

MASHA *(to her husband)*: Haven't you gone yet?

MEDVEDENKO *(feeling guilty)*: What do you want? They won't give me a horse!

MASHA *(with bitter vexation, through her teeth)*: I wish I'd never lay eyes on you again!

(The chair is placed at the left. PAULINA, MASHA *and* DORN *sit down at the side;* MEDVEDENKO, *saddened, sits away from the rest.)*

DORN: All these changes! You've made a study out of the parlor.

MASHA: Konstantine feels more comfortable working in here. He can go out into the garden to think.

(The night watchman taps.)

SORIN: Where is my sister?

DORN: She went to the station to get Trigorin. She'll be home soon.

SORIN: If you thought it necessary to send for my sister, I must be very sick. *(After a moment)* What a predicament— I'm very sick and I don't get any medicine.

DORN: And what would you like to take? Valerian drops? Bicarbonate? Quinine?

SORIN: He's at it again, lecturing. Oh, dear! *(He points to the couch.)* Is that bed for me?

PAULINA: It's for you, Uncle Peter.

SORIN: Thank you.

DORN *(hums)*: "The moon appears in the sky at night . . ."[43]

SORIN: I'd like to give Konstantine an idea for a story. It ought to be called *L'homme qui a voulu*—"The Man Who Wanted." Long ago, when I was young, I wanted to become a writer—and I didn't become one. I wanted to be able to express myself—and I made such a mess of that. . . . (*Mimicking himself*) "And so on . . . as I was saying . . . you know what I mean . . . you know . . . that is not to say . . . et cetera . . ." And I repeated everything I said, sweated over it. I wanted to get married—and I didn't. I wanted to live in the city—and here I am, ending up my life in the country.

DORN: I wanted to become a civil service official and I did become *just* that.

SORIN (*laughing*): That wasn't one of my goals; that just happened.

DORN: To express discontent with life at the age of sixty-two implies a certain lack of proportion, you must admit.

SORIN: He's so stubborn! Don't you understand that I want to live?

DORN: That's not a consideration. According to the law of nature, every life must come to an end.

SORIN: You're so damned self-satisfied. You've had your fill, and that's why you look on life with indifference. All the same, you're just as afraid to die as I am.

DORN: Fear of death is an animal fear. One must suppress it. Only religious people, terrified by their sins, have any reason for fearing death. Well, you're not religious . . . and what possible sins could you have committed? Furthermore, for twenty-five years you've belonged body and soul to the civil service . . . and that's that.

SORIN (*laughing*): Twenty-eight . . .

(KONSTANTINE *enters and sits down on a little stool at* SORIN's *feet*. MASHA *looks at him intently*.)

DORN: We are preventing Konstantine from working.
KONSTANTINE: Oh, no, not at all.

(*Pause*.)

MEDVEDENKO: Do you mind if I ask you a question, doctor? Which foreign city did you like the best?
DORN: Genoa.
KONSTANTINE: Why Genoa?
DORN: There are marvelous crowds in the street. In the eve-

ning, when one comes out of one's hotel, the street is filled with people. You wander through the crowd, down one street, down another, aimlessly, you move with it, you become part of it, and you begin to think that there's only one collective soul . . . just like the one Nina represented in your play. By the way, where is she now? Where is she and how is she doing?

KONSTANTINE: I suppose she's all right.

DORN: I've heard she's leading quite a life for herself. What's she been up to?

KONSTANTINE: It's a long, long story, doctor.

DORN: To make a long story short . . .

(Pause.)

KONSTANTINE: She ran away from home and joined Trigorin. You knew that?

DORN: Yes.

KONSTANTINE: She had a child. The child died. Trigorin got tired of her, and he came back to his old attachments, as we knew he would. But, after all, he never really did break away. He simply wandered from one to the other, spinelessly. As far as I know, Nina's personal life has been a failure.

DORN: And the theater?

KONSTANTINE: Even worse, I think. She began acting in a provincial theater, near Moscow, then she left for the provinces. At the time, I was always with her, I followed her everywhere, I went where she went. She always tried leading roles, but she was a ham, she acted in bad taste, she screamed too much, she was too busy. Sometimes you could see by a gesture that she had talent; her death scenes were good, but her good moments were few and far between.

DORN: So she does have some talent all the same?

KONSTANTINE: That's hard to say. I guess she does. I went to see her, but she wouldn't have anything more to do with me; they didn't even let me go up to her hotel room. I understood how she felt, so I didn't insist. *(Pause)* What else do you want me to say? Later, when I came back here, she began to write to me. They were warm, intelligent, interesting letters. She didn't complain but I could tell she was miserable; every line sick, strained, nervous; and her imagination was a bit confused. She always signed her letters "The Sea Gull." As in Pushkin's "The Sea Maiden,"⁴⁴ the miller kept saying he was a crow, she herself kept repeating over and over that she was a sea gull. Now, she's here.

DORN: Here, where?

KONSTANTINE: In town, at the hotel. About five days ago she took a room there. I tried to go and see her, so did Masha, but she won't see anyone. Semyon says he saw her out walking yesterday afternoon about a mile or so from here.

MEDVEDENKO: Yes, I met her. She was on her way back to town. I said hello and I asked her why she didn't come to visit us. She said she would come.

KONSTANTINE: She won't. *(Pause)* Her father and stepmother don't want to see her any more. They locked the gates to their property. They've posted guards all around to prevent her from getting in. *(He goes with the doctor toward the writing table.)* How easy it is to be a philosopher on paper, doctor, and how hard it is in real life.

SORIN: She was a charming girl.

DORN: I beg your pardon?

SORIN: I said she was charming. Civil Service Officer Sorin was quite in love with her for a time.

DORN: The old lecher.

(SHAMRAYEV's laughter can be heard.)

PAULINA: I think they're arriving from the station.

KONSTANTINE: Yes, I hear Mama's voice. . . .

(Enter ARKADINA, TRIGORIN and, behind them, SHAMRAYEV.)

SHAMRAYEV *(entering)*: We're all getting old, we're falling apart day by day: you alone, dear lady, always remain young, beautifully dressed, vivacious, alluring. . . .

ARKADINA: You want to bring me bad luck again, you tiresome creature!

TRIGORIN *(to* SORIN*)*: Hello, Uncle Peter! Still sick? You bad boy. *(Seeing* MASHA, *joyfully)* Masha!

MASHA: You recognized me? *(She shakes his hand.)*

TRIGORIN: Married?

MASHA: Since forever.

TRIGORIN: Happy? (*He greets* DORN *and* MEDVEDENKO, *then approaches* KONSTANTINE *hesitatingly.*) Irina tells me you have forgotten the past and are no longer angry.

(KONSTANTINE *holds out his hand.*)

ARKADINA (*to her son*): Boris has brought the magazine with your new story in it. (*She goes out.*)

KONSTANTINE (*taking the book from* TRIGORIN's *hands*): Thank you. That was kind of you.

(*They sit down.*)

TRIGORIN: Your admirers send you their greetings. They're quite interested in you; they ask me how you are, your age, whether you're dark or fair; they imagine, I can't think why, that you're probably not young any more. And nobody knows your real name, only the pseudonym. You're as mysterious as the man in the iron mask.

KONSTANTINE: Are you staying long?

TRIGORIN: No, I'm thinking of going back to Moscow tomorrow. I must go. I have to finish a story quickly, and I've promised something to a quarterly. It's still the same old hectic life. (*While they speak*, MASHA *and* PAULINA *lay out a card table;* SHAMRAYEV *lights candles and brings up chairs. They take a game of lotto out of the bureau.*) The weather's not been very kind to me. It's a ferocious wind. Tomorrow morning, if it's calm enough, I'll go out on the lake to fish. And I'll get a chance to see the spot again where you did your play . . . do you still remember? I've got an idea for a story that's almost ready; all I have to do is refresh my memory about the place.

MASHA (*to her father*): Lend my husband a horse. He has to get home.

SHAMRAYEV (*imitating her*): A horse . . . he has to get home. . . . (*Severely*) You could have seen yourself: the horses have just returned from the station. I can't send them out again.

MASHA: But there are other horses. (*Seeing that her father*

doesn't wish to answer) You're impossible. Try to get anything from you . . .

MEDVEDENKO: I'll walk, Masha, really. . . .

PAULINA *(sighing)*: Walk, in this weather . . . *(She sits down
at the card table.)* Come on. . . .

MEDVEDENKO: It's not far . . . only four miles. Bye. . . . *(He
kisses his wife.)* Bye, Mother. . . . *(His mother-in-law gives
him her hand as if it were a chore for her; he kisses it.)* I
wouldn't have bothered anybody if it weren't for the
baby. . . . *(He waves to everybody.)* Good-bye. *(He goes
out, walking guiltily.)*

SHAMRAYEV: He'll make those four miles. He's not a general.

PAULINA *(knocks on the table)*: Come on, please. Let's not
waste any time. Supper will be ready soon. Let's play one
round.

   *(SHAMRAYEV, MASHA and DORN sit down around the
   table.)*

ARKADINA *(to TRIGORIN)*: During the long autumn evenings,
they play lotto[45] to pass the time. Look, it's an old set.
Mother used it when we were children. Shall we have a
game before supper? *(She and TRIGORIN sit at the table.)*
It's a boring game but you get used to it. *(She gives everyone three cards.)*

KONSTANTINE *(leafing through the magazine)*: He reread his
own story. But he didn't even cut the pages on mine. *(He
puts the magazine on the desk, goes to the door at the left;
passing next to his mother, he kisses her on the forehead.)*

ARKADINA: Do you want to play, Konstantine?

KONSTANTINE: No, thanks, it doesn't interest me. . . . I'm
going for a walk. *(He goes out.)*

ARKADINA: The kitty is ten kopecks. Would you put in for me,
doctor?

DORN: Your wish is my command.

MASHA: Everybody's put in. I'll begin. Twenty-two!

ARKADINA: There it is!

MASHA: Three!

DORN: So far so good.

MASHA: Everybody got three? Eight! Twenty-one! One!

SHAMRAYEV: Not so fast.

ARKADINA: They gave me such a send-off at Kharkov,[46] my last engagement. Lord, I'm still dizzy from it!

MASHA: Thirty-four!

(In the wings, the sound of a melancholy waltz.)

ARKADINA: The students gave me an ovation. Three baskets of flowers, two wreaths and this . . . *(She takes off a brooch and shoves it on the table.)*

SHAMRAYEV: That is what one calls a real object. . . .

MASHA: Fifty!

DORN: Fifty? Really?

ARKADINA: I had a stunning dress on. You can say what you like, but when it comes to dressing, you can search the world over—it's hard to find my equal.

PAULINA: Konstantine's playing. The poor boy's depressed.

SHAMRAYEV: They say terrible things about him in the papers.

MASHA: Seventy-seven!

ARKADINA: Why pay attention?

TRIGORIN: He's unlucky. He hasn't mastered a style of his own yet. It's strange, vague, he just raves on. No living characters.

MASHA: Eleven!

ARKADINA *(turning to* SORIN*)*: Peter dear, are you bored? *(Pause)* He's fast asleep.

DORN: The civil service is asleep.

MASHA: Seven! Ninety!

TRIGORIN: If I lived in a house like this, near a lake, would I have become a writer? I would have suppressed this passion in myself and devoted myself to fishing, and that's that.

MASHA: Twenty-eight!

TRIGORIN: To catch a perch or a bass . . . that's ecstasy!

DORN: And I believe in Konstantine. He has something! Without any doubt! He thinks in images; what he writes is colorful, striking. I feel something there. Only it's a pity he doesn't have a definite purpose. What he writes is simply impressionistic. And impressions don't go far enough. Irina, how do you like having a writer for a son?

ARKADINA: Imagine, I haven't read anything of his yet! I never have any time.

MASHA: Twenty-six!

(KONSTANTINE *enters quietly and goes to his desk.*)

SHAMRAYEV (*to* TRIGORIN): Trigorin, here's something that belongs to you.

TRIGORIN: What is it?

SHAMRAYEV: Konstantine killed a sea gull and you asked to have it stuffed.

TRIGORIN: I don't remember that! (*Reflecting*) I don't remember!

MASHA: Sixty-six! One!

KONSTANTINE (*opens the window and listens*): It's so dark! I don't know why I feel so strange.

ARKADINA: Konstantine, shut the window, there's a draft.

(KONSTANTINE *shuts the window.*)

MASHA: Eighty-eight!

TRIGORIN: Game!

ARKADINA (*gaily*): Bravo! Bravo!

SHAMRAYEV: Bravo!

ARKADINA: This man is always lucky in everything. (*She gets up.*) Now, come to supper. Our great man hasn't had a bite to eat all day. After supper, we'll continue. (*To her son*) Konstantine, leave your manuscripts alone and come to supper.

KONSTANTINE: No, Mama, I'm not hungry.

ARKADINA: As you like. (*She wakes* SORIN.) Peter dear, come to supper. (*Taking* SHAMRAYEV'S *arm*) I'll tell you about my ovation at Kharkov. . . .

(PAULINA *snuffs out the candles on the table, then, with* DORN'S *help, pushes* SORIN'S *wheelchair. Everybody goes out at the left.* KONSTANTINE, *seated at his desk, remains alone.*)

KONSTANTINE (*starts to write; he rushes over the preceding lines*): I talked so much about new forms, and now I feel as if I had slipped, little by little, into the conventional. (*He reads.*) "The sign on the wall proclaimed . . . a pale face framed by black hair . . ." Proclaimed, framed . . . that's flat. (*He strikes it out.*) I'll begin with the raindrop patter waking my hero, and cut the rest. The description of the moonlight is long and labored. Trigorin has found his style, it's so easy for him now. He has the broken neck of a bottle lying glittering in the moonlight and the mill wheel casting a shadow . . . there you have the moonlit night. In my stories it's a shimmering light, twinkling stars, the sound of a piano in the distance, dying away in the sweet-scented air . . . it's agony. *(Pause)* Yes, I'm more and more convinced there are neither old forms nor new ones, only what comes straight from the heart, without any concern for form. *(A knock at the window)* What's that? *(He looks out the window.)* One can't see anything. *(He opens the glass door and looks into the garden. He calls out.)* Who's there? *(He goes out; his steps are heard on the terrace. A moment passes and he comes back with* NINA.*)* Nina! Nina!

(NINA *puts her head on* KONSTANTINE'S *chest and sobs quietly.)*

KONSTANTINE *(deeply moved)*: Nina! Nina! It's you, you. . . . I felt it all day . . . I had a terrible feeling all day . . . I was so uneasy all day. *(Takes off her talma.)* [47] Oh, my dear sweet Nina, you're here. Let's not cry, we mustn't. . . .

NINA: Is anyone here?

KONSTANTINE: Nobody.

NINA: Lock the doors before they come.

KONSTANTINE: Nobody will come.

NINA: I know Arkadina is here. Lock the doors.

KONSTANTINE *(locks the door to the right and goes to the one at the left)*: This one has no key. I'll barricade it with a chair. *(He pushes an armchair in front of the door.)* Don't worry. Nobody will come in.

NINA *(looking at him intently)*: Let me look at you. *(She looks around.)* It feels so good, it's warm. This used to be the parlor. . . . Have I changed a great deal?

KONSTANTINE: Yes, you're thinner and your eyes are so much bigger. Nina, it's so strange to see you. Why wouldn't you see me? Why didn't you come before? I know you've been here for a week. I went to town several times a day to try to see you. I stood under your window like a beggar.

NINA: I was afraid you might hate me. Every night I dream that you're looking at me without recognizing me. If you only knew! Since I arrived, I've been wandering around here, near the lake. I've been right near your house several times and I didn't dare come in. Please let's sit down. (*They sit down.*) Let's sit and talk. Oh, let's talk. It's so nice, warm and comfortable in here. . . . Do you hear the wind? Turgenev said somewhere: "Happy is he who at such a time has a roof over his head, a warm place." I am a sea gull. No, that's not what I meant. (*She rubs her forehead.*) Where was I? Yes . . . Turgenev . . . "May God help all those wanderers who have no home."[48] Ah, well . . . (*She sobs.*)

KONSTANTINE: Nina, you're crying again! Nina!

NINA: It's nothing. It makes me feel better. I haven't cried for two years. Late last evening I went down into the garden to see if our stage was still standing. It was there. I began to cry for the first time in two years. It's as if a weight had lifted somewhere inside of me. You see, I'm not crying any more. (*She takes his hand.*) So, you have become a writer, and I'm an actress. Here we are, caught in the whirlpool. . . . I was a happy little child, in the morning I awoke singing, I loved you, I had dreams of glory, and now? Tomorrow, early in the morning, I'll go to Yelets,[49] third class, with the peasants, and at Yelets some ignorant merchant will pursue me with his affections. Isn't life vulgar!

KONSTANTINE: Why go to Yelets?

NINA: I signed a contract for a winter tour. It's time to go.

KONSTANTINE: Nina, I cursed you, hated you, I tore up your letters and your pictures, but every moment I knew I was attached to you forever. I can't ever stop loving you. Since I lost you forever, since they began publishing my work, my life has been unbearable. I'm suffering. My youth has suddenly left me, and I feel eighty years old. I cry out for you. I worship the ground you walk on. I see your face everywhere . . . this tender smile that lighted up the happiest moments of my life.

NINA (*disturbed*): Why does he say these things to me, why does he . . .

KONSTANTINE: I'm alone . . . no affection to warm me. I'm deathly cold. All that I write is dry, hard, colorless. Stay here with me, Nina, I beg of you, or let me go with you!

(NINA *puts her cape on swiftly.*) Nina, why? Why? For heaven's sake, Nina, Nina . . . (*He watches her dress.*)

(*Pause.*)

NINA: My carriage is near the little door. Don't come with me . . . , I'll find my way. . . . (*Through her tears*) Give me a glass of water.

KONSTANTINE (*pouring*): Where are you going now?

NINA: To town. (*Pause*) Is Arkadina here?

KONSTANTINE: Yes. My uncle was sick this week; we telegraphed her to come.

NINA: Why do you tell me you worship the ground I walk on? I ought to be killed. (*She holds onto the table.*) I'm so tired! If only I could rest . . . rest . . . (*She raises her head.*) I am a sea gull . . . no . . . I am an actress. Of course! (*She hears the laughter of* ARKADINA *and* TRIGORIN, *listens, then runs to the door at left and looks through the keyhole.*) He's here, he, too. (*Coming back to* KONSTANTINE) Of course . . . It's not important . . . Yes . . . He didn't believe in the theater, he laughed at my dreams, and little by little I stopped believing, too, and I lost my courage. And with that, the strain of love, jealousy, constant anxiety about the baby . . . I didn't know what to do with my hands, how to stand on a stage, how to use my voice. You can't imagine what it is to know you're acting badly. I'm a sea gull. No, that's not it. . . . Do you remember, one day you killed a sea gull? A man passed by there, he saw it, and took its life, accidentally, because he had nothing better to do. It's an idea for a short story. No, that's not it. . . . (*Rubs her forehead.*) What was I saying? I was talking about the theater. I'm not like that any more. I'm a good actress now. I'm good. I act with joy, I'm drunk with power on stage, and think I'm marvelous. And now that I'm sure, I can't stop walking, and thinking, thinking, feeling, my strength growing with each day. . . . Now I know, I understand, Konstantine, that the essential thing in our profession, be it acting or writing, what matters is not fame or glory or anything else I dreamed about, but how to endure, to know how to bear one's cross and to have faith. I have faith and it all doesn't hurt so much any more, and when I think about my vocation, I'm not afraid of life any more.

KONSTANTINE *(sadly)*: You have found your way, you know where you're going, while I am floating in a chaos of dreams and images, without knowing why I write and what it's for. I don't have any faith, and I don't know what my vocation is.

NINA *(listening intently)*: Shhh . . . I'm going. *Adieu.* When I've become a great actress, come and see me. Will you promise? And now . . . *(She squeezes his hand.)* It's already late. I can't stand up . . . I'm exhausted. I'm hungry.

KONSTANTINE: Stay. I'll bring you some supper. . . .

NINA: No, no . . . Don't come with me. I'll find the way. . . . So, she brought him with her. So what? When you see Trigorin, don't say anything. I love him, I love him more than ever . . . that is an idea for a story. I love him, I love him passionately. I love him desperately. How nice it was in the old days, Konstantine. Do you remember? Life was simple, warm, joyous, pure, feelings were like flowers, tender and graceful. . . . Do you remember? *(She recites.)* "Mankind and the animals, lions, eagles and partridges, horned deer, geese, spiders, silent fish inhabiting the sea, starfish and those creatures invisible to the naked eye—in short, in a word, all living things, all living things, all living things, having run their sad course, are extinct. Eons have passed since a living soul has stirred on the earth's surface. And this poor moon shines its light in vain. In the meadows the cranes no longer waken and the May beetles' murmur is silent in the limes. . . ." *(She throws herself into* KONSTANTINE's *arms and then leaves, running out through the open glass door.)*

KONSTANTINE *(after a pause)*: They mustn't see her in the garden, mustn't tell Mama. That might upset Mama. . . . *(For two minutes he silently tears up all of his manuscripts and throws them under the table. Then he opens the door at the right and goes out.)*

DORN *(trying to open the door)*: Strange. The door seems locked. *(He enters and puts the armchair in place.)* Obstacle course.

(Enter ARKADINA, PAULINA, *behind them* YAKOV, *carrying bottles, and* MASHA, *then* SHAMRAYEV *and* TRIGORIN.)

ARKADINA: Put the bottles of red wine and the beer for Boris right here on the table. We're going to gamble and drink. Places, gentlemen.

PAULINA (*to* YAKOV): Bring the tea right away. (*She lights the candles and sits at the card table.*)

SHAMRAYEV (*leading* TRIGORIN *to the cupboard*): Here's the object I was mentioning a while ago. (*He takes out the stuffed sea gull.*) Here's what you ordered.

TRIGORIN (*looking at the sea gull*): I don't remember! (*A moment of reflection*) I don't remember!

(*In the wings, a shot rings out. Everyone shudders.*)

ARKADINA (*frightened*): What's that?

DORN: Nothing. Something must have exploded in my medicine kit. Don't worry. (*He goes out and returns a moment later.*) That was what it was. A bottle of ether blew up. (DORN *hums.*) "Again I stand before you, enchanted . . ." [50]

ARKADINA (*sitting down in front of the table*): Oh, how frightened I was. It reminded me of . . . (*She covers her face with her hands.*) Everything went black around me. . . .

DORN (*leafing through a journal; to* TRIGORIN): Two months ago, there was an article, a letter from America, and I'd like to ask you about it. . . . (*He takes* TRIGORIN *around the waist toward the footlights.*) It's a question that interests me a great deal. . . . (*Lower, sotto voce*) Get Irina out of here. The fact is that Konstantine has shot himself. . . .

CURTAIN

AFTERWORD

Seventy years after its first performances, *The Sea Gull* has become one of the world's best loved plays. People of the theater, actors and directors, approach this play with love and awe. It is a work intimately concerned with the creative process and the creative imagination: writers and actors see in it a mirror of their own lives. Like all great works of art, *The Sea Gull* contains mysteries and ambiguities that can never be fully resolved. There is no single way to interpret *The Sea Gull,* and a measure of its importance as a play is the mystery at the heart of its conception. Also, and for good reasons, the play rarely succeeds totally on stage—great love breeds overweening passion and more crimes are committed in the name of passionate involvement than in other realms. It is exceedingly difficult to maintain a proper balance of all the elements in the play.

Essentially *The Sea Gull* is a play of character. Its ten major characters are of almost equal importance. They represent a curious cross section of life, artistic and mundane. As does the title of the play, each of the characters has a symbolic role and represents an alternative in life. Konstantine Treplev is the young writer seeking for a valid form of creation. Boris Trigorin is the established writer, obsessed with his work, successful but not great, and fully cognizant of his limitations. Nina Zarechnaya is the young actress who aspires to a difficult art and learns that the secret of her métier is not genius but endurance, that all artists and performers must learn to endure in their lives as well as in their professions. Irina Arkadina is the successful artiste, a woman who feeds on the adulation of her entourage and who somehow manages to triumph despite her ruthless egotism.

These four characters form the backbone of the play. Konstantine founders as Nina finds strength. Trigorin is weak but basks in Arkadina's strength. Konstantine loves his mother as he does Nina, desperately. Nina falls in love with Trigorin and he uses her for his own literary devices, as a means to knowledge, discarding her and returning to Arkadina when he has had enough of her. The love Nina and Arkadina bear toward Trigorin helps destroy Konstantine.

These four characters are intimately linked throughout the play. Nina aspires to Arkadina's place in the world of the theater. By the end of the play we realize that she may even become a better actress, though she, too, may succumb to the false brilliance of the climate she inhabits. Konstantine could never become another Trigorin. His genius is more inspired, his talent less controllable. Trigorin is a professional, Konstantine an inspired amateur who loves his métier too much to be canny enough to succeed in it. Here we have two generations: the established and the aspiring. Each of the characters mirrors the others. They are played off against each other in both their loves and their art. Nina's sensibilities are wounded by Trigorin. She learns, as Arkadina must have learned before her, that love is a matter of possession and strength. The women who have this knowledge are stronger than their men.

The other characters mesh fascinatingly with the creative foursome at the forefront of the play. Masha represents the dispossessed, always wondering about the true nature of her identity. She is most probably Paulina's daughter by Dorn. Although she never speculates about her origin consciously, she is aware of a mystery, and her tragedy is that she can never find her niche in life. Her life is symbolized in the unhappy love she holds for Konstantine and the unfulfilled marriage she makes with Medvedenko. She tells her story to Trigorin: if he should write about it, there might be a purpose to her existence. Masha is as unfulfilled as her mother, Paulina, who has loved Dr. Dorn for some thirty years, remaining faithful to him as well as married to her boorish husband, Shamrayev. Masha and Paulina are muted echoes of Nina and Arkadina. Masha loses Konstantine to Nina. Paulina loses Dorn to the world at large. Medvedenko, the schoolteacher, the comic foil of the play, is a kindly man, loyal and dependable, if pedantic and limited, insensitive to the needs of a woman like Masha. He loves his wife and child and never senses the truth of his life. Shamrayev is as egotistical and hard as Arkadina and is the only character of the play evenly matched with her. Shamrayev and Paulina are as absurdly mated as Medvedenko and Masha. Neither of the men could ever comprehend the frustrated yearning of his wife's heart.

Dorn, the doctor, and Sorin, the man of the law courts—the first sensitive and worldly, the second now old and doddering, trying pitifully to indulge in the creature comforts of life to convince himself that he has lived—are also intimately involved in the play. Dorn is the would-be artist, the man of fine sensibilities, the only one capable of appreciating Konstantine's potential worth. Sorin is the would-be writer or public speaker, who never did anything with his life and lives on fine-cushioned regrets.

The Sea Gull is an enmeshed web of unfulfilled relationships. Dorn will never legalize his relationship with Paulina. Sorin will never feel he has lived. Shamrayev can never satisfy his thirst for nouveau-riche renown. Trigorin can never feel he is a great writer. Konstantine, most deprived of all, losing his mother's love, never quite able to comprehend his need of her, abandoned by Nina for his mother's lover, without a strong enough desire to live, without the compulsiveness that makes an artist through habit, loses his faith and commits suicide. Paulina can never possess Dorn exclusively, Masha will never know Konstantine's love, Arkadina can never possess Trigorin fully and Nina loses him to a more comfortable relationship with her rival. Yet, in all of this loss, Arkadina and Nina do have a measure of triumph. Arkadina never admits defeat and she is saved from being a villain by her positive yea-saying to the trivialities of life. Cornered, in danger of losing Trigorin to an immature love, she fights like a savage animal to maintain her status quo. Her solipsism is admirable.

Of all the characters, it is Nina who learns from life. She loses Trigorin and her child but she gains a métier. She begins the play as an awkward, extravagant young actress with a minimal talent but by the end she has learned enough of life to throw herself into her art totally. She is at the forefront of the play. Trigorin conceives his story of the sea gull for her— the victim, plucked from her state of innocence by the passing writer, deflowered by life, sacrificed, disillusioned before her time. But what Trigorin could never have known was that Nina would survive him and go on to become an artist. The sea gull is an ironic symbol, for it is really Konstantine who is sacrificed to the egotism of those who surround him. Nina survives the symbol as Konstantine cannot.

Too much has been made of the poetic quality of *The Sea Gull* and it has thus often been performed as in a trance. Chekhov himself urged the actors of the first production—in St. Petersburg in 1896 at the Alexandrinski Theater—to play the play naturally: ". . . The essential thing, my friends—is to avoid the theatrical . . . everything must be simple . . . completely simple . . . These are simple, ordinary people. . . ." Of course, Chekhov was reacting to a declamatory style of acting prevalent at the time, but this same admonition retains its validity today. It would seem to us that Chekhov meant that the rhythm and the tone of ordinary life should be respected when performing the play: life is both absurdly comic and tragic, almost at the same moment, and the play would benefit enormously from a respect for the changes of mood which constitute everyday existence. It is true that *The Sea Gull* is a poetic play, but its poetry is of the essence and in its implications rather than in the performing surface. Like all of Chekhov's comedies—and this is the name he chose for them —*The Sea Gull* is an amalgam of a tragic sensibility expressed in terms of the comic absurdity so abundant in modern life. The essential problem in realizing the play scenically is the maintaining of as many of its ironies as evidently as possible. Each of the characters must play off and balance with the others.

For instance, when Stanislavski first played Trigorin in 1898, at the newly formed Art Theater of Moscow, he interpreted him as somewhat of a dandy. Chekhov, who was given to utterances in trenchant, laconic images, insisted that he wear threadbare clothes. He praised Stanislavski's performance but maintained that it wasn't the character he wrote. When pressed to comment, he replied: "He wears baggy checked pants and has holes in his shoes." Chekhov showed Stanislavski how Trigorin smoked a cigar. The charade proposed by Chekhov to Stanislavski abundantly justifies the irony that Nina and Arkadina should have fallen in love with such a man. When Stanislavski played Trigorin in white trousers and bathing slippers, an irony was missed, namely, that they had fallen in love with his image and were unable to see him as he really was. Chekhov seems to be suggesting throughout his work that love is a mysterious force that cannot choose the object of its passion. *The Sea Gull* makes the point clearly that love is both the salvation and the destruction of a human being's existence and that art is in some mysterious way the salvation of those who create and that they hoard their love and channel it into their work. It is the Ninas, the Trigorins and the Arkadinas who live and endure. Be they great or only second rate, it matters not, for they have conquered the secret of life in both their lives and their professions. The rest are but dissatisfied spectators of the world, as are Dorn and Sorin, or servants of those they love, such as Medvedenko and Paulina, boorish tyrants such as Shamrayev and sacrificed lovers such as Masha and Konstantine.

Certain aspects of *The Sea Gull* were never explained by Chekhov and will probably always remain ambiguous. Konstantine's play is either a foolish prose poem by a very young writer or else a modern conception with a spark of genius. We can be sure that it is unsophisticated, but we cannot be sure it does not present a new and accurate vision of life. It may be interpreted by Nina as a misunderstood work by a very young genius or, more plausibly, as the ravings of an irritated young man. At any rate, it is an awkward piece of work and it does embarrass those who first listen to it. People of the theater tend to regard it with awe and to misunderstand its ambiguities and sonorities as those of genius.

It will also never be abundantly clear whether Nina has a great talent or not. Arkadina is not a great actress, either, but she has conquered her métier. She is a personality even more than she is an actress. Trigorin is a professional writer of the second rank who is obsessed by his inferiority to Turgenev and Tolstoy, but we can never be certain of the true worth of his work. For we know these artists as people and Chekhov was infinitely wise in choosing fascinating people who were also artists of the second rank. In the theater it is very difficult to portray great artists. We may only sense their greatness and we are only concerned with them as people and not as artists. And the truth Chekhov maintained is that these highly creative people are very highly destructive in their own lives, as silly as anyone else, trivial as children, tragically adolescent and abundantly capable of joy and sorrow.

Legend has it that Noel Coward was irritated by *The Sea Gull* with its symbol neatly stuffed over the mantelpiece of the last act, silently proclaiming: "I am the title, I am the title, I am the title!" *The Sea Gull* contains more flaws in its mechanism than any of the three plays that followed it. It was the work of a writer who was in a state of transition and searching for the secret of his own métier. There is too much exposition. The fourth act contains long sections recounting what has happened to Nina during the time she ran away with Trigorin. All of the events as they unfold before us occur before and after the major moments of the play, almost as they do in classical French tragedy. We never see Trigorin and Nina in their life together.

The tone of the play is frequently ambiguous. Konstantine's play in the first act, Arkadina's two scenes in the third, first with her son, placating and pleading with him not to kill himself, and then with her lover, placating and pleading with him not to leave her, are certainly serious scenes. Yet they contain moments of the most absurd comedy, of the rhythm of farce. The two major scenes of the third act (one might even wish to include the preceding vignette, with Sorin begging Arkadina to give Konstantine money) are so richly comic that they very nearly threaten to upset the balance of the play, and it is usually in these scenes that performances go haywire.

Yet how subtle and beautiful the juxtapositions of the play are! Act One begins with Medvedenko and Masha. She is dressed in black, in mourning for her life. Act Four begins with the same two characters, now married, now both mourning for their lives. In Act Three Sorin first asks Arkadina to give Konstantine money; a moment later, Konstantine asks her to give money to support Sorin in the country. The lotto game in Act Four, with its numbers spit forth by Masha like ironic commentaries on life, is beautifully constructed in staccato outbursts. Konstantine wanders in and out of the scene like a sputtering shadow. And Trigorin, lucky as always, wins the lotto game and symbolically closes Konstantine out after Konstantine has refused to play the game—of life. So much of the action of the play is both realistic, plausible and yet ingeniously symbolic. At the end, Nina and Konstantine are momentarily reunited, brought back to the scene of their literary crime, she to live again the moments of the beginning of her awareness of life, he to realize how much he has lost. All of the characters are brought back to the first scene of the play. Trigorin comes to see the stage again and note local color for the details of his forthcoming short story.

Along the tenuous line of the play there have been many comic outbursts. Arkadina has been pitted against Shamrayev, Sorin against Dorn, Masha against Medvedenko. The play ends *in medias res,* at a seemingly trivial moment of life, after dinner, in the drawing room. The characters resume their lives and only Dorn knows that Konstantine has shot himself and that their lives have thus irrevocably changed. We are suspended at a moment when the symbolic action of the play is over. Unwieldy, of many moods and many three-dimensional characters, *The Sea Gull* is a difficult, emotion-charged, exuberant, brilliantly felt work of art. To know it is to love it, to be attracted and mystified by it, perhaps as Trigorin is by Nina, for at the base of the play is the mystery of human love and attraction. "Is it the magic of the lake?" asks Dorn. There is so much love and so little wisdom in the world. Thus we have one of the most accurate visions of modern life by one of the finest sensibilities ever to have attempted to make life palpitate meaningfully upon the stage.

NOTES

First performance: October 17, 1896, Alexandrinski Theater, St. Petersburg. First published: in RUSSIAN THOUGHT, December, 1896. First performance at the Moscow Art Theater: December 17, 1898.

1. In the original text: six versts. A verst equals .66 mile. Six versts equal 3.96 miles.

2. Nikolai Alexeyevich Nekrasov (1821–1878), a Russian lyric poet; poet laureate of the poor.

3. Eleonora Duse (1859–1924), Italian actress who has come to symbolize the utmost refinement in the art of acting.

4. Alexandre Dumas fils' *Camille* (1852), dramatized from his novel. One of the great roles for a flamboyant and subtle actress.

5. A Russian play by B. M. Markevich (1822–1884). Chekhov wrote a parody of the play, which remains unpublished. It represented the kind of slipshod drama that Chekhov particularly disliked.

6. The reaction of Guy de Maupassant (1850–1893) to the Eiffel Tower came at the end of his life, for it was built in 1889 on the site of the Champ-de-Mars.

7. The original expression, *Kievski meshchanin,* refers to someone in the lower middle class. It is a pejorative idiom, with the connotation of narrow-mindedness and philistinism easily attached to it.

8. Count Leo Nikolayevich Tolstoi (1828–1910) did not particularly admire the plays of Chekhov, though he had a certain fondness for the one-act farce *The Boor.*

9. Emile Zola (1840–1902) would represent an earthier talent than Trigorin's. Though his reputation in Chekhov's time might have been on a par with Tolstoy's, his work hardly shares that distinction today. The kind of realism he aimed for in his work would have been admired by Trigorin.

10. Heine's *"Zwei Grenadieren"* is known by the music Schumann composed for it, just the sort of bravura piece Sorin would love.

11. This kind of aroma-rama, a most modern touch, helps to make Konstantine's play seem more ridiculous than need be, and yet it lends a kind of magic realism to the proceedings that also makes the play fascinating.

12. A quote from a poem by Nekrasov: "She Had a Heavy Cross to Bear," 1856.

13. A quote from a poem by V. I. Krassov: "Stanzas," 1840.

14. A rich agricultural center in the Ukraine. Gogol was born nearby.

15. Rasplyuyev is the Sganarelle to Krechinski's Don Juan in *Krechinski's Wedding* (1854), a play by Alexander Suk-hovo-Kobylin (1817–1903). For a description of the comedy, see Marc Slonim's *Russian Theatre from the Empire to the Soviets* (New York: Collier Books, 1961), pp. 72–73.

16. Prov Sadovski (1818–1872) was the founder of a theatrical dynasty of actors who were associated with the Moscow Maly Theater. He was discovered by the actor Shchepkin and became famous for his interpretations of Molière, Gogol and Ostrovski.

17. The original text is a garbled Latin expression: *"De gustibus aut bene aut nihil,"* which in turn is a confusion of two other expressions: *"De gustibus non disputandum est"* (There is no disputing tastes) and *"De mortuis aut bene aut nihil"* (Say nothing but good about the dead). Chekhov slyly suggests thereby that Shamrayev is not a very cultivated man. Elsewhere in the plays, Kulygin (*The Three Sisters*) spouts Latin expressions ad nauseam and Natasha (also *The Three Sisters*) speaks atrocious schoolgirl French.

18. The Russian translation distorts the Shakespearean original a bit. Konstantine's response in Russian is more direct: "Why did you give yourself up to vice, look for love in an abyss of crime?" He is, of course, referring to Arkadina's

liaison with Trigorin and she does not miss the cruel allusion he is making, for they are playing at being Hamlet and Gertrude in their own lives. Arkadina hated his father.

19. The "partridges" *(kuropatki)* seem a little out of place with the other impressive beasties; it is impossible to know whether this was an effect calculated to produce unexpected humor in the sophisticated.

20. Also known as "ignis fatuus" or "friar's lantern," a flitting phosphorescent light seen at night, chiefly over marshy ground, and supposed to be due to spontaneous combustion of gas from decomposed organic matter.

21. Konstantine's play may have been an opportunity for Chekhov to satirize the work of the Symbolist-Decadent school, which had just come to prominence at the time.

22. The red spots were first created for the Moscow Art Theater production by I. I. Geppert, the stage manager, an effect which had already been used in another play. Stanislavski and Nemirovich-Danchenko took the stage directions of Chekhov very seriously and began an entire tradition of a background of meaningful and literal sounds to accompany the action as a form of realistic musical obbligato. This tradition, when relentlessly practiced, often obscures what is happening on stage and detracts from the subtle values of the stage moment.

23. The original reference is to the Latin Jupiter, from a Latin proverb: "Jupiter, you're angry; therefore, you're wrong." Dorn is a very cultivated gentleman. Arkadina is a very excitable woman.

24. Medvedenko is a gentle and unconsciously humorous pedant.

25. In French in the original text; a universal theater expression meaning the young leading male role.

26. An old superstition states that a sudden unpredictable silence in a conversation, especially at twenty minutes before or past the hour, means that an angel is hovering and passing overhead. This is the climactic moment of the first act. Chekhov's plays are filled with indications that a pause in the stage action should take place. As they were originally conceived, the pauses were of many different kinds. A fascinating discussion of them may be found in Stanislavski's production book (London: Dennis Dobson, Ltd., 1952), pp. 113–116.

One of the most expressive devices which Stanislavsky makes use of in the play with particular frequency and variety is the pause. According to Nemirovich-Danchenko "a way was being discovered in the mise-en-scènes of *The Sea Gull* for rendering the pauses both vital and dynamic; they were either used to convey the feeling of relaxation fron the tension of a previous scene, or to prepare the way for a coming emotional climax, or again to maintain a long silence charged with dramatic significance. . . . A pause that was not dead, but capable of . . . holding the audience in a state of suspense, or deepening the emotions of the characters, or accompanied by sound effects deepening the mood." To Stanislavsky a pause never means a total absence of scenic action: it is merely one of its special forms, a form which is usually filled with other scenic elements, such as gesture, timing, movement or musical sounds. The pauses, above all, serve the purpose of laying special emphasis on big scenic moments while their varied use causes that slowing up of the rhythm of the performance which the producer wanted to effect and which is characteristic of the scenic style of the production. . . . The duration of Stanislavsky's pauses differs considerably: their amplitude (to use Stanislavsky's term) varies from a tiny pause, a little pause, a pause of five seconds, ten seconds, fifteen seconds, ten plus five seconds, ten plus ten seconds, fifteen plus, a long pause and a very long pause. Their number (over one hundred) and their role in the scenic movement and in the conduct of the dialogue is exceptionally great. . . . In some individual cases, the pause, being filled with an important (from the point of view of the advancement of the plot) action of a character, revealing his or her intense emotional state of mind, renders the given scene particularly significant by the very fact of concentrating the attention of the audience on this action. . . . On other occasions the pause serves the purpose of setting off the dramatic character of a situation, of compelling the audience to dwell on some scene which is characteristic of the life of the characters in the play; of emphasizing some specially significant gesture or some special piece of acting of the performer; of underlining a moment in the play which, from the point of view of the plot, is of particular importance. . . .

The angel of silence is a very long pause and allows all of the characters to become aware of the very first instant of Trigorin's and Nina's incipient relationship.

27. Siebel's aria from Gounod's *Faust*. Dorn's humming generally has a very specific comment to make. Here he is pooh-poohing Masha's melodramatic assertions. It is very similar to our use of "Hearts and Flowers" to ridicule someone who is making a fool of himself with ridiculous aspirations.

28. Chekhov's characters are fond of French expressions. She fancies herself *comme il faut* (correct) in all matters of chic.

29. Maupassant's narratives have remained fashionable reading although they are no longer admired today as much as they were at that time. This one is a macabre tale included in *La Maison Tellier* (1881); *Sur l'eau* was also the title of some notes and sketches that he wrote after a cruise in the Mediterranean. Arkadina was probably reading the tale.

30. Many passages in Chekhov's work have been cut for artistic reasons or because of altercations with the censor. Specific reference to Arkadina's liaison with Trigorin were toned down to pacify the censor. This little passage, omitted from the original published version, is so pleasant that it adds a lovely stage moment and was effectively performed by the APA company—which is why it is included here.

31. Edward Gibbon (1737–1794), the English historian of the decline and fall of the Roman Empire; Herbert Spencer (1820–1903), the evolutionary philosopher, predating Darwin. Medvedenko reads voraciously but without much discrimination.

32. An old-fashioned nerve sedative as common then as aspirin is today and with the same all-purpose placebo usage.

33. A garden shrub having small, fragrant purple flowers.

34. Poprishchin is the hero of Gogol's *Diary of a Madman*.

35. Turgenev (1818–1883) wrote his novel *Fathers and Children* (known mostly as *Fathers and Sons*) in 1862; it still has the reputation of a masterpiece. Turgenev's reputation is especially high abroad and it is to Chekhov's credit that his literary allusions are so subtly and accurately drawn. Trigorin lacked Turgenev's "finesse."

36. The original reference is to Agamemnon and being drawn along in a chariot. The antiquated reference is no longer readily actable.

37., 38. These were two of the explicit passages cut by the censor.

39. A nineteenth-century French melodrama, which has been forgotten. Chekhov's fondness for obscure French works led him to use one as partial basis for one of his own one-act plays, *The Wedding*.

40. One of the best hotels in Moscow until a few years ago.

41. The owner's name is used as an address.

42. Actually a pood. One pood equals 36.113 pounds.

43. Dorn comments on Sorin's somber mood by singing an old song.

44. Pushkin's (1799–1837) "The Sea Maiden" ("Rusalka") is a romantic poem. The "undine" becomes one of the central images of *Uncle Vanya*.

45. Lotto is old-fashioned bingo, but the same principle holds: five squares in a row must be covered. The counters placed over the numbers in lotto are generally made of wood. Since nothing in Chekhov's plays is without significance, it would be interesting to know why the numbers that Masha calls off were chosen. They seem to be ironic, abstract commentaries on Arkadina's boasting.

46. One of the major cities of the Ukraine.

47. A cape with a hood, named for the celebrated French tragedian Talma (1763–1826). One of Talma's great contributions to theater custom was the insistence on accuracy of costume. It is also nicely ironic for Nina to appear to Konstantine in such a cape.

48. Quotes from Turgenev's novel *Rudin*.

49. A Russian town south of Moscow.

50. See note 13.

Uncle Vanya

Scenes from Country Life in Four Acts

CHARACTERS

SEREBRYAKOV, ALEXANDER,
   a retired professor

YELENA,
   his wife, age 27

SOFIA (SONYA),
   his daughter by a first marriage

VOINITSKI, MARIA,
   widow of an important official, mother of the professor's
   first wife

VOINITSKI, IVAN (VANYA),
   her son

ASTROV, MIKHAIL,
   a doctor

TELYEGIN, ILYA (WAFFLES),
   a poor landlord

MARINA,
   an old nurse

A WORKMAN

The scene is SEREBRYAKOV'*s country estate.*

ACT ONE

> *The garden. We see the terrace and part of the garden. Under an old poplar tree in the pathway, a table is set for tea. A bench and some chairs. A guitar lies on one of the chairs next to the bench. Not far from the table is a swing. It is getting on toward three o'clock. It is a gray day.*

MARINA (*a stout old lady, sits by the samovar, knitting a stocking;* ASTROV *walks up and down in front of her;* MARINA *fills his glass*): Have something to drink, my dear.

ASTROV (*accepting the glass*): I don't really feel like it.

MARINA: You might like a little vodka, perhaps?

ASTROV: No. I don't drink vodka every day. It's stifling here. (*Pause*) Marina, how long have we known each other?

MARINA (*thinking about it*): How long? God help me to remember. . . . You came here, to the country . . . when was it? Sonya's mother was still alive. You came to us for two winters in her time. . . . Well, then, it was eleven years ago. (*Pondering*) And it may even be longer. . . .

ASTROV: Have I changed much since then?

MARINA: Oh, yes. You were young and handsome then. Now you're getting older. You're not so handsome any more. And what's more, you drink vodka.

ASTROV: Yes . . . In the course of the last ten years I've become another man. You know why? I'm overworked, Marina. I'm on my feet from morning till night, I get no rest. And late at night I lie under the blankets afraid I'll get dragged off to see a patient. In all the time we've known each other, I've never had one free day. No wonder I'm growing old. And my life is boring, stupid and grubby . . . it drags you down. I'm surrounded by misfits; you live around them for two or three years and without your knowing it, you become a misfit, too. There's no escaping it. *(Twirling his moustache)* You see I've grown a big moustache . . . a silly moustache. I've become a character, Marina. Oh, as far as I know I haven't become stupid; thank God I still have my wits about me, but I don't feel things any more. I don't know how, but I don't care about anything. I don't want anything. I don't love anybody. You're probably the only one I really love. *(Kisses her on the head.)* I had a nurse like you when I was a child.

MARINA: Would you like something to eat?

ASTROV: No. I went to Malitskoye the third week of Lent, during the epidemic. It was typhus. People were lying side by side in the huts . . . such filth, stench and smoke. There were calves running around on the floor among the sick . . . and pigs right there. I had my hands full all day. I never sat down, didn't have anything to eat or drink, and when I came home I still couldn't rest. They brought in a railroad man. I put him on the table to operate on him and he went and died on me under the chloroform. So, just when I didn't want it to happen, I started to feel things again and my conscience bothered me, as if I had deliberately killed him. I sat down and shut my eyes . . . and this is what went through my mind: I wondered if the people who live one or two hundred years from now, the ones we're paving the way for now, would remember us with a kind word. You know they won't, Marina!

MARINA: The people won't remember, but God will.

ASTROV: Thank you for that. That was well said.

(Enter VOINITSKI.*)*

VOINITSKI *(comes out of the house; he fell asleep after lunch and looks a little rumpled; sits on the bench and straightens his fancy necktie)*: Yes . . . *(A pause)* Ah, yes . . .

ASTROV: Sleep well?

VOINITSKI: Yes . . . very well. *(He yawns.)* Ever since the professor has been living here with his wife, life has been out of joint. We have no time to sleep, we eat all sorts of spicy things for lunch and dinner, we drink wine. . . . It's not healthy! We never used to have a free moment, Sonya and I worked—you can say that again. And now only Sonya works—I eat, drink and sleep. . . . It's no good!

MARINA *(shaking her head):* Such goings on! The professor gets up at noon and the samovar whistles all morning while everybody waits for him. When they weren't here, we always used to eat around noon, like everybody else, and now we have to wait till nearly seven. At night the professor reads and writes, and suddenly he rings around two o'clock in the morning. . . . What do you think, my dear? He wants tea! Wake up the servants! Start up the samovar! Such goings on!

ASTROV: Do you think they'll stay on here for long?

VOINITSKI *(whistles):* A hundred years. The professor has decided to settle down here.

MARINA: You see. The samovar has been out on the table for two hours now, and they've gone for a walk.

VOINITSKI: Calm yourself. They're coming, they're coming. . . .

(Voices are heard; from the other end of the garden, returning from their walk, come SEREBRYAKOV, YELENA, SONYA and TELYEGIN.)

SEREBRYAKOV: Excellent, excellent . . . A beautiful view.

TELYEGIN: It's remarkable, your excellency.

SONYA: Tomorrow we're going into the woods, Papa. Want to come?

VOINITSKI: Let's have some tea, ladies and gentlemen!

SEREBRYAKOV: My friends, would you be so kind as to have my tea brought to me in my study? I still have much to accomplish today.

SONYA: You'll love the woods. . . .

(YELENA, SEREBRYAKOV and SONYA go into the house. TELYEGIN goes to the table and sits down near MARINA.)

VOINITSKI: It is hot and stifling, but our renowned professor is wearing an overcoat and galoshes, with an umbrella and gloves.

ASTROV: Which means he takes care of himself.

VOINITSKI: How lovely she is! How beautiful! In all my life I've never seen a more beautiful woman.

TELYEGIN: Whenever I ride in the countryside, Marina, or walk in the shade of your garden, or gaze at this table, I know the meaning of bliss! The weather is enchanting, the birds are singing, we live in peace and harmony . . . what more could we want? *(Accepting the tea he is served)* I thank you from the bottom of my heart!

VOINITSKI *(dreamily)*: What eyes . . . wonderful woman!

ASTROV: Tell us something, Ivan.

VOINITSKI *(listlessly)*: What shall I tell you?

ASTROV: Isn't anything new?

VOINITSKI: No. All old hat. I'm just as I have been, or worse yet. I'm getting lazy; I just go about grumbling like an old bear. My old parrot of a mother, *Maman,* is still squawking about the emancipation of women; she has one foot in the grave, and the other in those smart notebooks of hers that pontificate about the dawn of a new life.

ASTROV: And the professor?

VOINITSKI: As usual, the professor sits in his study and writes from early morning until late at night. "His mind straining, his brow knitting, his odes he's writing, and there's no praise forthcoming." [1] Poor paper! He really ought to be writing his autobiography. There's a marvelous subject! A retired professor, you understand, an old fossil, a professorial rat—he has gout, rheumatism, migraine headaches; his liver is swollen with jealousy and envy—and this little rat lives on the estate of his first wife, lives there against his will because he hasn't enough in his pockets to live in the city. He's forever complaining about his misfortune, though if the truth be known, he is extraordinarily fortunate. *(Nervously)* Just think of it, what good fortune! The son of an ordinary sexton, a scholarship student; he gets his teaching degree and becomes a professor, and is now known as his excellency, son-in-law of a senator, and so on and so forth. All that is unimportant, however. But listen to this: this man, who for twenty-five years has been reading and writing about art, and in all that time has never understood anything about art, has for twenty-five years been hashing over other people's ideas about realism, naturalism and all that nonsense; for twenty-five years he has been reading and writing about what intelligent people already know and about what stupid people don't want to know—which means that for twenty-five years he's been taking nothing and making nothing out of it. And with it all, what conceit! What pretention! He retired, and no living soul knows anything at all about him, he's so completely unknown; which means that for twenty-five years he's been trespassing on other people's property. And look at him—he struts around like some kind of god on earth!

ASTROV: And you envy him.

VOINITSKI: Yes, I envy him! The success he has with women! No Don Juan ever had such complete success. His first wife, my sister, a beautiful, gentle creature, pure as that blue sky up there, noble, generous, who had more admirers than he had pupils—she loved him as only pure angels can love beings as pure and beautiful as themselves. My mother, his mother-in-law, adores him still, and he still puts the terror of the Lord into her. His second wife, a beautiful and clever woman—you just saw her—married him when he was already old, and she gave him her youth, her beauty, her freedom, her brilliance. And for what? Why?

ASTROV: Is she faithful to the professor?

VOINITSKI: Unfortunately, yes.

ASTROV: Why unfortunately?

VOINITSKI: Because that faithfulness is false to the marrow. Full of sound and fury but no logic. To betray an old husband whom one cannot bear—that is immoral; to seek to stifle one's passing youth and one's emotions—that is not immoral.

TELYEGIN (*in a tearful voice*): Vanya, I don't like it when you say such things. Really, you must know that he who deceives his wife or husband is of course an unfaithful person and may very well betray his own country!

VOINITSKI (*annoyed*): Dry up, Waffles!

TELYEGIN: Pardon me, Vanya. My own wife betrayed me with another man on the day after our marriage, just because of my unattractive appearance. But I did not forsake my duties. I still love her and I am faithful to her. I help her as much as I can and have given her my possessions for the education of the children she had by the other man. I have lost my happiness, but I have kept my pride. And she? Her youth has already passed her by, her beauty, according to the laws of nature, has faded, and the other man is dead. . . . What has she got left?

(Enter SONYA and YELENA; a moment later, MARIA, with a book; she sits and reads; she is served tea and she drinks it without looking up.)

SONYA *(in a hurry, to MARINA)*: Some peasants have come, Marina. Go see what they want, and I'll tend to the tea.

(She pours some tea. MARINA leaves. YELENA takes her tea and drinks it; then she sits in the swing.)

ASTROV *(to YELENA)*: I've come to see your husband. You wrote to say he was very ill, rheumatism and what all, and now it seems he's in the pink of health.

YELENA: Yesterday evening he was quite broken up, complaining about a pain in his legs, but today he seems all right.

ASTROV: And I came all this way as fast as I could. Well, so what, it's not the first time. Just for that, I'll stay with you until tomorrow morning and get some good sleep at least —*quantum satis*[2]

SONYA: How wonderful. You so seldom spend a night with us. You probably haven't had any dinner.

ASTROV: No, I haven't.

SONYA: Then you can stay and have dinner with us then. These days, we dine at around seven. *(She drinks.)* The tea is cold!

TELYEGIN: The temperature of the samovar has diminished considerably.

YELENA: That's all right, Ivan, we'll drink it cold.

TELYEGIN: Pardon me . . . I'm not Ivan, I am Ilya Ilyich— Ilya Ilyich Telyegin—or, as some people call me because of my pock-marked face, Waffles. I baptized Sonya, over there, and his excellency, your husband, knows me very well. I'm living with you now on this estate, and if you deign to take notice, I have dinner with you every day.

SONYA: Ilya Telyegin is our helper, our right hand. *(Tenderly)* Give me your glass, Godfather, I'll pour you some more tea.

MARIA: Ah!

SONYA: What is it, Grandmother?

MARIA: I forgot to tell Alexander . . . I must be losing my memory. Today I received a letter from Pavel in Kharkov; he sent his new pamphlet.

ASTROV: Is it interesting?

MARIA: Interesting, but somewhat strange. He refutes what he himself defended seven years ago. It's awful!

VOINITSKI: There's nothing awful about it at all. Drink your tea, *Maman*.

MARIA: But I want to talk!

VOINITSKI: We've been talking for fifty years now, talking and reading pamphlets. It's time we stopped.

MARIA: Why is it objectionable to you to listen when I speak? Excuse me, Jean, but in the last year you've changed so much that I positively don't know you. You were a man of definite convictions, an enlightened person. . . .

VOINITSKI: Oh, yes! I was an enlightened person, and I shed light on nobody. . . . *(A pause)* I was an enlightened person. A positively poisonous pleasantry! I'm forty-seven years old now. Until last year I tried, just like you, purposely to obscure my eyes with all your pedantry, so as not to see life as it really is—and I thought I was doing the right thing. But now, if you only knew! I can't sleep nights, I'm so annoyed and resentful at how stupidly I've let time slip by, when I might have had everything that is now denied me in my old age!

SONYA: How boring you are, Uncle Vanya!

MARIA *(to her son)*: It's as though you were denying your former convictions. They're not to blame, it's you. You've forgotten that convictions by themselves are nothing, so much dead wood. You've got to do something about them.

VOINITSKI: Do something? Not everybody can be a perpetual-motion[3] writing machine like your Herr Professor.

MARIA: What do you mean by that?

SONYA *(imploring)*: Grandmother! Uncle Vanya! Please!

VOINITSKI: I'll shut up. I'll shut up and I'll say I'm sorry.

(Pause.)

YELENA: What lovely weather we're having today . . . not too hot. . . .

(Pause.)

VOINITSKI: Lovely weather to hang oneself . . .

(TELYEGIN *strums on his guitar.* MARINA *goes around the back of the house and calls the chickens.)*

MARINA: Here, chick, chick, chick . . .

SONYA: What did the peasants want?

MARINA: Same as usual; they're interested in that piece of fallow land. Here, chick, chick, chick . . .

SONYA: Which one are you after?

MARINA: The speckly one has gone off with her chicks; the crows might get them. . . .

(*She goes out.* TELYEGIN *plays a polka; everybody listens silently; a* WORKMAN *enters.)*

WORKMAN: Is the doctor here? *(To* ASTROV) Excuse me, Dr. Astrov, we've come over for you.

ASTROV: Who wants me?

WORKMAN: The people at the factory.

ASTROV *(annoyed)*: Thank you very much. What can I do? I have to go. . . . *(Looks for his cap.)* It's annoying, damn it.

SONYA: That's really too bad. . . . Come back and eat after you're finished at the factory.

ASTROV: No, it'll be too late. Now where? Where, oh, where did I put it? *(To the* WORKMAN) In that case, would you be so good as to get me a glass of vodka, my good fellow? *(The* WORKMAN *goes out.)* Where . . . where, oh, where did it go? . . . *(Finding his cap)* In one of Ostrovski's[4] plays there was a man with a big moustache and small capabilities . . . that's me. Well, my dear people, I have the honor . . . *(To* YELENA) If you and Sofia ever have time to drop in at my place, I'd be very happy. I don't have a big estate, some eighty acres or so, but if it should interest you, there's a model farm and a nursery the like of which you won't find for hundreds of miles around. And next to my place you'll find the state forestry. The forester there is an old man and he's usually sick, so I generally run the place.

YELENA: I've already been told that you love the forest very much. That does render a great service, but doesn't it interfere with your real vocation? You *are* a doctor.

ASTROV: Only God knows what our real vocation is.

YELENA: And is it interesting?

ASTROV: Yes. It's interesting work.

VOINITSKI *(ironically)*: *Very!*

YELENA *(to* ASTROV*)*: You're still a young man; you don't look . . . well, thirty-six or thirty-seven at the most. . . . It can't be as interesting as all that. Just forests and more forests. I should think it would be monotonous.

SONYA: No, it's extraordinarily interesting. Every year Mikhail plants new trees and he's already received a bronze medal and a diploma. He does everything he can to save the old forests from being destroyed. Just listen to what he says, you'll agree completely. He says that the forests make the world a more beautiful place to live in, they teach people to understand what beauty is and they inspire them with noble thoughts. Forests help to temper the climate. In other countries, where the climate is milder, less time is spent in the struggle with nature, and so you find people who are gentle and tender; beautiful people, easy-going and sensitive, with refined speech and graceful movements. The arts and sciences flourish in such countries, their philosophy is not depressing and their attitude to women is full of a refined nobility. . . .

VOINITSKI *(smiling)*: Bravo, bravo! It's all very nice, but not terribly convincing, so . . . *(to* ASTROV*)* you will excuse me, my friend, if I continue to burn wood in my stove and build my barns of wood.

ASTROV: You may burn peat hair⁵ in your stove and build your barns of stone. Oh, well, you can cut a tree down if you have to, but why ruin the forest? The Russian forests are trembling under the ax, millions of trees are dying, the homes of birds and beasts are being destroyed, rivers are getting shallow and drying up, wonderful landscapes are disappearing, never to return, and all because people in the forest haven't sense enough to stoop down and pick up the peat from the ground. *(To* YELENA*)*: Don't you think I'm right, madame? You'd have to be a complete barbarian to burn such beauty in your own stove, to destroy what you cannot create. Man was given a mind and creative powers to make more of what he was given. But until now, he hasn't created, he's only destroyed. There are fewer and fewer forests, the rivers are drying up, wild game is becoming extinct, the climate is spoiled and every day the earth gets poorer and uglier. *(To* VOINITSKI) You look ironically at me and everything I say seems trivial to you —you think I'm some sort of crank—but when I walk in a wood that I have saved from destruction, or when I listen to the rustling sounds of a young forest planted with my own hands, I realize that I have power over the elements somehow, and if a thousand years from now man will be happy, then I'll have a part in that, too. When I plant a birch tree and I see it getting green and swaying with the wind, my soul is filled with pride and I . . . *(Seeing the* WORKMAN, *who enters with a glass of vodka on a tray)* Well . . . *(Drinks.)* It's time for me to go. All this probably doesn't make much sense anyway. I have the honor to bid you good afternoon. *(Goes toward the house.)*

SONYA *(takes him by the arm and they go together)*: When will you come to us again?

ASTROV: I don't know.

SONYA: In another month, perhaps?

> (ASTROV *and* SONYA *go into the house;* MARIA *and* TELYEGIN *stay at the table;* YELENA *and* VOINITSKI *go toward the terrace.)*

YELENA: Oh, Ivan, you were just impossible again. Was there any need to get upset with Maria and go on about perpetual-motion writing machines? And at lunch today you argued with Alexander again. How petty!

VOINITSKI: But what if I hate him!

YELENA: Alexander is not to be hated, he's just like everybody else. He's no worse than you are.

VOINITSKI: If you could only see your face, how you move . . . What a lazy life! What indolence!

YELENA: And how bored I am with it! Everybody's against my husband, everybody looks on me with pity: she's unhappy, she has an elderly husband! This sympathy everybody has for me, how well I understand it! It's the way Astrov just said it: you all destroy the forests thoughtlessly, and soon nothing will be left on earth. In the same way you destroy each other, and soon, thanks to you, nothing will be left on earth, no loyalty, no purity, no capacity for self-sacrifice. Why can't you look at a woman with indifference if she isn't yours? Why? The doctor was right: because in all of you there is a demon of destruction. You have no pity—neither for the forests, for the birds, for women nor for one another.

VOINITSKI: I don't like this philosophizing!

(Pause.)

YELENA: The doctor has a tired, nerve-wracked face. It's an interesting face. Obviously Sonya is attracted to him. She's fallen in love with him and I understand her. He's been here three times since we came, but I'm shy and I haven't spoken to him; I haven't been very nice to him. He must be thinking I'm not very nice. You know, Ivan, the reason why you and I are such friends is because we're both of us such tiresome, boring people! So tiresome! Don't look at me like that, I don't like it.

VOINITSKI: How can I look at you in any other way, if I love you? You are my joy, my life, my youth! I know my chances for a little reciprocation are infinitesimal, almost nil, but I don't want anything at all, only let me look at you, listen to your voice. . . .

YELENA: Quiet, somebody might hear you.

(They go toward the house.)

VOINITSKI *(goes to her)*: Let me tell you of my love, don't persecute me—that alone will be a great happiness for me. . . .

YELENA: This is unbearable. . . .

(Both go into the house. TELYEGIN strums on the strings and plays a polka; MARIA jots something down in the margins of her pamphlet.)

CURTAIN

ACT
TWO

> *The dining room of the* SEREBRYAKOV
> *estate. It is late at night. The night
> watchman is heard tapping*[6] *in the gar-
> den.* SEREBRYAKOV *sits in an armchair
> next to the open window, dozing.* YEL-
> ENA *sits next to him, also dozing.*

SEREBRYAKOV *(coming to)*: Who's there? Sonya, is it you?

YELENA: It's me.

SEREBRYAKOV: You, Lyenochka . . . What an unbearable pain!

YELENA: Your foot warmer has fallen on the floor. *(Covering his legs)* I'll go shut the window, Alexander.

SEREBRYAKOV: No, I'm suffocating. I just dozed off a moment ago and I dreamed that my left leg belonged to somebody else. I woke up with this unbearable pain. No, it's not gout, it's probably rheumatism. What time is it now?

YELENA: Twelve-twenty.

(Pause.)

SEREBRYAKOV: In the morning, go into the library and see if we have the Batyushkov.[7] It seems to me we have it.

YELENA: What?

SEBEBRYAKOV: Will you look for the Batyushkov in the morn-ing. I remember we had a copy. Now, why do you suppose I'm breathing so heavily?

YELENA: You're tired. You haven't slept for two nights.

SEREBRYAKOV: They say that Turgenev developed angina pectoris[8] after the gout. I'm afraid I may have the same thing. Damned, detestable old age. Damn it. When I be-

84

came old, I became repulsive to myself. And you all must find me repulsive to look at.

YELENA: You take such a tone when you talk about your old age . . . as if it were our fault.

SEREBRYAKOV: And I'm especially repulsive to you. (YELENA *gets up and sits farther away from him.*) You're right, of course. I'm not stupid. I understand. You're young, healthy, good looking—you want to live—and I'm an old man, almost a corpse. Do you really think I don't understand? Of course, it's stupid of me to go on living. Just be patient, I'll soon set you all free. I haven't long to drag myself about.

YELENA: I'm exhausted. For God's sake, keep quiet.

SEREBRYAKOV: It appears that thanks to me you're all exhausted, bored, ruining your youth. Only I take pleasure and satisfaction in life. Of course!

YELENA: Keep quiet! You're torturing me!

SEREBRYAKOV: I'm torturing you all. Of course.

YELENA (*through tears*): It's unbearable! Tell me what you want of me.

SEREBRYAKOV: Nothing.

YELENA: Well, then, keep quiet. I ask you.

SEREBRYAKOV: A strange thing . . . When Ivan or his old idiot mother, Maria, are talking, everyone listens, but if I utter a single word, then everyone begins to feel unhappy. Even my voice is repulsive. All right, I admit it, I'm repulsive, I am an egotist, despot . . . but don't you think that in my old age I have some right to egotism? Don't I actually deserve it? I ask you, have I not the right to a peaceful old age and to the consideration of my people?

YELENA: No one is disputing your rights. (*The wind batters the shutters.*) The wind has come up. I'll shut the window. (*She shuts it.*) It's going to rain. . . . Nobody is disputing your rights.

(*Pause. The night watchman taps and sings a song.*)

SEREBRYAKOV: All your life you work for art, you get accustomed to your study, to your audience, to the esteem of your venerable colleagues . . . and suddenly, for no conceivable reason, you find yourself in a mausoleum; every day you see nothing but stupid people, and listen to idle conversation. . . . I want to live. I love success, fame, the approbation of the crowd . . . and here—it's like being in exile. Every minute you long for the past, you watch others succeeding, you fear death. . . . I can't bear it! I haven't the strength! And here they don't even want to forgive me my old age!

YELENA: Wait, have patience: in five or six years I'll be old, too.

(Enter SONYA.)

SONYA: Papa, you had us send for Dr. Astrov, and when he came you refused to see him. That's not nice. To trouble people for no reason at all . . .

SEREBRYAKOV: What is your Astrov to me? He understands medicine as well as I do astronomy.

SONYA: You would ask the entire faculty of medicine to come and treat your gout.

SEREBRYAKOV: I cannot bear to speak to that fool.

SONYA: As you like. *(Sits down.)* It's all the same to me.

SEREBRYAKOV: What time is it now?

YELENA: After midnight.

SEREBRYAKOV: I'm suffocating! Sonya, give me some of those pills on the table!

SONYA: Right away. *(Brings him a bottle of pills.)*

SEREBRYAKOV *(exasperated)*: Those aren't the ones! One can't ask you for anything!

SONYA: Please don't be so capricious. Maybe some people like it, but spare me, please! I don't like it. I don't have the time. I have to get up early tomorrow to mow the hay.

(Enter VOINITSKI in a dressing gown, with a candle.)

VOINITSKI: There's a storm gathering outside. *(Lightning)* Did you see that! Hélène and Sonya, go to sleep, I'll take your place!

SEREBRYAKOV *(frightened)*: No, no! Don't leave me alone with him! No. He'll talk me under the table!

VOINITSKI: But they must get some rest! They haven't slept for two nights.

SEREBRYAKOV: They may go and sleep, but you go with

them. I thank you. I beg of you. For the sake of our former friendship, don't protest. We'll talk later.

VOINITSKI (*smiling ironically*): Our former friendship . . . former . . .

SONYA: Keep quiet, Uncle Vanya.

SEREBRYAKOV (*to his wife*): My dear, don't leave me alone with him! He'll talk me under the table.

VOINITSKI: This is becoming rather ridiculous.

(*Enter* MARINA *with a candle.*)

SONYA: Go and lie down, Marina. It's terribly late.

MARINA: The samovar hasn't been cleared from the table yet. It's easy to say go lie down.

SEREBRYAKOV: They are all not sleeping, they are exhausted. Only I am in a state of bliss.

MARINA (*goes to* SEREBRYAKOV; *tenderly*): What is it, my dear? Are we not feeling well? I have a pain in my legs, too; how they ache. (*Arranges the foot warmer.*) You've had this illness for a long time. Sonya's mother, may she rest in peace, used to kill herself looking after you night and day. She loved you so. . . . (*Pause*) Old people are like little children—they want to be pitied, only nobody pities old folks. (*Kisses* SEREBRYAKOV *on his shoulder.*) Let's go, my dear; to bed. Come along, little fellow. I'll bring you some linden tea to drink, to warm your feet. . . . I'll pray to God for you. . . .

SEREBRYAKOV (*touched*): Let's go, Marina.

MARINA: I have such a pain in my legs, such a pain! (*Leads him out, together with* SONYA.) Vera used to grieve so, she was always crying—you were only a tiny little thing then, Sonya. . . . Come, come, my dear. . . .

(SEREBRYAKOV, SONYA *and* MARINA *go out.*)

YELENA: I'm worn out with him. I can barely stand up.

VOINITSKI: You with him, and I with myself. I haven't slept for three nights.

YELENA: There's something rotten in this house. Your mother hates everything except her pamphlets and the professor; the professor is irritated, he doesn't trust me, and he's afraid of you; Sonya is angry with her father and hasn't spoken to me for two weeks now; you hate my husband and openly disdain your mother; I'm irritated and so many times today I've been on the verge of tears. . . . There's something rotten in this house.

VOINITSKI: Stop the philosophy!

YELENA: Ivan, you're a well-educated and intelligent man, and I should think you would understand that the world is not being ruined by crimes and fires, but by hate and hostility, all this petty squabbling. You mustn't grumble all the time; help us to make peace among ourselves.

VOINITSKI: First help me to make peace with myself. My darling . . . (*Bends down to her hand.*)

YELENA: Stop! (*Takes her hand away.*) Go away!

VOINITSKI: The rain will be over soon, and everything in nature is refreshed and breathes more lightly. Only I am not refreshed by the storm. Night and day, my thoughts suffocate me, haunting me with my hopelessly wasted life. I have never lived. The past was stupidly spent on nothing, and the present is abominable in its absurdity. There you have my life and my love; what can I do with them, what is to be done? My feelings are slowly dying of it, like a ray of sun swallowed into a pit; and I, too, am dying.

YELENA: When you talk to me of your love, I feel numb and I don't know what to say. Forgive me, I have nothing to say to you. (*Wishing to leave*) Good night.

VOINITSKI (*barring her way*): If you only knew how I suffer, knowing that there is another life in this house beside mine wasting away—your life! What are you waiting for? What damned philosophy is holding you back? If you would only realize . . . only just realize . . .

YELENA (*looking intently at him*): Ivan, you're drunk!

VOINITSKI: That may be, that may very well be.

YELENA: Where's the doctor?

VOINITSKI: He's here . . . spending the night. That may be . . . that may very well be . . . everything may just very well be!

YELENA: You were drinking today? Why?

VOINITSKI: It makes you think you're alive. . . . Don't interfere with me, Hélène!

YELENA: You never used to drink, and you never talked so much. . . . Go to sleep! You're boring me.

VOINITSKI (*squeezing her hand*): My darling . . . my wonderful one!

YELENA *(annoyed)*: Leave me alone. This is getting to be disgusting. *(Going out.)*

VOINITSKI *(alone)*: She's gone. . . . *(Pause)* Ten years ago, I used to see her at my poor sister's home. She was seventeen then, and I was thirty-seven. Why didn't I fall in love with her then and propose to her? It might have been possible then! And now she'd be my wife. . . . Yes . . . Now we would both be awakened by the storm; she would be afraid of the thunder, and I would hold her in my arms and whisper, "Don't be afraid, I'm here." Oh, wonderful thoughts, such nice thoughts, they make me laugh. . . . Oh, my God, my thoughts are all so confused. . . . Why am I old? Why doesn't she understand me? All those theories, that idle moralizing, her absurd, lazy thoughts about the world going to pot, are deeply distasteful to me. *(Pause)* Oh, how I've been cheated! I worshiped that professor, that pitiful gout-ridden creature, I worked for him like an ox; Sonya and I squeezed the last drop of sweat out of this estate. Like kulaks,[9] we sold the vegetable oil, dried peas and cottage cheese, though we didn't dare eat a crumb. We gathered in the kopecks by the thousands and sent them off to him! I was proud of him and all of his knowledge, I lived and breathed only him! Everything he read and uttered seemed like genius to me. . . . My God, and now? He's retired and the sum total of his life can be seen: after he goes not one page of his work will remain; he's completely unknown, he's a nobody! A soap bubble! And I've been swindled—I can see it now—stupidly swindled. . . .

(Enter ASTROV with a frock coat on, without a waistcoat or a necktie; he is a little tipsy; TELYEGIN comes after him, with his guitar.)

ASTROV: Play!

TELYEGIN: They're all asleep!

ASTROV: Play, I said! *(TELYEGIN plays quietly; to VOINITSKI)* You alone here? No ladies? *(Arms akimbo, sings quietly.)* "Gone is my stove, gone is my bed, Master has no roof over his head . . ."[10] The storm woke me. Quite a rain. What time is it now?

VOINITSKI: Who the hell knows?

ASTROV: I thought I heard Yelena's voice.

VOINITSKI: She was here a moment ago.

ASTROV: A splendid woman. (*Looking at the bottles on the table*) Medicine. What a lot of prescriptions! From Kharkov, from Moscow, from Tula . . .[11] All those cities bothered by his gout. Is he sick or is he pretending?

VOINITSKI: He's sick.

(*Pause.*)

ASTROV: Why so sad today? Is it the professor you're upset about, or what?

VOINITSKI: Leave me alone.

ASTROV: Or is it that you're in love with the professor's wife.

VOINITSKI: She is my friend.

ASTROV: Already?

VOINITSKI: What do you mean by "already"?

ASTROV: A woman becomes a man's "friend" only in a certain sequence: first she's an acquaintance, then a lover, and only then does she become a "friend."

VOINITSKI: That is a vulgar philosophy.

ASTROV: What? Oh, yes . . . I must confess . . . I am becoming vulgar. As you can see, I'm a little high. As a rule, I drink only once a month. When I'm in this state, I become insolent and impertinent in the extreme. I'm afraid of nothing! I undertake the most difficult operations and I do them perfectly; I draw up the wildest plans for the future. When I get like this I don't think of myself as a crank and I'm convinced I am bringing the greatest benefits to mankind . . . the greatest! When I get like this, I evolve my own philosophical system and all of you, my friends, seem to me to be just so many small insects . . . microbes. (*To* TELYEGIN) Waffles, play!

TELYEGIN: I would be only too glad to accommodate you, my friend, but you must remember—everybody in the house is sleeping!

ASTROV: Play, I said! (TELYEGIN *plays quietly.*) We need a drink. C'mon, I think we still have some cognac left in there. When it's light, we'll go over to my place. *Shell* we? I have an assistant who never says "shall we" but always *"shell* we." Terrible fellow. *Shell* we? (*Seeing* SONYA *approaching*) Excuse me, I don't have a necktie on. (*Exits quickly;* TELYEGIN *goes after him.*)

SONYA: Well, Uncle Vanya, you've been drinking again with the doctor. The two gay blades have been having a friendly old time together. Well, he's always like that, but what's got into you? At your age, it doesn't become you at all.

VOINITSKI: Age has nothing to do with it. When life isn't real to you, you live on illusions. It's better than nothing.

SONYA: The hay's all been mowed, it rains every day and it's all rotting . . . and you talk about illusions. You've completely given up this estate. I work alone, and I just haven't any strength left. . . . *(Startled)* Uncle, there are tears in your eyes!

VOINITSKI: What tears? It's nothing . . . nonsense. . . . Just now you looked at me just like your poor mother used to. My dear . . . *(Avidly kisses her hands and face.)* My sister . . . my dear sister . . . Where is she now? If she only knew! Ah, if she only knew!

SONYA: What? Knew what, Uncle?

VOINITSKI: It's too painful, no good . . . nothing. . . . Later . . . It's nothing at all. . . . I'll go. *(He goes.)*

SONYA *(knocks at the door)*: Mikhail! Aren't you asleep? May I see you a moment!

ASTROV *(from the other side of the door)*: Right away! *(Enters after a short time; he has put his waistcoat and necktie back on.)* What can I do for you?

SONYA: You go drink if you like, if you don't think it's repulsive, but please, don't give my uncle anything to drink. It's bad for him.

ASTROV: All right. We won't drink any more. *(Pause)* I'm leaving here now. What's done is done. By the time the horses are harnessed, it will be light out.

SONYA: It's raining. Stay until morning.

ASTROV: The storm is passing over, we're getting only the edge of it. I'm going. Please, don't write me any more to ask me to attend to your father. I tell him it's gout, and he says it's rheumatism; I ask him to lie down and he sits up. Today he wouldn't even talk to me at all.

SONYA: He's spoiled. *(She looks in the sideboard.)* Would you like to have a snack?

ASTROV: Perhaps I will.

SONYA: I like having a bite to eat at night. I think there's something in the sideboard. I've heard he had a lot of success with women during his lifetime; they spoiled him. Have some cheese.

(Both stand at the sideboard and eat.)

ASTROV: I haven't had anything to eat all day, just been drinking. Your father's a hard nut to crack. *(Takes a bottle out of the sideboard.)* May I? *(Has a glassful.)* There's nobody here right now, so we can speak frankly. You know, I couldn't live a single month in your house, breathing in this atmosphere. . . . Your father, always taken up with his gout and his books; Uncle Vanya and his melancholia; your grandmother, plus your stepmother . . .

SONYA: What about my stepmother?

ASTROV: You know, everything about people ought to be beautiful: their faces, their clothes, their souls, their thoughts. She's beautiful, no arguing that, but . . . see how she eats, sleeps, walks about bewitching everybody with her beauty—well, that's all there is to it. She has no responsibilities, other people work for her. . . . You know I'm right? An idle life can't be a pure one. *(Pause)* Oh, maybe I'm making the case too strong. Like your Uncle Vanya, I'm not satisfied with life. We're both becoming grumblers.

SONYA: You're not satisfied with your life?

ASTROV: Oh, I love life in general, but our life, our provincial, narrow, Russian life—that's what I can't stand. I have contempt for it with all the strength in my soul. As for my own personal life, God knows there's absolutely nothing good about it. You know how you feel when you're walking through a dark forest at night and there's a light far in the distance; you don't notice your fatigue or the darkness or the sharp sting of the branches beating against your face. . . . I work—that you know—as no one else in the district does, and I keep getting beaten down by fate, but I don't stop, sometimes I suffer from it unbearably, and there's no light in the distance for me. I don't expect anything for myself any more, I don't like people. . . . It's been a long time since I've loved anybody.

SONYA: Nobody?

ASTROV: Nobody. I can feel tenderly toward your old nurse, in memory of the old days. The peasants are all the same—

they're crude, they live in filth—and it's impossible to get along with educated people. They wear you out. All of your good neighbors think their frivolous thoughts, feel their frivolous feelings and see no farther than the end of their noses—they're stupid. And those who are cleverer and more important are hysterical types; they spend all their time analyzing and brooding . . . whining, hating, morbidly slandering; they come up alongside you, look at you askance and announce to the world, "Oh, this one's a psychopath!" or, "This one's a bag of wind!" And when they don't know what label to stick on your forehead, then they say, "He's a strange one, very strange!" *I* love the forests—that's strange; I don't eat meat—that's even stranger. A spontaneous, decent, open attitude to nature and to people—that we do not have any more . . . not at all! Not on your life! *(He is about to have a drink.)*

SONYA *(preventing him)*: No, please, I'm asking you not to drink any more.

ASTROV: Why not?

SONYA: It's not becoming to you! You're a refined person, you have such a gentle voice . . . and you're better than anyone else I know. You're a fine person. Why do you want to lower yourself, like ordinary people, who drink and play cards? Oh, don't do that, please! You keep saying that people don't create but only destroy; then why are you destroying yourself? It's not right, not right at all, I beg you, I implore you.

ASTROV *(stretching his hand to her)*: I won't drink any more.

SONYA: Give me your word.

ASTROV: My word of honor.

SONYA *(shaking his hand warmly)*: Thank you!

ASTROV: Basta!¹² I've sobered up. You see, I'm already sober and thus shall I remain to the end of my days. *(Looks at his watch.)* Well, let's continue. I tell you, my time has passed and it's too late for me now. . . . I've grown old from working too much, I've become common, I don't feel anything any more, I can't get attached to anyone any more. I don't love anybody . . . and I can't fall in love any more. I'm thrilled only by beauty. I'm not indifferent to it. It seems to me that if Yelena wanted to, she could turn my head in a day. . . . But that's not love, that's not affection. . . . *(Closes his hand over his eyes and shudders.)*

SONYA: What's the matter?

ASTROV: Nothing . . . At Lent one of my patients died under the chloroform.

SONYA: It's time you forgot about that. *(Pause)* Tell me, Mikhail . . . if I had a friend or a younger sister, and if you knew that she . . . well, let's say . . . she loved you, what would you think of that?

ASTROV *(shrugging his shoulders)*: I don't know. I don't think I'd think about it at all. I would give her to understand that I could not love her . . . my mind is not occupied with such things. Anyway, if I'm going, it's time to go. Good-bye, my dear, or we'll go on like this till morning. *(Shaking her hand)* I'll go through the drawing room, if I may. I'm afraid your Uncle Vanya might try to detain me. *(He goes out.)*

SONYA *(alone)*: He didn't say anything to me . . . his heart and soul are both still closed to me; then why do I feel such happiness? *(Laughs happily.)* I said to him: You're a refined, noble person, you have such a gentle voice. . . . Perhaps that was a little gauche of me? His voice trembles, it caresses me; I can still feel it. And when I talked to him about my younger sister, he didn't understand. . . . *(wringing her hands)* Oh, it's so awful, I'm not beautiful! I'm not beautiful! How awful! And I know I'm not beautiful, I know it, I know it. . . . Last Sunday, when we were coming out of church, I heard them talking about me, and one of the women said, "She's such a good girl, so kind, but it's a pity she's so plain. . . ." Plain.

(Enter YELENA.)

YELENA *(opening the window)*: The storm has passed. How good the air is! *(Pause)* Where's the doctor?

SONYA: He's gone.

(Pause.)

YELENA: Sophie!

SONYA: What?

YELENA: How long are you going to keep sulking? We've never done each other any harm, why must we be enemies? Enough is enough. . . .

SONYA: I myself wanted to . . . *(Embraces her.)* No more anger.

YELENA: That's better.

(Both are moved.)

SONYA: Is Papa in bed?

YELENA: No, he's sitting in the drawing room. . . . We haven't spoken to each other in a whole week. . . . God knows why. . . . *(Seeing the sideboard open)* What's that?

SONYA: Mikhail had something to eat.

YELENA: There's some wine. . . . Let's drink *bruderschaft.*[13]

SONYA: Let's.

YELENA: A loving cup . . . *(Fills the glass.)* That's better. Well, shall we . . . be friends?

SONYA: Friends. *(They drink and kiss one another.)* I've wanted to make peace for so long now, but somehow I was too ashamed. . . . *(She weeps.)*

YELENA: Why are you crying?

SONYA: No reason, just like that.

YELENA: Now, that's enough. . . . *(Cries.)* You silly thing, now I'm crying, too. . . . *(Pause)* You resented me because you thought I married your father for mercenary reasons. . . . If you believe in oaths, then I swear to you, I married him for love. I was infatuated with him—he was an educated and famous man. It wasn't real love, it was artificial, but it was real to me then. It's not my fault. But ever since our marriage, you haven't stopped accusing me with your sharp and suspicious eyes.

SONYA: Well, let's make peace! Let's forget.

YELENA: Don't look at people that way—it's not becoming to you. We have to believe in one another, otherwise life becomes impossible.

(Pause.)

SONYA: Tell me, honestly, as a friend: are you happy?

YELENA: No.

SONYA: I knew it. Just one more question. Tell me truthfully: would you have wished for a young husband?

YELENA: What a child you are! I would have, of course. *(Smiles.)* Ask me anything else, go ahead and ask. . . .

SONYA: Do you like the doctor?

YELENA: Yes, very much.

SONYA (*smiling*): I have a stupid expression on my face, don't I? He's just left, and I still hear his voice and his footsteps. I look at a dark window . . . and I see his face appear there. What do you think? . . . But I mustn't talk so loud, I'm ashamed. Let's go to my room. We can talk there. Do I seem stupid? Tell me . . . tell me something about him. . . .

YELENA: Like what?

SONYA: He's smart; he knows everything; he can do anything he wants. . . . He's a doctor and he plants forests. . . .

YELENA: It has nothing to do with forests or medicine. . . . My dear, you must understand, he has a kind of genius! You know what that means? Courage, an open mind, a broad outlook . . . As soon as he plants a tree, he's already imagining what will become of it in a thousand years, he's already dreaming about the happiness of mankind. Such people are rare, we must love them. . . . He drinks, sometimes he's crude . . . well, what of it? In Russia, a talented person cannot remain unspoiled. Just think what a life that doctor leads! The mud on the roads, the frosts, the snow-storms, the enormous distances, the crude, primitive people, poverty and disease everywhere around, and under such conditions and struggles day after day . . . it would be hard to keep oneself sober and unspoiled to the age of forty. . . . (*Kisses her.*) With all my heart, I wish you every happiness. . . . (*She gets up.*) I am a boring, unimportant person. . . . In my music, in my husband's home, in my romantic life—to put it bluntly, everywhere—I have always been a very unimportant person. As a matter of fact, Sonya, if you think about it, I'm very, very unhappy! (*She paces up and down.*) No happiness in this world for me. No! . . . Why are you laughing?

SONYA (*laughing, hiding her face*): I'm so happy . . . happy!

YELENA: I'd like to play the piano. . . . I'll play something for you right now.

SONYA: Oh, yes, do play. (*Embraces her.*) I can't sleep. Do play!

YELENA: In a moment. Your father isn't sleeping. When he's sick, music irritates him. Go and ask him. If he says it's all right, I'll play. Go on.

SONYA: Right away. (*She goes out.*)

(*The night watchman can be heard tapping in the garden.*)

YELENA: I haven't played for such a long time. I'll play and weep, weep like an idiot. (*Looking out the window*) Is that you tapping, Yefim?

VOICE OF THE WATCHMAN: It's me!

YELENA: Don't tap, the master's sick.

VOICE OF THE WATCHMAN: I'll go in a minute! (*Whistling*) Hey, you, Zhuchka, Malchik! Zhuchka!

(*Pause.*)

SONYA (*returning*): He says no!

CURTAIN

ACT
THREE

The drawing room of the SEREBRYAKOV
*house. Three doors: stage left, right and
center. Daytime. Early afternoon.*

We see VOINITSKI, SONYA *(she is seated)
and* YELENA *(she walks across the stage,
lost in thought).*

VOINITSKI: If you please, the Herr Professor has expressed
the desire that we gather in the sitting room at one o'clock
today. *(Looks at his watch.)* It's a quarter to. He wishes to
disclose something to the world.

YELENA: Probably something about business.

VOINITSKI: He hasn't got any business. He writes foolishness,
grumbles and envies everybody, that's all.

SONYA *(a tone of rebuke)*: Uncle!

VOINITSKI: Ah, well, so sorry. *(Points to* YELENA.*)* Just feast
your eyes: there she walks, swaying lazily about. How
nice! How very nice!

YELENA: Just buzzing away all day long . . . buzzing, buzzing.
Don't you ever get tired! *(Depressed suddenly)* I'm dying of
boredom, I don't know what to do with myself.

SONYA *(shrugging her shoulders)*: Isn't there enough work to
do? There's as much as you'd care to do.

YELENA: For instance?

SONYA: Right here on this farm, you could do some teaching
or nurse the sick. Isn't that enough to do? When you and
Father weren't here, Uncle Vanya and I went to market
ourselves to sell the flour.

YELENA: I don't know how. And it isn't interesting. It's only
in idealistic novels that people teach and nurse the sick,

but I can't, for no reason at all, suddenly up and nurse the sick and teach people, can I?

SONYA: What I don't understand is how you can avoid doing it. Wait awhile: you'll get used to it. *(Embracing her)* Don't be bored, dear. *(Grinning)* You're bored, you can't find a niche for yourself, but boredom and idleness are contagious. Look: Uncle Vanya does nothing and only follows you around like a shadow; I've left my work and come running to you, to talk. I've become so lazy, I can't stand myself! Dr. Astrov didn't visit us very often in the past, only once a month; to get him to come wasn't easy; but now he comes over every day, leaving his forests and medicine. You know, you're very probably a witch.

VOINITSKI: Why so languid? *(Agitated)* Well, my languorous one, my darling, be reasonable! In your veins flows the blood of water nymphs—be a water nymph! Let yourself go for once in your life, fall head over heels in love at first sight with any old water sprite—and jump in head first, so that the Herr Professor and all of us may throw up our hands in astonishment!

YELENA *(angrily)*: Leave me alone! How cruel this is! *(About to go)*

VOINITSKI *(not allowing her to)*: Well, then, my joy, please . . . excuse me. *(Kisses her hands.)* Truce.

YELENA: You must admit, even an angel couldn't bear up under this patiently.

VOINITSKI: As a token of peace and harmony, I'll bring you a bouquet of roses; I prepared them for you this morning . . . autumn roses—charming, sad roses. . . . *(He goes out.)*

SONYA: Autumn roses—charming, sad roses . . .

(Both of them look through the window.)

YELENA: It's already September. How will we ever live through the winter here! *(Pause)* Where is the doctor?

SONYA: He's in Uncle Vanya's room. He's writing something. I'm glad Uncle Vanya went out. I have something to say to you.

YELENA: About what?

SONYA: About what? *(Puts her head on* YELENA's *breast.)*

YELENA: There, there, come now. . . . *(Smoothes her hair.)* Enough.

SONYA: I'm not beautiful.

YELENA: You have beautiful hair.

SONYA: No! *(Turns around to look in the mirror.)* No! When a woman isn't beautiful, then they tell her, "You have beautiful eyes, you have beautiful hair. . . ." I've loved him for six years now, I love him more than my own mother; every moment I hear his voice, I feel the touch of his hand; I watch the door, expecting him; I always think he's about to come in. And you can see I always come to you to talk about him. Now he comes over here every day, but he doesn't look at me, he doesn't see me. . . . It's so unbearable! There's no hope for me, none! *(Despairing)* Oh, God, give me strength. . . . I prayed all night. . . . I often go to him, to say something to him, I look in his eyes. . . . I haven't any pride, no control. . . . I can't hold back; and yesterday I confessed to Uncle Vanya that I loved him . . . and all the servants know that I love him. Everybody knows.

YELENA: Does he know?

SONYA: No. He doesn't even notice me.

YELENA *(lost in thought)*: He's a strange man. . . . You know what? Let me talk to him. I'll carefully allude to it. . . . *(Pause)* Really, how long can you go without knowing? . . . Let me! (SONYA *nods her head in consent.*) Good. He either loves you or he doesn't. It's not hard to find out. Don't be embarrassed, don't be upset, my dear. I'll question him so carefully, he won't even notice. All we have to find out is yes or no. *(Pause)* If it's no, he shouldn't come here. Right? (SONYA *nods her head in consent.*) It's easier if you don't see him. Putting it off for another day is wrong; we must ask him right away. He intended to show me some of his drawings. . . . Go and tell him I want to see him.

SONYA *(very upset)*: You will tell me the whole truth?

YELENA: Yes, of course! I think the truth, whatever it is, is never quite so terrible as not knowing at all. Trust me, my dear.

SONYA: Yes . . . yes . . . I'll tell him you want to see his drawings. . . . *(She goes, and stops at the door.)* Not knowing is better . . . then there's still some hope. . . .

YELENA: What is it?

SONYA: Nothing. *(She goes out.)*

YELENA *(alone)*: There's nothing worse than knowing some-

body's secret and not being able to help them. *(Pondering)*
He's not in love with her—that's clear—but why doesn't
he marry her? She's not pretty, but for a country doctor,
at his age, she'd make an excellent wife. She's clever and
so good-hearted, a virgin. . . . Oh, well, that's not the
point. . . . *(Pause)* I understand the poor girl. The awful
boredom here . . . Instead of real people she's surrounded
by poor gray imitations, she hears only stupid banalities,
all they know how to do is eat, drink and sleep; but he
appears, and he's not like the others; he's handsome, interesting, fascinating, like some bright star on the horizon
. . . yielding to the charm of such a man, forgetting oneself. . . . I think I'm a bit attracted myself. Yes, when he's
not here, I'm bored; I catch myself smiling, when I think
of him. . . . That Uncle Vanya says I have an undine's
blood in my veins. "Let yourself go, for once in your
life. . . ." Well, maybe I should. . . . To fly away from all
of you like a free bird, away from all your sleepy faces,
from your conversations, to forget you exist on earth . . .
But I'm a coward, I'm shy. . . . My conscience would
torture me. . . . He comes over here every day, I can guess
why he's here, and already I feel guilty, ready to fall on
my knees before Sonya and excuse myself, weep. . . .

ASTROV *(comes in with his maps)*: Hello there! *(Shakes hands.)*
You want to see my drawings?

YELENA: Yesterday you promised to show me your work. . . .
Are you free?

ASTROV: Oh, yes. *(He stretches his maps out on the card table
and fastens them with tacks.)* Where were you born?

YELENA *(helping him)*: In Petersburg.

ASTROV: And where did you receive your education?

YELENA: At the conservatory.

ASTROV: This may not be very interesting for you. . . .

YELENA: Why? Of course, I don't know the country very
well, but I've read a good deal.

ASTROV: Here in the house I have my own table . . . in Ivan's
room. When I'm really tired out, utterly dead, then I drop
everything and come here to amuse myself with these things
for hours on end. . . . Ivan and Sonya draw up their accounts and I sit next to their table and mess around. I
feel warm and peaceful, the crickets chirp along. But I
don't allow myself this pleasure very often, only once a

month. . . . *(Pointing to the maps)* Now look over here. It's a map of our district as it was fifty years ago. The light and dark green sections stand for the forests; half of the area was occupied by forests at that time. Where you have the red lines cross-hatched over the green, there were elk and goats. . . . I've indicated both the flora and the fauna. On this lake there lived swans, geese, ducks, and as the old people say, that makes "a powerful lot of birds," as far as the eye can see, swarms of them flying about. Besides the villages and the small towns, you can see, here and there, scattered settlements, farms, secluded monasteries, water mills. . . . There's an abundance of cattle and horses. They're indicated in blue. For instance, this small rural district where the blue paint is thick: there were whole herds of horses, about three to each farm. *(Pause)* Now look farther down here. Here it is as it was twenty-five years ago. Already only one-third of the area was forest land. No more wild goats, still some elk. The green and blue sections are already paler. That's the way it goes. Now let's get on the third part: the map of the district as it is now. There are green sections here and there, but just in spots; the elk, the swans and the wood grouse have disappeared altogether. . . . As for the scattered settlements, the farms, the monasteries and the water mills—there's not even a trace of them. In general, the map shows a gradual and unmistakable decline, which will apparently come to an end in only another ten or fifteen years or so—completely. You will say that there are cultural reasons for all this, that the old life must naturally make way for the new. Yes, I understand; if in place of the forests that have been destroyed there were new highways and railroads, if there were factories, workshops and schools, the people would be healthier, richer and wiser; but nothing of the kind has happened! In the district there are the same swamps, mosquitoes, the same bad roads, the same poverty, typhus, diphtheria, fires. . . . Everything has degenerated as the result of a difficult struggle for existence; it has degenerated due to stagnation, ignorance, an utter lack of understanding. . . . When you're cold and hungry and sick, you grab at anything to save your life, to save your children, subconsciously, instinctively you clutch at anything that might stem your hunger or warm you up, you are capable of destroying everything without any thought for the future. . . . Almost everything has been destroyed, but nothing new has been created in its place. *(Coldly)* I can see by the expression on your face that this doesn't interest you.

YELENA: But I understand so little of it. . . .

ASTROV: It's not a question of understanding it; you're simply not interested.

YELENA: To be frank, my thoughts were elsewhere. Forgive me. I must conduct a little interrogation. I'm embarrassed; I don't know how to begin.

ASTROV: Interrogation?

YELENA: Yes, interrogation, but . . . it's quite innocent. Let's sit down. *(They sit down.)* It concerns a certain young individual. We will speak sincerely, as friends, without beating about the bush. We'll talk about it and then we'll forget what it was all about. All right?

ASTROV: All right.

YELENA: It concerns my stepdaughter, Sonya. Do you like her?

ASTROV: Yes, I have great respect for her.

YELENA: Do you like her as a woman?

ASTROV *(not right away)*: No.

YELENA: Only a few more words, and then we're done. You've noticed nothing?

ASTROV: Nothing.

YELENA *(Taking his hand)*: You don't love her, I can see it in your eyes. . . . She's suffering. . . . You must understand. . . . Stop coming here.

ASTROV *(gets up)*: I'm past all that . . . and I have no time. . . . *(Shrugging his shoulders)* When do I ever have time? *(He is embarrassed.)*

YELENA: Phew, what an unpleasant conversation! I'm as upset as if I'd been carrying around a great weight on my shoulders. Well, thank God, it's over. Let's forget it, let's act as if nothing had been said, and . . . go away. You're an intelligent man, you must understand. . . . *(Pause)* I'm even blushing.

ASTROV: If you had told me about this a month or two ago, I might perhaps have considered it, but now . . . *(Shrugs his shoulders.)* Well, if she suffering, then of course . . . There's only one thing I don't understand: why did you find it necessary to have this interrogation? *(Stares her in the eye and points a threatening finger.)* You sly creature!

YELENA: What does that mean?

ASTROV *(laughing)*: Sly creature! All right, Sonya is suffering, I grant you that, but then why this interrogation? *(Preventing her from speaking, agitated)* Now don't look so surprised, you know perfectly well why I come over here every day, why and because of whom I come—that you know perfectly well. Predatory creature, don't look at me like that, you can't fool a wise old owl. . . .

YELENA *(puzzled)*: Predatory? I don't understand you.

ASTROV: You pretty little fuzzy weasel . . . You need a victim! I haven't been doing anything for a whole month now. I've dropped everything, I stalk you greedily—and that pleases you so much, so very much. . . . But why? I'm conquered, you knew that without an interrogation. *(Folds his arms and bows his head.)* I submit. There, now eat me!

YELENA: You've gone out of your mind!

ASTROV *(laughing through his teeth)*: You're bashful. . . .

YELENA: Oh, I'm a great deal better than you think I am! I swear it! *(Wanting to go)*

ASTROV *(barring her way)*: I'm leaving here today, and I'll never be back again, but . . . *(Taking her by the hand, looking around)* Where can we see one another? Tell me quickly, where? *(Passionately)* What a marvelous, beautiful creature . . . One kiss . . . just let me kiss your sweet-smelling hair. . . .

YELENA: I swear to you . . .

ASTROV *(preventing her from speaking)*: Why do you swear? There's no need to swear! Superfluous words . . . no need . . . How beautiful! Such hands! *(Kisses her hands.)*

YELENA: Now that's enough . . . please go. . . . *(Withdraws her hands.)* You're forgetting yourself.

ASTROV: Just tell me where we can see each other tomorrow? *(Takes her by the waist.)* You see, this was inevitable; we must see each other.

   (Kisses her; at this moment, VOINITSKI enters with a bouquet of roses and stands at the door.)

YELENA *(not seeing* VOINITSKI*)*: Have pity on me . . . leave me alone. . . . *(Laying her head on* ASTROV'*s chest)* No! *(She tries to disengage herself.)*

ASTROV *(holding her by the waist)*: Come to the forest tomorrow . . . at two. . . . Yes? Say yes? You'll come.

YELENA *(seeing* VOINITSKI*)*: Let me go! *(Terribly embarrassed, she goes to the window.)* This is terrible!

VOINITSKI *(puts the bouquet of roses on the chair; upset, he wipes his face and the back of his neck with a handkerchief)*: It's nothing. . . . No . . . nothing . . .

ASTROV *(blustering)*: The weather wasn't bad today, my dear Ivan; in the morning it was cloudy, it certainly looked like it was going to rain, but now the sun is out again. One can't complain; it's been a splendid autumn . . . and the crops have been quite satisfactory. *(Rolling his maps up into a cylinder)* Except for one thing: the days have been getting shorter. . . . *(He goes out.)*

YELENA *(quickly goes to* VOINITSKI*)*: You must do everything in your power to get my husband and me out of here today! You hear? Today!

VOINITSKI *(wiping his face)*: What? Well . . . all right . . . Hélène, I saw everything, everything. . . .

YELENA *(nervously)*: Do you hear me? I must leave here today, without fail!

(Enter SEREBRYAKOV, SONYA, TELYEGIN *and* MARINA.*)*

TELYEGIN: I myself, your excellency, have not been entirely well. I've been sick for two days now. Something's the matter with my head. . . .

SEREBRYAKOV: Where is everybody? I don't like this house. It's some kind of labyrinth. Twenty-six huge rooms, all dispersed, and nobody can ever find anybody. *(Rings.)* Ask Maria and Yelena to be so kind as to come in.

YELENA: I'm here.

SEREBRYAKOV: Will you sit down, people, please.

SONYA *(goes to* YELENA, *impatiently)*: What did he say?

YELENA: Not now.

SONYA: You're trembling? Are you upset? *(Glances searchingly at her face.)* I understand. . . . He said he couldn't stay here any more . . . didn't he? *(Pause)* Tell me: didn't he?

(YELENA *nods her head.*)

SEREBRYAKOV (*to* TELYEGIN): One can get accustomed to ill health, come what may, but what I cannot bear is the routine of country life. It makes me feel as if I'd fallen off the earth onto another planet. Please be seated, people. Sonya! (SONYA *doesn't hear him. She stands with her head sadly fallen.*) Sonya! (*Pause*) She doesn't hear me. (*To* MARINA) And you, Marina, sit down. (MARINA *sits down and knits a sock.*) Thank you, everybody. Now lend me your ears, as they say. Attention, please! (*He laughs.*)

VOINITSKI (*upset*): Am I needed? May I go?

SEREBRYAKOV: No, no. I need you here most of all.

VOINITSKI: What do you want of me?

SEREBRYAKOV: "Want of you?" What are you so upset about? (*Pause*) If I've done you any wrong, then please forgive me.

VOINITSKI: Drop that tone. Let's get on with the matter. . . . What do you want?

(*Enter* MARIA.)

SEREBRYAKOV: Here's *Maman*. I'll begin, ladies and gentlemen. (*Pause*) Ladies and gentlemen. I have invited you here to announce to you that the inspector general[14] is arriving. However, joking aside, it's a serious matter. People, I've gathered you here to ask your help and advice, and, knowing your customary kindness, I hope to receive it. I am an educated man, always in my books, and I have always been a stranger to practical life. I cannot manage without the advice of experienced people, and so I ask you, Ivan, and you all, you, Ilya, and you, *Maman* . . . The fact is, *manet omnes una nox,* which means that we shall live as long as God deems it fit; I am old and sick, and so I must take the proper time to settle my affairs insofar as they concern my family. My life is over; I am not thinking of myself, but I have a young wife and an unmarried daughter. (*Pause*) To continue to live in the country is impossible for me. We were not cut out for it. But to have the means to live in the city on what we receive from this estate is impossible. Let us assume that we sell the forest, that would be an extraordinary measure to take, it cannot be repeated year after year. We must find an expedient which would guarantee us something permanent, a more or less definite sum of income. I have thought of one such expedient and I have the honor of proposing it to you for discussion. Passing over the details, I shall sketch for you a rough outline. Our estate yields on an average of not more than two percent. I propose to sell it. If we convert the money into interest-bearing securities, we should receive from four to five percent, and I think there would even be a surplus of a few thousand which would allow us to buy a small summer house in Finland.[15]

VOINITSKI: Wait . . . I think my ears are deceiving me. Repeat what you said.

SEREBRYAKOV: With the money we get, invest in interest-bearing securities, and with the surplus, what remains, buy a summer house in Finland.

VOINITSKI: Not Finland . . . You said something else.

SEREBRYAKOV: I propose to sell the estate.

VOINITSKI: That's it. Sell the estate: a magnificent, splendid idea. . . . And what do you propose that I and my old mother should do with ourselves, and what about Sonya?

SEREBRYAKOV: We will discuss all that in good time. Not everything at once.

VOINITSKI: Wait. Obviously, up until now, I've not had a drop of common sense. Up until now I was stupid enough to think that this estate belonged to Sonya. My poor dead father bought this estate as a dowry for my sister. Up till now I was naïve, I understood the law was not made for Turks, and so I thought the estate passed, after the death of my sister, to Sonya.

SEREBRYAKOV: Yes, the estate belongs to Sonya. Who disputes it? Without the approval of Sonya, I wouldn't undertake to sell it. The fact that I propose to sell it is all to Sonya's benefit.

VOINITSKI: This is inconceivable, absolutely inconceivable! Either I have gone stark, raving mad or . . . or . . .

MARIA: Jean, don't contradict Alexander. Truly, he knows better than we do what is right and what is wrong.

VOINITSKI: No, give me some water. (*He drinks.*) Say what you like, whatever you like!

SEREBRYAKOV: I don't understand what has upset you so. I

don't say that my proposal is ideal. If you do not find it suitable, then I will not insist.

(*Pause.*)

TELYEGIN (*embarrassed*): Your excellency, I feel not only reverence for learning, but also I feel somehow as if it were in the family. My brother Grigory Ilyich's wife's brother, perhaps you know him, Konstantin Trofimovich Lakedemonov, had a master's degree.

VOINITSKI: Wait, Waffles, we're busy. . . . Wait, later. . . . (*To* SEREBRYAKOV) Now ask him. This estate was bought from his uncle.

SEREBRYAKOV: But why should I ask him? What for?

VOINITSKI: This estate was bought long ago for ninety-five thousand. Uncle paid only seventy thousand, and there remained a debt of twenty-five thousand to pay. Now listen: the estate would not have been bought if I had not given up my inheritance in favor of my sister, whom I dearly loved. Is it not enough that I worked for ten years like a beast of burden and paid off the mortgage . . .

SEREBRYAKOV: I'm sorry I began this conversation.

VOINITSKI: The estate is free of debt and in order only because of my personal efforts. And now that I am old, they want to drive me out by the scruff of my neck!

SEREBRYAKOV: I don't understand what you're getting at!

VOINITSKI: For twenty-five years I managed this estate, I worked, I sent you money, like a conscientious steward, and not once in all that time did you thank me. All that time—in my youth and now—I received from you the pitiful sum of five hundred rubles a year—a beggar's wage!—and not once did you ever think of increasing it by even one ruble!

SEREBRYAKOV: Ivan, how could I have known? I'm not a practical man, and I don't understand these things. You could have added to it as much as you liked.

VOINITSKI: Why didn't I steal? Why didn't you all despise me for not stealing? That would have been only fair, and now I wouldn't be a beggar!

MARIA (*sternly*): Jean!

TELYEGIN (*excited*): Vanya, my friend, you mustn't, you really mustn't. . . . I'm trembling all over. . . . Why spoil good relations? (*Kisses him.*) You mustn't.

VOINITSKI: For twenty-five years I, with this mother of mine, like a mole, have been cooped up inside these four walls. . . . All of our thoughts and feelings were for you alone. In the daytime we spoke about you, about your work, we were proud of you, we uttered your name with reverence; we wasted our nights reading your magazines and books, which I now deeply despise!

TELYEGIN: You mustn't, Vanya, you really mustn't. . . . I can't stand it. . . .

SEREBRYAKOV (*angrily*): I don't understand what it is you want.

VOINITSKI: For us, you were a creature of a higher order, and I knew your articles by heart. . . . But now my eyes are opened! I see everything! You write about art, but you don't understand anything about art! All your work, which I loved, isn't worth a copper kopeck! You've made a fool of us!

SEREBRYAKOV: People! Can't you make him stop! I must get out of here!

YELENA: Ivan, I demand you keep quiet! Do you hear?

VOINITSKI: I will not keep quiet! (*Barring* SEREBRYAKOV's *way*) Wait, I have not finished! You have ruined my life! I have not lived, I have not lived! I have you to thank that I have destroyed and done away with the best years of my life! You are my worst enemy!

TELYEGIN: I can't bear it. . . . I cannot bear it for a moment. . . . I'm going. . . . (*Goes out very much upset.*)

SEREBRYAKOV: What do you want from me? What right do you have to speak to me in such a tone? Nonentity! If the estate is yours, then take it. . . . I don't need it!

YELENA: I'm leaving this hell this very minute! (*Shouts.*) I can't stand it any more!

VOINITSKI: I have spoiled my life! I was talented, intelligent, daring. . . . If I had lived a normal life, then I could have become some sort of Schopenhauer or a Dostoevski. . . .[16] I'm raving! I'm going out of my mind! Mother, I'm desperate! Mother!

MARIA (*sternly*): Listen to Alexander!

SONYA (*kneeling down before* MARINA *and huddling close to her*): Marina! Marina!

VOINITSKI: Mother! What shall I do? Never mind, don't tell me! I know what I must do! (*To* SEREBRYAKOV) You will remember me! *(Goes out by the middle door.* MARIA *goes after him.)*

SEREBRYAKOV: People, what is the meaning of this, after all? Take this raving lunatic away from me! I cannot live under the same roof with him! He lives here . . . *(points to the middle door)* almost by my side. . . . Let him move into the village, or to one of the cottages, or I shall leave. Stay in the same house with him I cannot. . . .

YELENA *(to her husband)*: We'll leave here today! Make the arrangements at once!

SEREBRYAKOV: Worthless individual!

SONYA *(remains on her knees, turning toward her father; nervously, through her tears)*: You must be merciful, Papa! Remember, when you were younger, Uncle Vanya and Grandmother used to spend their nights translating your books for you, copying your papers . . . every night, every single night! Uncle Vanya and I worked without rest, afraid to spend even a single kopeck on ourselves, and we sent it all to you. . . . We earned our keep. Oh, I'm not saying it's right, not right at all, but you must try to understand us, Papa. You must be merciful!

YELENA *(moved, to her husband)*: Alexander, for God's sake, make it up with him, I beg of you.

SEREBRYAKOV: Very well, I'll talk it over with him. . . . I'm not accusing him, I'm not angry, but, you must admit, his behavior has been somewhat strange. All right, I'll go to him. *(He goes out by the middle door.)*

YELENA: Be gentle with him, calm him. . . . *(*YELENA *goes out after him.)*

SONYA *(pressing close to* MARINA*)*: Marina! Marina!

MARINA: It's nothing, dear. The geese do cackle . . . and then they stop. They cackle . . . and they stop. . . .

SONYA: Marina!

MARINA *(caressing her hair)*: You're trembling as if you were out in the cold! Well, well, my little orphan, God is merciful. Some linden tea or some raspberry jam, and it will go away. . . . Don't grieve, my dear. . . . *(Looking at the middle door, angrily)* Go away, geese, a plague on you!

(A shot is heard behind the scenes. YELENA *screams;* SONYA *shudders.)*

Oh, you!

SEREBRYAKOV *(comes running in, reeling from fear)*: Restrain him! Hold him back! He's gone out of his mind!

(YELENA and VOINITSKI struggle at the door.)

YELENA *(trying to take the revolver from him)*: Give it to me! Give it to me, I tell you!

VOINITSKI: Leave me alone! Hélène, let me go! *(Freeing himself, running and looking around for SEREBRYAKOV)* Where is he? Oh, there he is! *(Shooting at him)* Bang! *(Pause)* Didn't get him? Missed again? *(Angrily)* Damn, damn . . . damn it to hell. . . . *(Throws the revolver on the floor and sits exhausted in the chair. SEREBRYAKOV is stunned; YELENA leans against the wall, fainting.)*

YELENA: Get me out of here! Take me away, kill me . . . but I can't stay here, I absolutely cannot!

VOINITSKI *(in despair)*: Oh, what am I doing! What am I doing!

SONYA *(quietly)*: Marina! Marina!

CURTAIN

ACT
FOUR

IVAN's *room; it is his bedroom as well
as the office of the estate. By the window
there is a large table with account books
and papers of all kinds, a writing desk,
bookcases and scales. A smaller table for*
ASTROV; *on this table there are drawing
equipment and paints; nearby is a portfolio. A birdcage with a starling in it.
On the wall is a map of Africa, which is
obviously of no use here. A huge divan,
upholstered in oilcloth. On the left, a
door leading to the rest of the house; on
the right, a door to a passageway; near
to the door at right lies a mat for the
peasants to wipe their feet on. It is an
autumn evening. All is quiet.*

TELYEGIN *and* MARINA *are seated, facing one another, winding the wool for
stockings.*

TELYEGIN: A little faster, Marina. They'll soon be calling to
say good-bye. They've already asked for the horses to be
brought.

MARINA (*trying to wind faster*): There's only a little left.

TELYEGIN: They're going to Kharkov. They're going to live
there.

MARINA: Good for them.

TELYEGIN: They're frightened. . . . Yelena said, "I won't spend
another hour in this place. . . . Let's go while the going is
good. . . . We'll live in Kharkov," she says, "we'll have a
look around and then we'll send for our things. . . ." They're

112

not taking much with them. You know, Marina, it wasn't their fate to live here. . . . Not their fate . . . Fatal predestination.

MARINA: Good for them. All that noise they've been making lately, the shooting . . . it's a shame!

TELYEGIN: Yes, a subject worthy of Aivazovski's[11] brush.

MARINA: It wasn't meant for my eyes. *(Pause)* Once again, we'll live as we did in the old days. In the morning we'll have tea at eight o'clock, lunch at one, we'll sit down to supper in the evening; everything in order, like at other people's homes . . . Christian-like. *(With a sigh)* I haven't eaten noodles for a long time now, sinner that I am.

TELYEGIN: Yes, it's been a long time since noodles have been prepared here. *(Pause)* A long time . . . This morning, Marina, I was walking through the village, when a shopkeeper shouted after me, "Hey, you, sponge!" Oh, that gave me a bitter feeling!

MARINA: Don't pay any notice, my dear. We're all sponges on God. You, Sonya, Ivan; none of you sit around without working, all of you work hard! All of you . . . Where's Sonya?

TELYEGIN: In the garden. They're all with the doctor, looking for Ivan. They're afraid he might have done himself some harm.

MARINA: And where is his pistol?

TELYEGIN *(whispering)*: I hid it in the cellar!

MARINA *(grinning)*: How sinful!

(VOINITSKI and ASTROV enter from outside.)

VOINITSKI: Leave me alone. *(To MARINA and TELYEGIN)* Get out of here, leave me alone, if only for an hour! I can't bear to be watched over.

TELYEGIN: Right away, Vanya. *(Tiptoeing out)*

MARINA: The geese go: honk, honk, honk! *(Gathering her wool and going)*

VOINITSKI: Leave me alone.

ASTROV: With the greatest satisfaction, I would long ago have needed to leave here, but, I repeat, I will not go until you give back what you took from me.

VOINITSKI: I took nothing from you.

ASTROV: Look, seriously . . . don't hold me back. I should have left long ago.

VOINITSKI: I took nothing from you.

(Both sit down.)

ASTROV: Really? Well, in that case, I'll wait a little longer, and then, pardon me, but we'll have to take stronger steps. We'll have to tie you up and search you. I'm telling you this in all seriousness.

VOINITSKI: As you wish. *(Pause)* To play the fool to such an extent: to shoot twice and miss both times. I'll never forgive myself!

ASTROV: If you had the inclination to shoot, why didn't you just put a bullet through your own head?

VOINITSKI *(shrugging his shoulders)*: Strange. I tried to kill somebody, but they don't arrest me, they don't bring me to trial. They must think I'm mad. *(Evil laugh)* I'm mad, but they are not mad who hide behind the mask of a professor, playing hocus-pocus, concealing their own mediocrity and stupidity, their shameful heartlessness. They are not mad who marry old men and then deceive them openly. I saw it, I saw how you kissed her!

ASTROV: Yes . . . I did. Here's what I think of you. *(Thumbs his nose at him.)*

VOINITSKI *(looking at the door)*: No, it's the earth which is mad to tolerate you!

ASTROV: How stupid!

VOINITSKI: Well, if I'm mad and irresponsible, I have the right to utter stupidities.

ASTROV: That's an old joke. You're not mad, you're just a queer duck. You're a clown. I used to think people like you were sick and abnormal, but now I'm of the opinion that yours is the normal state of man. To be a clown. You're perfectly normal.

VOINITSKI *(his hands covering his face)*: I'm so ashamed! If you only knew how ashamed I was! This sharp feeling of shame is worse than any pain. *(Depressed)* It's unbearable! *(Bending over the table)* What can I do with myself? What can I do?

ASTROV: Nothing.

VOINITSKI: Give me something to comfort me! Oh, my God

. . . I'm forty-seven years old; if I were to live till sixty, then I have thirteen years left. Long years! How can I live through these thirteen years? What will I do, how can I fill them? Oh, please understand . . . (*Compulsively squeezing* ASTROV's *hand*) You must understand, if I could only live out the remaining years of my life in some new way. To wake up some fine, clear morning and feel as if you could begin life anew, that the past is all forgotten, cleared away like smoke. (*He weeps.*) To start a new life . . . Tell me how to start . . . where shall I start. . . .

ASTROV (*angrily*): Oh, that's enough! That new life again! Our situation, yours and mine, is hopeless.

VOINITSKI: Is it?

ASTROV: I'm convinced of it.

VOINITSKI: Give me something to comfort me. . . . (*Pointing to his heart*) It burns inside me here.

ASTROV (*shouts angrily*): Stop it! (*Relenting*) Those who will live after us a hundred or two hundred years from now, and who will disdain us for having lived out our lives so stupidly and insipidly—they may perhaps find the way to be happy, but we . . . we have only one hope left. Our hope is that when we will be resting in our graves, we may perhaps be visited with dreams . . . even sweet ones. (*Sighing*) Yes, my friend. In all the district there were only two decent, intelligent men: you and I. But ten years of this philistine existence, this contemptible life, have done us in; its rotten fumes have poisoned our blood, and we have become as vulgar as somebody else. (*Agitated*) Now, don't try to talk me out of it. Give me back what you took from me.

VOINITSKI: I didn't take anything from you.

ASTROV: You took a jar of morphine from my medicine bag. (*Pause*) Listen, if you want so much to do yourself in, then go into the forest and shoot yourself there. But give me back the morphine, or there'll be talk about it, conjecture, they'll think I gave it to you. . . . I'll be having to come over and cut you open. . . . You think that's any fun?

(*Enter* SONYA.)

VOINITSKI: Leave me alone!

ASTROV (*to* SONYA): Sofia, your uncle made off with some

morphine from my medicine bag and he won't give it back to me. Tell him that's not . . . clever, in the long run. And I don't have time. I have to go.

SONYA: Uncle Vanya, did you take the morphine?

(Pause.)

ASTROV: He took it. I can vouch for that.

SONYA: Give it back. Why do you want to frighten us? *(Tenderly)* Give it back, Uncle Vanya! I may be no less unhappy than you are, only I refuse to despair. I bear it and I will continue to do so as long as I live. You must bear up, too. *(Pause)* Give it back! *(Kisses his hand.)* Dear, nice Uncle, my darling, give it back! *(She weeps.)* You're a good man, you will have pity on us and give it back. You must be patient, Uncle! Be patient!

VOINITSKI *(reaches into the table drawer and gives it to* ASTROV): Here, take it! *(To* SONYA) We've got to start working right away, quickly start something, or I won't be able to bear it . . . I won't be able to . . .

SONYA: Yes, yes, work. As soon as we see them off, we'll sit down to work. . . . *(She nervously sorts out the papers on the table.)* We've neglected everything.

ASTROV *(puts the jar in the medicine bag and fastens the straps)*: Now we can get under way.

YELENA *(enters)*: Are you here, Ivan? We're ready to go. . . . Go to Alexander, he wants to say something to you.

SONYA: Go, Uncle Vanya. *(Takes* VOINITSKI *by the arm.)* Let's go. Papa and you must make it up. You must.

*(*SONYA *and* VOINITSKI *go out.)*

YELENA: I'm going. *(Takes* ASTROV's *hand.)* Good-bye.

ASTROV: Already?

YELENA: The horses are harnessed.

ASTROV: Good-bye.

YELENA: You promised me you would leave here today.

ASTROV: I remember. I'm going right away. *(Pause)* Are you frightened? *(Takes her hand.)* Are you really so afraid?

YELENA: Yes.

ASTROV: Then stay! Eh? Tomorrow, in the forest . . .

YELENA: No . . . It's already decided. That's why I can bear

to look at you courageously, because the departure has
already been decided on. . . . I ask you for only one thing:
think better of me. I would wish you had respect for me.

ASTROV: Oh! *(Gesture of impatience)* Stay, do that, please.
You must realize, you have nothing in the world to do, you
have no aim in life, nothing to occupy your mind, and
sooner or later, it will make no difference, if you give way
to your feelings—it's inevitable. It would be better if it
didn't happen in Kharkov or in Kursk somewhere,[18] but
here, close to nature. . . . It's poetic here, at least, the
autumn itself is beautiful. . . . Here there are forest reserva-
tions, the dilapidated country houses they have in Turgenev's
novels.

YELENA: How ridiculous you are. . . . I'm angry with you . . .
but all the same, I'll remember you with pleasure. You're an
interesting, original man. We will never see each other
again, so why hide it? I'm even a little infatuated with you.
Well, then, let's shake hands and part friends. Think kindly
of me.

ASTROV *(shaking hands)*: Well, you might as well go. . . .
(Deep in thought) You seem like a fine, sincere person, but
. . . re really quite strange. You came here with your hus-
. . . d and everybody who was here working, running around
. . . building something or other was forced to drop his work
. . . spend the entire summer occupied with your husband's
. . . nd you. Both of you—he and you—infected us with
. . . leness. I was carried away; for a whole month I
. . . one anything and during all that time people have
. . . nd the peasants allowed their cattle to graze in
. . . planted forests. Thus, wherever you and your
. . . go, you bring about some destruction. I'm joking,
. . . , but all the same . . . Strange . . . I'm convinced
. . . ou had stayed, the devastation would have been
. . . us. It would have ruined me and no good would
. . . me of it for you, either. Well, you must go. *Finita la
commedia!* [19]

YELENA *(takes a pencil from his table and quickly conceals it)*:
I'll take this pencil to remember you by.

ASTROV: How strange. We were friends and suddenly, for no
reason at all, we'll never see each other again. It's the same
for everyone. Before anybody comes in, before Uncle Vanya
comes in with a bouquet, let me . . . allow me . . . to kiss

you good-bye. . . . All right? (*Kisses her on the cheek.*)
Well, now . . . that was nice.

YELENA: I wish you all the best. (*Glancing around*) Oh, well,
never mind, for once in my life! (*She embraces him impetu-
ously and then both separate quickly.*) I must go.

ASTROV: Go quickly. If the horses are harnessed, then you
must go.

YELENA: I think I hear them coming.

(*Both listen.*)

ASTROV: *Finita!*

(*Enter* SEREBRYAKOV, VOINITSKI, MARIA *with book,* TEL-
YEGIN *and* SONYA.)

SEREBRYAKOV (*to* VOINITSKI): Let bygones be bygones. After
all that has happened, I have lived through so much in
these last few hours and had so many thoughts that it seems
to me that I could write a whole treatise on how one must
live for the edification of posterity. I readily acce
apologies and I ask you to forgive me. Good-by
changes kisses with VOINITSKI *three times.*)

VOINITSKI: You will receive exactly what you received i
past. Everything will be as it was.

(YELENA *embraces* SONYA.)

SEREBRYAKOV (*kisses* MARIA'*s hands*): Maman . . .

MARIA (*kissing him*): Alexander, have yourself photog
and send me your picture. You know how dear yo
me.

TELYEGIN: Farewell, your excellency! Don't forget us!

SEREBRYAKOV (*after kissing his daughter*): Farewell .
well all! (*Taking* ASTROV'*s hand*) Thank you for your excellent company. . . . I respect your way of thinking, your
enthusiasm and your impulses, but allow an old man to
present, with his farewell salutations, only one observation:
one must work, people! One must do something! (*Bows to
everyone.*) My best to you all! (*He goes out.* MARIA *and*
SONYA *go after him.*)

VOINITSKI (*kisses* YELENA's *hand passionately*): Farewell . . .
Forgive me . . . We shall never see each other again.

YELENA (*moved*): Farewell, my dear. (*Kisses him on the head
and goes out.*)

ASTROV (*to* TELYEGIN): Waffles, while they're at it, tell them to
bring my horses round, too.

TELYEGIN: Yes, my friend. (*He goes out. Only* ASTROV *and*
VOINITSKI *remain.*)

ASTROV (*removing his paints from the table and putting them
in a valise*): Why aren't you seeing them off?

VOINITSKI: Let them go. I . . . I can't. . . . It's too painful for
me. I must get busy quickly with something. . . . Work . . .
work! (*He rummages among the papers on the table. Pause;
bells are heard.*)

ASTROV: They're going. The professor must be happy! You
couldn't get him back here for love or money.

MARINA (*coming in*): They've gone. (*Sits in the armchair and
knits a stocking.*)

SONYA (*enters*): They've gone. (*Wipes her eyes.*) May they live
and be well. (*To her uncle*) Well, Uncle Vanya, let's do
something.

VOINITSKI: To work, to work . . .

SONYA: It's been a very long time since we've sat together at
this table. (*She lights the lamp on the table.*) There seems
to be no ink. . . . (*Takes the inkstand and goes to the cupboard, filling it with ink.*) It makes me sad to see them gone.

MARIA (*slowly enters*): They've gone! (*Sits down and immerses
herself in her reading.*)

SONYA (*sits at the table and looks through the account book*):
Let's write, Uncle Vanya; first all the accounts. We've neglected them terribly. Today somebody wrote for his bill
again. Take your pen. You write one bill and I'll do another. . . .

VOINITSKI (*writes*): "Account . . . of Mr. . . ."

(*Both write silently.*)

MARINA (*yawning*): Ready to go bye-bye . . .

ASTROV: It's quiet here. Just pens scratching, crickets chirping,
it's warm and cozy. . . I don't want to leave here. (*Sound
of bells*) There come the horses. . . . All that remains is for
me to say good-bye to you, my friends, to say good-bye to

my table . . . and . . . go off! (*Puts his maps into a portfolio.*)

MARINA: Why are you fussing? Sit down.

ASTROV: I can't.

VOINITSKI (*writes*): "And the balance from your previous account is two hundred and seventy-five . . ."

(*A* WORKMAN *enters.*)

WORKMAN: Dr. Astrov, the horses are ready.

ASTROV: Very well. (ASTROV *gives him the medicine bag, his valise and portfolio.*) Here, take this. See you don't crush the portfolio.

WORKMAN: Yes, sir. (*Goes out.*)

ASTROV: Well . . . (*Starts saying good-bye.*)

SONYA: When will we see each other again?

ASTROV: Not before next summer, most probably. Hardly this winter . . . But if something were to happen, let me know. Then I'll come. (*Shakes hands.*) Thank you for the hospitality and your kindness . . . in a word, for everything. (*Goes to* MARINA *and kisses her on the head.*) Farewell, old lady.

MARINA: Are you leaving without tea?

ASTROV: I don't want any, Marina.

MARINA: Would you like to drink some vodka?

ASTROV (*undecided*): Perhaps . . . (MARINA *goes out; pause*) My carriage horse is beginning to limp. I noticed it again yesterday when Petrushka was taking him to water.

VOINITSKI: He needs to be reshod.

ASTROV: When I get to Rozhdestvennoye, I'll go to the blacksmith's. That's the only thing to do. (*He goes to the map of Africa and contemplates it.*) It must be so hot now in Africa . . . hot as hell!

VOINITSKI: Yes, very likely.

MARINA (*returning with a tray, on which there is glass of vodka and a piece of bread*): Have some. (ASTROV *drinks some vodka.*) To your health, my dear. (*A low bow*) And have a little bread with it.

ASTROV: No, it's fine as it is. . . . All the best to you! (*To* MARINA) Don't see me off, Marina. There's no need.

(*He goes.* SONYA *goes after him with a candle, to light his way.* MARINA *sits down in her armchair.*)

VOINITSKI *(writing)*: "Second of February, vegetable oil, twenty pounds . . . Sixteenth of February, vegetable oil again, twenty pounds . . . Buckwheat . . ."

(Pause. Sound of bells.)

MARINA: He's gone.

(Pause.)

SONYA *(returning, places the candle on the table)*: He's gone. . . .

VOINITSKI *(counting on the abacus and writing)*: So that makes fifteen . . . twenty-five . . .

(SONYA sits and writes.)

MARINA *(yawning)*: May the Lord forgive us all. . . .

(TELYEGIN enters on tiptoe, sits down near the door and quietly tunes his guitar.)

VOINITSKI *(to SONYA, smoothing her hair)*: My child, I'm so depressed! Oh, if you only knew how depressed I am!

SONYA: What can we do—we must live! *(Pause)* We'll live, Uncle Vanya. We shall live through a long, long succession of days and long, endless evenings; we will endure whatever fate has in store for us; we will work for others now and in our old age, we will not know the meaning of rest, and when our hour comes, we will die humbly, and beyond the grave we shall say that we suffered, that we wept, that it was a bitter life, and God will have pity on us; and both of us, Uncle, dear Uncle, will see a life which is bright, beautiful and fine, we shall rejoice and we shall look back at our present unhappiness with great tenderness, with a smile . . . and we shall rest. I believe it, Uncle, I believe it with all my heart and soul. . . . *(Kneels beside him and places her head on his hands; in a weary voice)* We shall rest! *(TELYEGIN plays his guitar quietly.)* We shall rest! We shall hear the angels, we shall see the heavens like bright diamonds, we shall see all the evils in the world and all of our suffering enveloped in the mercy which fills the world, and our lives will be quiet, tender and sweet as a caress. . . . I believe it, I do so believe it. . . . *(Wipes his tears away with a handkerchief.)* Poor, poor dear Uncle Vanya, you're weeping. . . . *(Through her own tears)* You've never known any joy in your life, but wait, Uncle Vanya just wait. . . . We shall rest. . . . *(She embraces him.)* We shall rest! *(The night watchman taps.* TELYEGIN *plays quietly;* MARIA *writes in the margins of her pamphlets;* MARINA *knits a stocking.)* We shall finally rest!

THE CURTAIN FALLS SLOWLY

AFTERWORD

Uncle Vanya is the most concise of Chekhov's plays. This is probably because it is an adaptation of his earlier work *The Wood Demon,* and a careful study of both plays reveals that Chekhov tried to keep as much as possible of the earlier play when he remade its image. It is very likely that he revised it in 1890, shortly after its unhappy debut at the Abramova Theater in Moscow in December, 1889, and not, as has been thought for a long time, after *The Sea Gull* and his return to the theater.

Uncle Vanya is a distillation of *The Wood Demon* with a change in focus. There are only five major characters in the play. The "Wood Demon" role of the earlier play, Mikhail Krushchev, became Dr. Astrov in the revision. The title role was transferred to Uncle Vanya, the simple, downtrodden loyal retainer who has sacrificed the best years of his life to a dream. As steward of the estate of the celebrated writer-scholar Serebryakov, he has been rewarded for his labors with a totally inadequate salary and the life of an ambiguous slave. Vanya, like so many of Chekhov's characters, could have seen himself as another Schopenhauer or Dostoevski, but through an innate laziness of character, lack of focus and ambition, he has lived a life of symbiotic achievement only. He fell in love with the professor's life and also, ironically enough, with the professor's wife, Yelena. Professor Serebryakov possesses everything that Vanya would wish to own. Vanya could never possess a beauty such as Yelena and he must content himself with her friendship. Actually Yelena is very much like Vanya. She married the professor because she was dazzled by his intellect; he was for her the symbol of a great man. She has sacrificed her beauty and her youth to him. Vanya and Yelena are great friends because they recognize in each other similarities of temperament and weak-

123

nesses common to them both. Like an alter ego, Vanya irritates her throughout the play. At the end, when she leaves, significantly it is Vanya she kisses good-bye with the most authentic emotion.

The potential hero of this play that lacks heroes is Astrov. In *The Wood Demon* he was a young man (Krushchev) who loved the forests and wished to conserve the national heritage. He was also a doctor, a young idealist of the kind that Russian life destroyed under the pressure of long years of hard work and disillusionment. Astrov is Krushchev ten years later, a man with a great spirit who has been broken by the vulgar life he has had to lead. His sensibilities have been blunted by the exigencies of his difficult life. He is at a dangerous turning point of his existence, ready to abandon all of the ideals he has lived for. He knows he is alive because he is still extraordinarily sensitive to beauty. Despite himself, he falls in love with Yelena; his essential nobility of character attracts her. She has long since become disillusioned with her cantankerous, hypochondriacal husband and Astrov is the only man she has met who possesses the integrity she yearns for. He neglects his practice by coming to hover near her. She deflects him from the course of his life as a magnet would an iron filing. Their attraction is the grand passion but neither quite has the temperament to live up to it. For Astrov has a slothful side to his nature—he is as melancholy as Vanya—and Yelena herself suffers from the same apathy of the soul.

The other individuals of the play gravitate toward these three major characters who are so much alike. Sonya has great love in her heart and is capable of toil, loyalty and devotion. She is not beautiful and she knows it. She loves Astrov with all her girlish heart, defending his idealistic notions about the forests and admiring him unquestioningly. More than Uncle Vanya, she is the symbol of the downtrodden. It is her aria that closes the play. She consoles Vanya for his misfortunes and hopes against hope that their endless toil will lead to a better future life in the world beyond. Her resignation is beautiful and her acceptance of life, though based on innocent blindness, is the noblest aspect of the play. She is the only nonridiculous character, lacking the others' solipsism and selfishness.

Serebryakov, everybody's great man, is a foolish, vain, elderly pedant; he is one of those fortunate few who, by innate breeding, horse sense and canniness, have managed to fascinate most of the men and women in his entourage. Yelena was capable of marrying him, Vanya's bluestocking of a mother reveres his genius, and even when he is old and complaining, he manages to make everything around him work only for him. He brings out the masochist in everyone.

Waffles is a silhouette of Vanya. He is a crotchety parasite, a disappointed man who, due to his physical attributes, has never been a favorite with the ladies. Abandoned by his wife on their wedding day, he has nevertheless helped support the children she had by the other man. Waffles has admired the erudition of the professor from far off and esteems him as much as Vanya once did. The only essential difference between them is that Waffles never could revolt against his life. He accepts his downtrodden status and maintains his illusions intact.

Thus we have a galaxy of characters who, from the most selfless to the most selfish, gravitate toward the selfish. Sonya, Astrov, Waffles, Vanya, Maria Voinitski, all worship at the altar of either Yelena or her husband or both. After experiencing this play, one wonders whether Chekhov meant us to believe that in this imperfect world the most unworthy are those who triumph. Yet even the most self-absorbed of the characters contains within himself the seeds of his degradation. Serebryakov can never be convinced that he is loved and Yelena feels the uselessness of her existence. By her faith, it is only Sonya who remains unscathed. And one wonders how deep her faith was meant to be and whether she expresses it only as a consolation to Vanya for his desperate situation at the end of the play. Speculation about Chekhov's characters is perhaps ultimately idle, for one returns always to the spectacle of a disabused sensibility with a razor-sharp eye and an unpitying glance. Chekhov's compassion sacrifices neither accuracy nor vision in its objective view of human foibles. He once said that he wrote with an icy heart. One can never improve upon the trenchant images Chekhov used.

Uncle Vanya comes to one marvelous comic boil. Chekhov saw that the silliest of conflagrations, the most trivial of arguments, could effectively symbolize the meaning of an entire life. In *Uncle Vanya*, all roads lead to the third act, to the moment in which Vanya tries to kill the professor. When Serebryakov decides that he can no longer live at the estate in the country, that he must sell it and buy a summer house in Finland, he does not reckon with the fact that he is sacrificing Vanya and his old mother, that they will have nowhere to go. Vanya, outraged, suddenly realizes fully that he has wasted twenty-five years of his life in service to this worthless man. One must also add that this realization, which is foreshadowed from the very first scenes of the play, is further aggravated by Vanya's catching Yelena and Astrov embracing. The fury he must sublimate at this moment is unleashed on the professor. He tries to kill Serebryakov and fails. Even murder is not Vanya's forte. The murder scene ends in a dreadful comic fizzle.

It is a measure of Chekhov's subtle scaffolding of the architecture of the play that Vanya himself is never aware that his murder attempt comes as much from his disappointment in catching Yelena with Astrov as it does from his imminent danger of losing his home. The action of *Uncle Vanya* is so subtly set up that it seems as if no action has transpired. Critics have treated us to formulae such as "indirect action," and it is still a commonplace to believe that nothing happens in Chekhov's plays. This is so far from the truth as to become irritating. What happens in Chekhov's plays is, as in life, very often beneath the surface. It explodes to the surface at the most inopportune and the wildest moments. Chekhov simply imitated the absurd rhythm of life when he wrote his plays. The explosive moment of *Uncle Vanya* is beautifully achieved, having been led to inexorably by the most plausible series of events. As in French classical tragedy, they do not always occur on stage. Sonya loves Astrov and asks Yelena to be her go-between with him, in a manner of speaking. Yelena seizes this opportunity to make sure that Astrov is in love with her. She knows instinctively that Astrov could not love Sonya. When Astrov is maneuvered into declaring his love for Yelena, Vanya discovers them together. It is precisely at the next theatrical beat that the professor announces his desire to sell the estate. Vanya explodes, tries to kill him, and fails. The professor decides to leave, hastened in his decision by Yelena, who cannot bear to remain where she has caused so much devastation.

To appreciate the beauty and simplicity of this construction, one need only see what Chekhov had made of *The Wood Demon*. In the earlier play, Sonya loved Krushchev and he returned her love. She was a beautiful young singer, somewhat precious, and by the end of the play they were united and ready to marry. Vanya was named George in *The Wood Demon* and his disappointment in the professor and in his life led him to commit suicide. Act Three ended with that suicide. After it, Yelena fled to Waffles' mill, where she remained until she had the courage to return to the professor. It was her return that motivated a joyously happy ending to the play. The last act of *The Wood Demon* is as different from the last act of *Uncle Vanya* as comedy is to tragedy. *The Wood Demon* ends in a delightful midsummer night's dream of united lovers; *Uncle Vanya's* last act is a long, sinuous elegy of departure. In the earlier play, Yelena was blamed by everyone for being an immoral woman. The opprobrium of the play settled on her. Her innocence was proved at the end of the play and the moral of the work seemed to be that the beautiful of the world were on trial before those who misjudged them. The Wood Demon tried to save the forests but human beings were in even greater danger because of inner hates and turmoils. It was a play of Tolstoyan moral rectitude. Chekhov saw the destructive vengefulness of society, much as Ibsen did, and spoke out sharply against it.

Uncle Vanya is a very different play. Chekhov united the characters in tighter relationships. He chose to have Sonya and Yelena in love with the same man. This single element of the plot served to unite the entire play. Sonya was no longer the marvelous young bluestocking, but the hard-working Cinderella whose love is as real as her lack of physical beauty. *Uncle Vanya* is a more aesthetic experience than its predecessor. It is as intimately connected with the experience of beauty, spiritual as well as physical, but it is stated without any attempt at a moral judgment. Beauty is depicted as a quality as well as an effect, a defect as well as an attribute. Those who perceive beauty are in danger of being dominated by it. It is as elusive as life. It is infinitely desirable but brings neither happiness nor fulfillment. Yet how much human beings strive to attain it! The quest for beauty, physical as well as spiritual, reflected as well as innate, is perhaps the true subject of *Uncle Vanya*.

By changing Sonya's character, by enhancing the love plot and, finally, by having Vanya fail in his murder attempt but not commit suicide, Chekhov chanced on a comic device that would embody the entire feeling of futility that the play needed to convey. Vanya's hit and miss is one of the finest moments of modern theater because it symbolizes the entire meaning of the play in one futile action. Nothing in the play changes essentially. The Astrovs and the Yelenas of this world were never meant for each other. They never cared enough. Through fear, apathy, loneliness, sloth of the soul, people's lives must be lived out in quiet desperation. Even Sonya's magnificent soliloquy at the end of the play may be interpreted as an ironic subterfuge, a means of consoling poor Vanya, whom Sonya loves and respects, for the essential meaninglessness of their existence.

When the play was first produced at the Moscow Art Theater, Astrov was undoubtedly the hero of the play. The Pirogov Congress, a conference of doctors, attended a performance. The doctors saw themselves in Astrov, his destiny was theirs; they were the anonymous humble workers of Russia who toiled for a better world that might never come. They were touched by his plight to the point of tears. It was the work of a doctor for a world of doctors.

Uncle Vanya is a play that makes everyone cry once in a while. Perhaps we may also have the courage to play it for comedy, as Chekhov intended, to play it "naturally," without sentimentality. As Chekhov said to Stanislavski (who played Astrov): "Astrov whistles! Vanya cries, but Astrov whistles." There are those who lament and those who sublimate. Vanya, Yelena, Serebryakov and Waffles are those who lament. Marina, the elderly nurse Chekhov invented for the play when he suppressed several of the richest characters in *The Wood Demon,* carries on nobly. And so do Sonya and Astrov. And were it possible to lift the veil of sentimentality that hangs over most productions of the play, one might even be able to see some of Sonya's callousness and Yelena's deep feeling. It is Yelena who is most probably the spirit of Chekhov within the play, even more so than Astrov. Like Madame Bovary, she is the character who best represents her author—the beautiful human being who wonders about her role in life, the dispossessed. It is amazing that Chekhov was able to distill so much meaning into the lives of six closely interrelated characters. Few plays in the modern repertory are so tightly wound, so sparsely and yet so richly inhabited. *Uncle Vanya* is Chekhov's neatest masterpiece.

NOTES

First performed by provincial Russian companies in the provinces, 1897, shortly after its first publication, in St. Petersburg, also 1897, in a collection of Chekhov's plays.
First performance at the Moscow Art Theater: October 26, 1899.

1. Vanya quotes from a satire, *Other People's Views*, by I. Dimitriev (1760–1837). The hero of the work has no talent for writing poetry. Chekhov's literary allusions are very sly.

2. Dr. Astrov spouts Latin to impress the ladies.

3. Vanya uses the Latin expression *perpetuum mobile* to refer to the professor's compulsive scholarship.

4. Alexander Ostrovski (1823–1866), one of Russia's most prolific playwrights, depicted many typical social types of his day, especially "the *samodurs* (willful, absurdly despotic, intellectually and morally limited egoists) who did as they pleased and trampled on human dignity and freedom." (See Marc Slonim's *Russian Theatre from the Empire to the Soviets* [New York: Collier Books, 1961], pp. 77–82.) One of the major themes of *Uncle Vanya* is this same despotic exploitation.

5. A highly organic soil, more than fifty percent combustible, composed of partially decayed vegetable matter found in marshy or damp regions, which is cut and then dried for use as fuel.

6. Russian watchmen tapped a stick against a board to warn thieves that they would be apprehended. The night

129

watchman's tapping is an atmospheric element that both begins and ends the second act of *Uncle Vanya*.

7. K. N. Batyushkov (1787–1855) is a Russian poet who was much admired by Pushkin. His major work is *The Death of Tasso*.

8. A severe pain of the heart muscle due to a coronary artery disease.

9. The kulaks were comparatively wealthy peasants who employed hired labor or possessed farm machinery. They were often stingy and given to usury.

10. A popular song of the time.

11. A railroad and metal-working center due south of Moscow.

12. Chekhov used fewer Italian expressions in his text than French; he traveled to Italy as well as France.

13. This lovely German expression is known in English as a loving cup, with the two persons drinking from the same cup and locking arms to do so.

14. Gogol's (1809–1852) celebrated comedy *The Inspector General*, or *Revizor* (1836), is a literary reminiscence dear to the heart of our pedant. In the play, the mayor gathers everyone together to announce the imminent arrival of a government inspector. Serebryakov realizes that he, too, by summoning everyone together, is generating quite a bit of suspense, and he loves doing it.

15. Finland was at that time a grand duchy of the Russian Empire. It did not achieve independence until 1917. The professor meant a region near St. Petersburg.

16. Schopenhauer (1788–1860) and Dostoevski (1821–1881) were undoubtedly chosen for their status as misunderstood geniuses, especially the former, whose pessimistic philosophy is embodied in *The World as Will and Idea* (1819). Vanya's paralysis of the will is the source of his great unhappiness.

17. I. K. Aivazovski (1817–1900) was a painter of seascapes and naval battles.

18. An industrial and railroad center north of Kharkov and south of Moscow.

19. See Note 12.

The Three Sisters

A Drama in Four Acts

CHARACTERS

PROZOROV, ANDREY SERGEYEVICH

NATALYA IVANOVNA,
  his fiancée, and later his wife

OLGA
MASHA } his sisters
IRINA

KULYGIN, FYODOR ILYICH,
  a schoolmaster, MASHA's husband

VERSHININ, ALEXANDER IGNATYEVICH,
  a lieutenant colonel and battery commander

TUSENBACH, NIKOLAI LVOVICH,
  the baron, a lieutenant

SOLYONY, VASSILI VASSILIEVICH,
  a captain second class

CHEBUTYKIN, IVAN ROMANOVICH,
  an army doctor

FEDOTIK, ALEXEY PETROVICH,
  a second lieutenant

RODÉ, VLADIMIR KARLOVICH,
  a second lieutenant

FERAPONT,
  a guard at the county council, an old man

ANFISA,
  an eighty-year-old nurse

The action takes place at a county seat
in the provinces.

ACT
ONE

The PROZOROV *house. A drawing room with columns, behind which one may see the ballroom. Noon. Outside it is sunny, fine weather. In the ballroom, the table is being set for lunch.*

OLGA, *in the blue uniform of the girls'-school teachers, corrects her students' notebooks while standing up and walking about.* MASHA *is seated, dressed in black, her hat on her knees, reading a book.* IRINA, *a study in white, stands absorbed in her thoughts.*

OLGA: Father died just one year ago today, the fifth of May, your saint's day,[1] Irina. It was very cold out, it was snowing. I thought I wouldn't survive it; you were lying there unconscious, as if you were dead. But now a year has passed, and we think about it calmly, and you are here, all in white again, you look radiant. (*The clock strikes twelve.*) The clock struck then just as now. (*Pause*) I remember when they took Father's coffin away, there was music, in the cemetery they fired a salute. He was a general, he commanded a brigade, yet there weren't many people there. One must remember that it was raining. It was raining very hard, there was snow on the ground.

IRINA: Why think about that any more!

(*Behind the columns, near the table in the ballroom,* BARON TUSENBACH, CHEBUTYKIN *and* SOLYONY *appear.*)

OLGA: It's warm today, we can keep the windows wide open, but the birch trees haven't any leaves yet. Father received the command of the brigade here and left Moscow with us eleven years ago, and I remember quite well that it was also early May, Moscow was already in flower, it was warm and bathed in sunshine. Eleven years ago, and I remember everything, as if we had left there yesterday. My God! This morning I awoke, I saw all the bright light, I saw it was spring, my heart burst with joy and I had the most passionate desire to return home.

CHEBUTYKIN: You can say that again!

TUSENBACH: That's nonsense, of course.

(MASHA, *deep in her book, quietly whistles a tune.*)

OLGA: Stop whistling, Masha! How can you do that! *(Pause)* Because I spend all my days at the school and I give private lessons later, I have a continual headache and I have such thoughts, I might as well be an old lady. It's true, these four years now, since I've been at the school, I feel that day by day, drop by drop, the strength of my youth is just draining away. Only one dream is growing and is invading every moment. . . .

IRINA: To go to Moscow. Sell the house, finish with everything here and go. . . .

OLGA: Yes! As soon as possible, to Moscow.

(CHEBUTYKIN *and* TUSENBACH *laugh.*)

IRINA: Our brother will probably become a professor and, at any rate, will not live here. Only poor Masha is stopping us. . . .

OLGA: Masha will come to Moscow to spend the summers, every year.

(MASHA *whistles a popular tune softly.*)

IRINA: God grant it will all come out right. *(Looking out the window)* It's beautiful today. I don't know why I feel so happy today! This morning, when I remembered it was my saint's day, I was suddenly filled with joy, and I remembered my childhood when Mama was still alive. And such marvelous thoughts excited me, such thoughts!

OLGA: You are radiant today. It makes you even more beautiful! And Masha is beautiful, too. And Andrey would be handsome if he hadn't gotten so fat; it doesn't suit him. I've grown older, I've grown thin, perhaps because I'm always cross with the girls at school. Now, today, when I'm free, and I'm at home, I don't have a headache, and I feel younger than yesterday. I'm only twenty-eight years old. . . . God's in his Heaven, all's right with the world, but it seems to me that if I were to get married and stay at home all the time, things would go better. *(Pause)* I would have loved my husband.

TUSENBACH *(to* SOLYONY*)*: You talk too much nonsense; I've had enough of listening to you. . . . *(Entering the drawing room)* I forgot to tell you. Today you'll be visited by our new battery commander, Vershinin. *(He sits down at the piano.)*

OLGA: Well, is that so? That's very nice.

IRINA: Is he an old man?

TUSENBACH: No, not too. At the most, forty or forty-five. *(He plays softly.)* He seems like a very nice fellow. Not stupid, that's for sure. Only, he talks too much.

IRINA: And is he an interesting man?

TUSENBACH: Yes, rather, only he has a wife, a mother-in-law and two little girls. Besides, it's already his second wife. He pays visits and tells everybody that he has a wife and two little girls. He'll tell you, too. His wife is some kind of crazy woman, she wears her hair in long girlish pigtails, she uses a lot of high-flown language, full of philosophizing, and tries frequently to commit suicide, to all appearances just to annoy her husband. I for one would long ago have left such a creature, but he bears up and just goes around complaining.

SOLYONY *(coming from the ballroom to the drawing room with* CHEBUTYKIN*)*: With only one hand I can only lift about fifty pounds,[2] but with two I can manage even more than two hundred pounds. I conclude from this that two men are stronger than one alone, not twice but three times stronger and more . . .

CHEBUTYKIN *(reads the newspaper while he walks)*: To prevent hair falling out . . . four point two five drams of

naphthalene to each half bottle of alcohol, in solution . . .
use daily . . . (*He takes his notebook out.*) I must make a
note of that! (*To* SOLYONY) To come back to what I was
saying to you, you cork up the bottle and insert a glass
tube through it. Then you take a little pinch of the simplest,
ordinary alum . . .

IRINA: Ivan Romanovich, dear Ivan Romanovich!

CHEBUTYKIN: Yes, my little girl, yes, my joy?

IRINA: Tell me, why do I feel so happy today? As if I were
sailing along with the great blue sky above me, with great
white birds flying. Why should this be? Why?

CHEBUTYKIN (*kissing both her hands tenderly*): My little
white bird . . .

IRINA: Today, when I awoke, got up, washed, I suddenly had
the impression that everything in the world had become
clear to me, and that I knew how one had to live. Dear
Ivan Romanovich, now I know everything. Man must
work, work by the sweat of his brow, whoever he may be;
that is the ultimate meaning and the goal of his existence,
his happiness, his joy. How good it is to be a worker who
gets up at dawn and goes out and breaks stones in the
street, or a shepherd, or a teacher who teaches children,
or a locomotive driver. My God, anything, it is better to
be a beast, an ox, or simply a horse, if only to work, than
a young lady who gets up at noon, takes her coffee in bed,
then spends two hours getting dressed. . . . Oh, that's terrible! You know the way you get thirsty on a hot day:
that's how I desire to work. And if I don't get up early in
the morning, and I don't work . . . take your friendship
away from me, Ivan Romanovich.

CHEBUTYKIN (*gently*): I'll take it away from you, I'll take it
away.

OLGA: Father got us used to getting up at seven o'clock. Now
Irina wakes up at seven and remains in bed until at least
nine, just thinking. And with such a serious face! (*She
laughs.*)

IRINA: You're so used to thinking of me as a little girl that
it astonishes you to see me with a serious expression on
my face. I'm twenty years old now!

TUSENBACH: The yearning for work, my God, how I understand that! I have never worked at anything in all my life.
I was born in Petersburg,[3] a cold and idle place, into a

family that never knew work or worry. I remember when I was returning home from military school, the valet took off my boots while I was playing around and my mother looked at me with ecstasy, and was astonished that others should look at me differently. They always protected me from work, only it's doubtful they will succeed forever, very doubtful! The time has come, something enormous has begun, a big strong storm is headed our way, it is coming ahead, it is already quite near, and it will soon blow over our society and sweep away the idleness, the complacence, the rotten boredom the prejudice against work. I shall work, but in some twenty-five or thirty years, every man will work. Every one!

CHEBUTYKIN: *I* shall not work.

TUSENBACH: Oh, you, you don't count.

SOLYONY: In twenty-five years you won't be in this world any more, thank God. In two or three years you'll die of a stroke, or I shall lose my temper and shoot a bullet in your head, my little angel. (*He takes a flask of perfume out of his pocket and douses his chest and hands.*)

CHEBUTYKIN (*laughs*): But it's a fact, I've never really done anything. Since I left the university, I've not lifted a finger, not even read, not a single book, nothing but newspapers. (*He takes another newspaper out of his pocket.*) There . . . I know, from the papers, that there was once, for example, a certain Dobrolyubov,[4] but what he might have written . . . no idea. Only God knows. (*Knocking is heard from the floor below.*) Ah, so . . . They're calling me from downstairs, somebody's calling me. I'll be back right away . . . in a moment. (*He goes quickly, combing his beard.*)

IRINA: He's up to something again.

TUSENBACH: That's for sure. He left with such a solemn face that he'll certainly be back with a present for you.

IRINA: Oh, how annoying.

OLGA: Yes, it's awful. He never stops making *faux pas*.

MASHA: "On the curved shore, a green oak stands, around the oak, golden strands . . . Around the oak, golden strands . . ."[5] (*She gets up, humming softly.*)

OLGA: You're not in a good mood today, Masha.

(MASHA *hums while she puts on her hat.*)

OLGA: Where are you going?

MASHA: Home.

IRINA: That's strange.

TUSENBACH: Leaving on your sister's saint's day!

MASHA: So what . . . I'll be back tonight. Good-bye, my dear. (*She kisses* IRINA.) Once again, I wish you health and happiness. In the old days, when Father was still alive, on a birthday we had thirty or forty officers to the house, it was noisy, and today there are only one and a half people, it's as quiet as the desert, I'm going. . . . I'm melancholy today, depressed, you mustn't listen to me. (*Laughing through her tears*) We'll talk later; until then, my darling, I'll go off somewhere or other.

IRINA (*displeased*): Well, really . . .

OLGA (*tears in her eyes*): I understand you, Masha.

SOLYONY: When a man begins to philosophize, that leads to philoso-sophistry,[6] or just sophistry; but if it's a woman who begins to philosophize, or two women, then I'll bite my tongue.

MASHA: What do you mean by that, you terribly frightening man?

SOLYONY: Nothing. "Before he'd time to cry out, the bear had sought him out." [7]

MASHA (*to* OLGA, *annoyed*): Stop sniffling!

(*Enter* ANFISA *and* FERAPONT *with a cake.*)

ANFISA: This way, little father. Come in, your feet are quite clean. (*To* IRINA) It comes from the county council, from Protopopov, Mikhail Ivanovich . . . a cake.

IRINA: Thank you. Will you thank him for me. (*Accepts the cake.*)

FERAPONT: What?

IRINA (*louder*): Tell him thank you from me.

OLGA: Nurse, give him a piece of cake. Go, Ferapont, go, they'll give you a piece of cake.

FERAPONT: What?

ANFISA: Come, little father, Ferapont Spiridonovich, come. . . . (*She goes out with* FERAPONT.)

MASHA: I don't like this Protopopov, this Mikhail Poptapich, or Ivanich. We mustn't invite him here.

IRINA: I didn't invite him.
MASHA: Then it's all right.

(Enter CHEBUTYKIN, *followed by an orderly carrying a silver samovar;³ buzz of surprise and discontent.)*

OLGA *(covering her face with both hands)*: A samovar! It's terrible! *(She goes to the table in the ballroom.)*
IRINA: Ivan Romanovich, my dear, what's got into you!
TUSENBACH *(laughs)*: I told you so.
MASHA: Ivan Romanovich, that's shameless!
CHEBUTYKIN: My darlings, my sweets, you're all I have, you're the most precious to me in all the world, I'll soon be sixty years old, I'm old, a miserable old bachelor. All that is good in me is the love I bear for you, and if it weren't for you, I would have quit this world a long time ago now. . . . *(To* IRINA) My dear, my child, I've known you since the day you were born. I carried you in my arms. I loved your poor mother so. . . .
IRINA: But why give such expensive presents!
CHEBUTYKIN *(through his tears, angrily)*: So expensive . . . Oh, you! Now that's quite enough! *(To the orderly)* Put the samovar down there. *(Imitating* IRINA) Expensive presents . . .

(The orderly takes the samovar into the ballroom.)

ANFISA *(crossing the drawing room)*: My children, the colonel nobody knows! He has already taken his cap off, my little ones, he is coming in. Anyushka, be very nice, be polite. . . . *(Going out)* And it's been time for lunch now for ever so long. Heavens . . .
TUSENBACH: It must be Vershinin.

(Enter VERSHININ.)

TUSENBACH: Lieutenant Colonel Vershinin!
VERSHININ *(to* MASHA *and* IRINA): Allow me to present myself: Vershinin. I am very, very happy finally to be among you. How grown up you've gotten! Tsk! Tsk!
IRINA: Please sit down. This is a pleasure.
VERSHININ *(gaily)*: I am so delighted! Now, there were three

sisters? I remember that there were three little girls. I no
longer remember their faces, but that your father, Colonel
Prozorov, had three little girls, that I remember very clearly, I saw you, with my own eyes. How time flies. Ay-yay-
yay, how it flies!

TUSENBACH: Alexander Ignatyevich comes from Moscow.

IRINA: From Moscow? You come from Moscow?

VERSHININ: Yes, from there. Your poor father commanded a
battery there, and I was an officer in the same brigade. (*To*
MASHA) I think I remember your face a little.

MASHA: And I don't remember you at all!

IRINA: Olya! Olya! (*She calls in the direction of the ballroom.*)
Olya, come here!

(OLGA *comes from the ballroom into the drawing room.*)

IRINA: Colonel Vershinin has just arrived from Moscow.

VERSHININ: So, you must be Olga Sergeyevna, the eldest . . .
And you are Maria . . . and you Irina, the youngest. . . .

OLGA: You are from Moscow?

VERSHININ: Yes. I studied in Moscow and I began my service
in Moscow, I was stationed there for a long time; finally I
was named commander of the battery here—and here I
am, as you can see. I don't really remember you, I remember only that you were three sisters. Your father has remained engraved in my memory, I have only to shut my
eyes to remember him as if he were still alive. I came to
your home, sometimes, in Moscow.

OLGA: I thought I remembered everybody and now suddenly . . .

VERSHININ: My name is Alexander Ignatyevich. . . .

IRINA: Alexander Ignatyevich, you come from Moscow . . .
what a surprise!

OLGA: We're going to move there.

IRINA: We hope to get there by autumn. It's our home, we
were born there . . . on old Basmanny Street. . . .

(*Both laugh joyously.*)

MASHA: They're quite surprised to see a fellow countryman,
from home. (*Briskly*) Now I remember! You recall, Olya,
they said there was someone at our house called "the

lovesick major." You were a lieutenant then and you were in love, and everybody was teasing you by calling you major, for some reason or other. . . .

VERSHININ (*laughing*): That's it, that's right . . . the lovesick major . . . exactly.

MASHA: You only wore a moustache then. . . . Oh, how old you've gotten! (*Almost in tears*) How you have grown older!

VERSHININ: Yes, when they called me the lovesick major, I was still quite young, I was in love. Now it's not like that.

OLGA: But you don't have a single gray hair. You have grown older, but you're not yet old.

VERSHININ: Yet I'm almost forty-three years old. Did you leave Moscow long ago?

IRINA: Eleven years. But don't cry so, Masha, you're a silly girl . . . (*through her tears*) or I'll start crying, too.

MASHA: It's nothing. And where did you live?

VERSHININ: On old Basmanny Street.

OLGA: And so did we. . . .

VERSHININ: For a time I lived on Nemetsky Street. From Nemetsky Street I went to the Red Barracks. There is a gloomy bridge on the way, you can hear the water flowing under the bridge. A man alone there feels very sad. (*Pause*) Here the river is so wide, so splendid! It's marvelous!

OLGA: Yes, only it's cold here, cold and full of mosquitoes. . . .

VERSHININ: Oh, don't say that! The climate here is excellent, fine, a real Russian climate. There are the forests, the rivers . . . and the birches, too. Dear modest birch trees, I prefer them to all other trees. Life is good here. There is only one thing I find strange, it is that the station is located thirteen miles[9] away or more . . . and nobody knows why that should be.

SOLYONY: I know why that is. (*Everybody looks at him.*) Because if the station were quite nearby, it would not be far away, and if it were far away, then it wouldn't be nearby.

(*Embarrassed silence.*)

TUSENBACH: Vassili Vassilievich, you are a joker.

OLGA: Now I remember you also. Yes, I do remember you.

VERSHININ: I knew your mother.

CHEBUTYKIN: She was an excellent woman, may she rest in peace.

IRINA: Mama is buried in Moscow.

OLGA: Yes, in the cemetery at Novo-Devichy . . .[10]

MASHA: Imagine, I have begun to forget her face. That's how they'll forget us, too. We'll be forgotten.

VERSHININ: Yes. We shall be forgotten. That's our fate, nothing to do about it. What today seems important, serious, heavy with consequence—well, a moment will come when it will be forgotten, when it will be of no importance. (*Pause*) And it's curious—we cannot know today what one day will be considered great or important, mediocre or ridiculous. Did not the discoveries of Copernicus or, let's say, Columbus seem at first to be useless, ridiculous, while people took the silly nonsense of a thoroughly ordinary nobody for truth itself. It may also be that our present way of life will one day be considered strange, uncomfortable, unintelligent, insufficiently pure, and who knows, even sinful. . . .

TUSENBACH: Who knows? It may also be that it will be said of our life that it did not lack grandeur and it will be thought of with respect. Today we have neither torture nor executioners nor invasions, but, all the same, how much suffering there is!

SOLYONY (*in a sharp voice*): Tsip, tsip, tsip . . . The baron would gladly do without his porridge, provided he be allowed to philosophize.

TUSENBACH: Vassili Vassilievich, I would like you to leave me alone. (*He changes position.*) Finally it becomes annoying.

SOLYONY: Tsip, tsip, tsip . . .

TUSENBACH (*to* VERSHININ): The suffering one can observe now—and there is so much of it!—proves all the same that society has attained a certain moral level.

VERSHININ: Yes, of course, of course.

CHEBUTYKIN: You just said, baron, that one would say of your life that it did not lack grandeur; but all the same, men are quite small. . . . (*He gets up.*) Look how small I am. It is as a consolation to me that you must say that my life did not lack grandeur, that's quite obvious.

(*Offstage, someone plays a violin.*)

MASHA: It's Andrey, our brother, who's playing.

IRINA: He's our scholar. He will probably become a professor. Papa was a military man, and his son chose an academic career.

MASHA: It was Papa's wish.

OLGA: We teased him terribly today. He's a little in love, it seems.

IRINA: With a girl from around here. She'll probably come and see us today.

MASHA: My God, how she dresses! It's not that her dresses are ugly or outmoded, but they're really pitiful. A bizarre skirt, a glaring color, somewhat yellow, with one of those vulgar little fringes, and a red blouse. And well-washed cheeks, scrubbed, scrubbed! Andrey isn't in love, I couldn't believe that, he has some taste, it's simply to tease us, to play around. I heard yesterday that she was going to marry Protopopov, the chairman of the local council. That would be just perfect. . . . (*In the direction of the side door*) Andrey, come here, dear, for a moment!

(*Enter* ANDREY.)

OLGA: It's my brother, Andrey Sergeyich.

VERSHININ: Vershinin.

ANDREY: Prozorov. (*He wipes the sweat from his face.*) You're the new battery commander?

OLGA: Imagine, Alexander Ignatyevich comes from Moscow.

ANDREY: Oh, yes? Well, I congratulate you. Now my little sisters will not give you a moment's peace.

VERSHININ: I've already taken advantage of your sisters' patience.

IRINA: Look at this little picture frame that Andrey gave me today! (*She shows off the little frame.*) He made it himself.

VERSHININ (*looking at the frame and not knowing what to say*): Yes . . . it's an object . . .

IRINA: And the little frame over the piano, he made that one, too.

(ANDREY *makes a gesture and goes off.*)

OLGA: He's our scholar, and he plays the violin, and he makes all sorts of little gadgets; in short, he's a jack of all trades.

Andrey, don't go! He always has a way of going off. Come here!

(MASHA *and* IRINA *take him by the arms and bring him back, laughing.*)

MASHA: Come, come!

ANDREY: Will you leave me alone!

MASHA: How funny he is! They used to call Alexander Ignatyevich the lovesick major, and he didn't get angry.

VERSHININ: Not at all!

MASHA: I'm going to call you the lovesick violinist!

IRINA: Or the lovesick professor.

OLGA: He's in love! Andriucha is in love!

IRINA (*applauding*): Bravo! Bravo! Encore! Andriucha is in love!

CHEBUTYKIN (*comes over to* ANDREY *from behind and takes his waist in both hands*): For love alone, nature put us on earth! (*He bursts out laughing; he still has a newspaper in his hands.*)

ANDREY: All right, that's enough, enough. . . . (*Wiping his face*) I didn't sleep all night, and now I'm, as they say, not quite myself; I read till four in the morning, then I went to bed, but it was no good. I thought of one thing and another, and daylight comes early now, the sun literally streams into your room. I hope while I'm here this summer, I'll get to translate a book from English.

VERSHININ: You read English?

ANDREY: Yes. Father—the Kingdom of Heaven be his—oppressed us with education. It's strange and silly, but I am obliged to admit that after his death I started to fill out, and in one year I really have gotten fat, as if my body had been liberated from a burden. Thanks to Father, my sisters and I know French, German and English, and Irina even knows Italian. But at what a price!

MASHA: In this town, to know three languages is a useless luxury. Rather than a luxury, a useless appendage, something like a sixth finger. We know many superfluous things.

VERSHININ: Well, now! (*He laughs.*) You know many superfluous things! It seems to me that there doesn't exist and cannot exist any town so sad and morose for there to be no need for cultivated and intelligent people. Let us admit that among the hundred thousand inhabitants of this old-fashioned and uncultured town, there would only be three such as you. It goes without saying that you could not vanquish the ignorant masses around you; little by little, as you advance in life, you will be obliged to yield and to be swallowed up in the crowd of a hundred thousand human beings; life will stifle you, but you will all the same not have disappeared without having exerted an influence; of women like you, there will be after you perhaps only six, then twelve, and so on, until finally you will become the majority. In two or three hundred years life on earth will be unimaginably beautiful, amazing, astonishing. Man has need of that life and if it doesn't yet exist, he must sense it, wait for it and dream of it, prepare to receive it, and to achieve that he must see and know more than our grandfathers and fathers saw or knew. (*He laughs.*) And you complain of knowing too many superfluous things.

MASHA (*takes off her hat*): I'm staying to lunch.

IRINA (*sighing*): We should all write this down, really. . . .

(ANDREY *is no longer there; he has gone out unnoticed.*)

TUSENBACH: You say that in a great many years, life on earth will be beautiful, astonishing. That's true. But to participate in this life from today on, even from afar, one must prepare for it, one must work. . . .

VERSHININ (*getting up*): Yes. You do have a lot of flowers! (*Looking all around him*) And the house is so lovely. I envy you! I've spent my whole life dragging around apartments with two chairs, a divan and stoves that are always smoking. What I have always missed in this life are flowers like these. . . . (*He rubs his hands.*) Ah! so what!

TUSENBACH: Yes, one must work. You must be saying to yourself: this German is becoming sentimental. But I am, on my word of honor, as Russian as they come and I don't even speak German. My father was orthodox. . . .

(*Pause.*)

VERSHININ (*pacing the stage*): I often wonder: if one were to start life all over again, and this time deliberately? If one were to live one's life as one does a rough draft, and then live it again for good! Well, each of us, I think, would above all try not to repeat himself and to create different surroundings, a house full of flowers like this one, full of light. . . . I have a wife, two little girls, and my wife is a woman with poor health, etcetera, etcetera. Well, if I were to begin my life over again, I would not get married . . . no, no, I wouldn't!

(*Enter* KULYGIN *in the uniform of a high school teacher.*)

KULYGIN (*goes to* IRINA): My dear sister, allow me to bring you congratulations on your saint's day and to wish you, with all my heart, health and all that a young girl of your age could wish for. And then to make a present to you of this book. (*He gives her a book.*) The history of our school for the last fifty years, composed by me. It's not much, I did it to pass the time, but read it all the same. Good day, ladies, good day, gentlemen! (*To* VERSHININ) Kulygin, professor at the high school. (*To* IRINA) You will find in this volume the list of all those who have graduated from our school in the last fifty years. *Feci quod potui, faciant meliora potentes.*[11] (*He kisses* MASHA.)

IRINA: But you already gave me this book for Easter.

KUULYGIN (*laughs*): Not possible! Then give it back, or rather give it to the colonel. Take it, my colonel. . . . You'll read it one day when you have nothing better to do.

VERSHININ: I thank you. (*He gets ready to leave.*) I am extremely glad to have met you.

OLGA: Are you leaving? But no, no!

IRINA: You will stay to lunch. Please do.

OLGA: You would give us great pleasure.

VERSHININ (*bowing*): I think I have fallen in here on a family occasion. Excuse me, I didn't know it, I haven't offered my best wishes. . . . (*He passes with* OLGA *into the ballroom.*)

KULYGIN: Today is the Lord's day, a day of rest; let us rest then, distract ourselves, each according to his age and his situation. We will have to take the carpets up in summer and store them until winter . . . dust them or put them in mothballs. . . . The Romans were healthy because they knew how to work, and also to rest, and they had *mens sana in corpore sano*. Their life flowed according to definite forms. Our director says: the principal thing in each life is its form. . . . That which loses its form is finished, and it is thus in our daily life as well. (*He takes* MASHA *by the waist, laughing.*) Masha loves me. My wife loves me. And the drapes will join the rugs. . . . I am happy today, in a charming mood. Masha, at four o'clock we're expected at the director's house. They are organizing an excursion of the teaching body, with their families.

MASHA: I won't go.

KULYGIN (*chagrined*): My dear Masha, why?

MASHA: We'll talk about it later. . . . (*Annoyed*) All right, I'll go, leave me alone, will you. . . . (*She goes off.*)

KULYGIN: And then we'll pass the evening at the director's house. Despite his defective state of health, this man strives above all to be sociable. He is an excellent man, a noble soul. An admirable man. Yesterday, after the council meeting, he said to me, "I'm tired, Fyodor Ilyich! I am tired!" (*He looks at the clock and then at his watch.*) Your clock is seven minutes fast. Yes, he said to me, "I am tired!"

(*Behind the scene, the violin-playing is heard.*)

OLGA: People, come along, lunch is served! We have a saint's day pie! [12]

KULYGIN: Ah, my dear, dear Olga! Yesterday I worked till eleven o'clock in the evening, I got tired, and today I feel happy! (*He goes into the ballroom and approaches the table.*) My dear . . .

CHEBUTYKIN (*puts the newspaper in his pocket and combs his beard*): A saint's day pie? Now that's just perfect.

MASHA (*to* CHEBUTYKIN, *severely*): Only look: don't you drink anything today. You hear me? It's bad for you.

CHEBUTYKIN: Really! That's a thing of the past. I am cured of that. It's been two years since I've been on a binge. (*Impatiently*) Besides, what harm could it do, my dear!

MASHA: All the same, don't you dare drink. Don't you dare. *Angrily, but so that her husband cannot hear*) Damn it. We'll have to go and be bored for another entire evening at the director's house!

TUSENBACH: If I were you, I wouldn't go . . . that's all there is to it.

CHEBUTYKIN: Just don't go, my dear.

MASHA: Don't go . . . that's easy to say. Damn this life, it's unbearable. . . . (*She passes into the ballroom.*)

CHEBUTYKIN (*goes up to her*): Come on now!

SOLYONY (*going through the ballroom*): Tsip, tsip, tsip . . .

TUSENBACH: That's enough, Vassili Vassilievich. Enough!

SOLYONY: Tsip, tsip, tsip . . .

KULYGIN (*gaily*): To your health, my colonel. I am a pedagogue, and in this house I'm just like one of the family, Masha's husband. . . . She is good, a very good person. . . .

VERSHININ: I'd like to have a glass of that dark vodka. . . . (*He drinks.*) To your health! (*To* OLGA) I am so glad to be here in your home! . . .

(IRINA *and* TUSENBACH *remain in the drawing room.*)

IRINA: Masha's not in a good mood today. She was married at eighteen, when her husband seemed to her the most intelligent of all men. It's not that way any more. He is the kindest of men, but not the most intelligent.

OLGA (*impatiently*): Andrey, will you come here, already!

ANDREY (*backstage*): I'm coming. (*He enters and goes to the table.*)

TUSENBACH: What are you thinking about?

IRINA: Nothing. I don't like your Solyony, and I'm afraid of him. He only utters stupidities. . . .

TUSENBACH: He's a strange man. I'm sorry for him, and he annoys me, but I'm more sorry for him. I think he's very shy. . . . When we're alone together, then he behaves well and intelligently, but as soon as there's company, he begins to be rude, and he starts acting wild and woolly. Don't go in, let them be seated at the table. Allow me to spend a moment by your side. What are you thinking about? (*Pause*) You're twenty years old, I'm not yet thirty. How many years ahead of us, a long, long row of days filled with my love for you.

IRINA: Nikolai Lvovich, don't talk to me about love.

TUSENBACH (*not listening to her*): I have such a thirst for life, for struggle, for work, and this thirst gets all mixed up in my heart with my love for you, Irina, and as luck would have it, you are beautiful and so life seems to me to be beautiful! What are you thinking of?

IRINA: You say life is beautiful. Yes, but what if it only seems so! For us, the three sisters, it has not yet been so beautiful, it has stifled us like a bad weed. . . . My tears are flowing, I shouldn't . . . *(She wipes her face rapidly and smiles.)* One must work, work, work. If we are not happy, if we see the dark side of life, it means that we do not know the meaning of work. We have come down from people who had contempt for work. . . .

(Enter NATALYA IVANOVNA; she is wearing a pink dress with a green belt.)

NATASHA: They're already at table. . . . I'm late. . . . *(She throws a furtive glance at the mirror, arranging herself.)* I think my hairdo isn't so bad. . . . *(Perceiving IRINA)* Irina Sergeyevna, I congratulate you! *(She embraces her heartily, for a long time.)* You have many guests, I'm really embarrassed. . . . Good day, baron!

OLGA *(entering the drawing room)*: Ah, there is Natalya Ivanovna. Good day, my dear!

(They embrace.)

NATASHA: Happy saint's day. You have so much company, I'm terribly embarrassed.

OLGA: Don't think of it, we're among friends. *(In a low voice, ominously)* What is this green belt here! My darling, that doesn't go very well!

NATASHA: Is that a bad sign?

OLGA: No, only they don't go together . . . it looks strange. . . .

NATASHA *(in a tearful voice)*: You think so; but it really isn't green, it's rather a neutral color.

(She follows OLGA into the ballroom. In the ballroom, they sit down at table; there is no one now in the drawing room.)

KULYGIN: I wish for you, Irina, a nice fiancé, a pleasant fellow. It is time for you to take a husband.

CHEBUTYKIN: Natalya Ivanovna, for you, too, I wish a nice little fiancé.

KULYGIN: Natalya Ivanovna already has one little fiancé.

MASHA *(knocks with her fork on her plate)*: I'll take one of those little glasses! What a great life! What the hell!

KULYGIN: You deserve a zero in conduct.

VERSHININ: The liquor is delicious. What is it made of?

SOLYONY: Cockroaches.

IRINA *(moaning)*: Ugh! How disgusting!

OLGA: For supper there'll be a roast turkey and an apple pie. Thank God I'm home all day and tonight, too. . . . Come back this evening, too, people. . . .

VERSHININ: May I be allowed to come, me, too?

IRINA: Please do.

NATASHA: They're so nice and easy in this house.

CHEBUTYKIN: "Nature put us here for love alone, my dear!" *(He laughs.)*

ANDREY *(annoyed)*: Stop it, everybody! Haven't you had enough yet?

(FEDOTIK and RODÉ enter with a large basket of flowers.)

FEDOTIK: But they're already at table!

RODÉ *(in a loud voice and lisping)*: At table? Ah, yes, already having lunch at table. . . .

FEDOTIK: Wait a moment! *(He takes a photo.)* One! Just one moment more . . . *(He takes another.)* Two! Now you can go on!

(They take the basket and enter the ballroom, where they are received noisily.)

RODÉ *(in a loud voice)*: Happy saint's day and the best, the very best! The weather is superb today, just marvelous. All this morning I've been walking around with the high school students. I'm teaching them gymnastics.

FEDOTIK: You may move, Irina Sergeyevna, you may! *(He takes a photo.)* You look nice today. *(He takes a top out of his pocket.)* By the way, here's a top . . . it makes an extraordinary hum.

IRINA: It's charming!

MASHA: "On the curved shore, a green oak stands, around the oak, golden strands . . . Around the oak, golden strands . . ." *(Moaning)* Why do I keep repeating that? This refrain has been haunting me ever since this morning. . . .

KULYGIN: We're thirteen at table!

RODÉ (*in a strong voice*): Come now, do you believe in these superstitions?

(*Laughter.*)

KULYGIN: Thirteen at table, that means there are lovers here. Could it be possible, by any chance, that it is you, Ivan Romanovich. . . .

(*Laughter.*)

CHEBUTYKIN: I'm an old sinner; what could be putting Natalya Ivanovna in such a state of confusion, I absolutely cannot imagine.

(*Loud laughter;* NATASHA *runs out of the ballroom.* ANDREY *follows her.*)

ANDREY: Please don't pay any attention. One moment, wait, please. . . .

NATASHA: I'm ashamed. . . . I don't know what's happening to me—and them, they're making fun of me. It's bad upbringing to leave the table, but I couldn't help it . . . I couldn't. . . . (*She covers her face with her hands.*)

ANDREY: My darling, I beg of you, please calm yourself. I assure you, they're only joking, nicely. My darling, my little one, they're all very good people who have a heart and who love us, you and me. Come close to the window, they won't see us. . . . (*He glances behind him.*)

NATASHA: I'm not used to being in company!

ANDREY: Ah, youth, beautiful, marvelous youth! My darling, my dear girl, don't be so upset. . . . Believe in me, trust me. . . . I am so happy, my heart is filled with love, with joy. . . . Oh, no, they don't see us! No, they don't see us! Why, why have I fallen in love with you, when did it begin to happen? Ah! I understand none of it. My darling, my pure little girl, be my wife! I love you, as I have never loved anyone.

(*They embrace. Two officers enter. On seeing the couple embracing, they stare, stupefied.*)

CURTAIN

ACT TWO

Same decor as the preceding act. Eight o'clock in the evening. Backstage, from the street, one hears, ever so lightly, the sounds of an accordion. There is no light.

Enter NATALYA IVANOVNA, *in a housecoat, carrying a candle; she advances and stops at the door that leads to* ANDREY'S *room.*

NATASHA: What are you doing, Andriucha? Are you reading? No, it's nothing, I was only . . . *(She goes and opens another door, and after a glance at the room, shuts it again.)* I was looking to see if anybody left any lights on. . . .

ANDREY *(enters, a book in his hand)*: What is it, Natasha?

NATASHA: I was seeing if any lights were left on. Now it's carnival week,[13] the servants are not themselves, you have to keep watch everywhere, to avoid trouble. Last night I came into the dining room at midnight and I found a candle burning. Who lit it—that I'll never find out. *(She puts her candle down.)* What time is it?

ANDREY *(looks at his watch)*: Eight-fifteen.

NATASHA: And Olga and Irina still haven't come home. Poor dears, always working. Olga is at the teachers' meeting, Irina at the telegraph office. . . . *(She sighs.)* This morning I said to your sister, "Take care of yourself, Irina, my angel." She doesn't even listen. You said eight-fifteen? I'm afraid our Bobik isn't well. Why is he always so cold? Yesterday he had a fever and today he's cold all over. . . . I'm so afraid!

ANDREY: It's nothing, Natasha. The little boy is fine.

152

NATASHA: All the same, I'd rather he was on a diet. I'm afraid. And this evening at around ten, the maskers are expected; if only they wouldn't come, Andriucha.

ANDREY: Really, I don't know what to say; they've been invited.

NATASHA: Today the little one wakes up in the morning, he looks at me and suddenly he smiles; he recognized me! "Bobik," I said to him, "good morning! Good morning, my darling!" And he began to laugh. Children understand everything, they understand so well, So, Andriucha, I'm going to tell them not to let the maskers[14] in.

ANDREY (*indecisive*): But that depends on my sisters. They are the mistresses of the house.

NATASHA: Them, too, I'll tell them, too. They're so nice. . . . (*Going off*) For supper I ordered some sour milk. The doctor says you should only have sour milk, or you'll never lose any weight. (*She stops.*) Bobik is all cold. I'm afraid he'll be cold in his room, most likely. Until the warm weather comes, we'd better move him somewhere to another room. For instance, to Irina's room, that's just what a child needs, it's not humid and there's sun all day. We must tell her. In the meantime she could share Olga's room. . . . At any rate, she's never there all day long, she only comes home to go to sleep. (*Pause*) My little Andriuchachanchik, you're not saying anything.

ANDREY: I was lost in my thoughts. Besides, there's nothing to say. . . .

NATASHA: Yes . . . I wanted to tell you something else. . . . Ah, yes, Ferapont, from the county council, is here, he was asking for you.

ANDREY (*yawns*): Tell him to come in.

(NATASHA *goes out.* ANDREY, *leaning over his candle into forgetfulness, reads his book. Enter* FERAPONT; *he wears an old threadbare overcoat with a raised collar and a scarf over his ears.*)

ANDREY: Good evening, my friend. What do you have to say to me?

FERAPONT: The chairman sends you a book and some papers. Here . . . (*He gives him a book and a large envelope.*)

ANDREY: Thank you. That's fine. Why do you come so late? It is after eight o'clock.

FERAPONT: What?

ANDREY *(louder)*: I say why do you come so late, after eight o'clock.

FERAPONT: Yes, sir. When I came, it was still light, but they didn't want to let me come in. The master is busy, they said. If that's the way they want it, if he's busy, he's busy. I can wait. I'm not in a hurry. *(Believing that* ANDREY *is asking him something)* What?

ANDREY: Nothing. *(Examining the book)* Tomorrow is Friday, the offices are closed, but I'll come all the same. . . . I'll find enough to occupy me. I'm bored at home. . . . *(Pause)* My dear old fellow, isn't it strange how it changes, how life deceives us! Today, out of boredom and not having anything to do, I took up this book with some old lectures at the university, and I began to laugh. . . . My God, I am secretary of the county council, the council whose president is Protopopov, I am its secretary, and all that I can hope for betterment is to become a member of the council! I, a member of the local rural council, I who dream every night that I am a professor at the University of Moscow, a celebrated scholar of whom all of Russia is proud!

FERAPONT: I don't know, I'm hard of hearing. . . .

ANDREY: If you could hear properly, I wouldn't perhaps have spoken to you. I must speak to someone, my wife doesn't understand me, my sisters somehow frighten me, I don't know why really, I'm afraid they'll make fun of me, shame me. . . . I don't drink, I don't like frequenting bars, but with what pleasure, I would like to go right now and spend an hour at Tiestov's[15] in Moscow or to the Moskovskaya Hotel, my dear fellow.

FERAPONT: A while ago at the council, a contractor was telling how in Moscow some big merchants were eating blini and that one of them who had eaten forty of them, died of it. Forty or fifty, I don't know any more. I don't remember.

ANDREY: In Moscow, you sit in an immense restaurant, you know nobody, and nobody knows you, and yet you don't feel ill at ease. And here, you know everybody, and everybody knows you, and you feel like a stranger, a stranger . . . a stranger and alone.

FERAPONT: What? *(Pause)* And the same contractor said—

unless he's lying—that they had laid a cable the whole length of Moscow.

ANDREY: Whatever for?

FERAPONT: I don't know. The contractor said so.

ANDREY: Stupid stories. (*He reads his book.*) Have you ever been in Moscow?

FERAPONT (*after a silence*): No. God didn't will it. (*Pause*) Shall I go?

ANDREY: You can go. Take care of yourself. (FERAPONT *goes.*) Take care of yourself. (*He reads.*) Tomorrow morning you'll come and get these papers. . . . Go. . . . (*Pause*) He's gone. (*Somebody rings.*) Yes, that's how it is. . . .

> (*He stretches and goes to his room without hurrying. In the wings, a nurse can be heard singing to a child while she cradles it. Enter* MASHA *and* VERSHININ. *During their conversation, the maid will light a lamp and some candles.*)

MASHA: I don't know. (*Pause*) I don't know. Evidently, habit plays a great part. After Father's death, for example, we couldn't get used to not having any more orderlies, but besides habit, what I'm saying seems to me simply fair. Perhaps elsewhere it isn't so, but in our town, the most honest, decent, best-educated men are the military.

VERSHININ: I'm thirsty. I should have liked some tea.

MASHA (*after a look at her watch*): They'll bring some soon. I was married when I was eighteen, and I was in awe of my husband because he was a professor, and I had just terminated my studies. He seemed to me then to be terribly wise, intelligent and important. Now it's not the same thing, unfortunately.

VERSHININ: So . . . I see.

MASHA: I'm not talking about my husband, I got accustomed to him, but among the civilians in general, there are so many gross, unkind, uncivilized men. Their rudeness troubles me, it wounds me, I suffer when I see a lack of finesse in a man, a lack of kindness and gentility. When I find myself in a milieu of professors, my husband's colleagues, I literally suffer.

VERSHININ: Yes . . . but it seems to me that with the military and the civilians, things are on the same level, at least in this town. On the same level! To listen to an intellectual, a civilian or a military man from here, he's sick of his wife, his home, his estate, his horses. . . . The Russian man has such a high-minded way of thinking, but tell me, why is it that in real life, he flies along at such a low level? Why?

MARSHA: Why?

VERSHININ: Why is he fed up with his children and his wife? And why can't his wife and children stand him?

MASHA: You're a little depressed today.

VERSHININ: That may be. I haven't eaten anything today since morning. And my girl is not too well, and when my little ones are ill, I am full of anxiety and eaten up by the remorse that they should have such a mother. Ah, if you had seen her today. What a nonentity! We began to quarrel beginning at seven o'clock in the morning. At nine o'clock I slammed the door and left. (*Pause*) I never speak of it, and, it's strange, I only complain to you. (*He kisses her hand.*) Don't be angry with me. I have no one else but you, you alone. . . .

(*Pause.*)

MASHA: What a noise in the chimney! Just before my father's death the wind also howled down the chimney. Exactly like that.

VERSHININ: Are you superstitious?

MASHA: Yes.

VERSHININ: How strange. (*He kisses her hand.*) You are a magnificent, marvelous woman! Magnificent, marvelous! It's dark here, but I can see your eyes shining.

MASHA (*moves to another chair*): Here it's lighter. . . .

VERSHININ: I love, I love, I love . . . I love your eyes, all your movements, which I dream about. . . . Magnificent, marvelous woman!

MASHA (*laughs softly*): When you speak to me in this way, it makes me laugh, even though it makes me afraid. Don't say it any more, I beg of you. (*In a low voice*) Oh, after all, go on. It's all the same to me. (*Covers her face with her hands.*) It's all the same to me. Someone's coming, speak about something else. . . .

(IRINA *and* TUSENBACH *come in from the ballroom.*)

TUSENBACH: I have three family names. My name is Baron
  Tusenbach-Krone-Altschauer, but I'm Russian and orthodox
  just like you. I've kept very few German characteristics,
  perhaps only the patience and stubbornness with which I
  bore you. I see you home every evening.

IRINA: I'm so tired!

TUSENBACH: And I'll come every evening to the telegraph
  office, to call for you and see you to the house for the next
  ten or twenty years, until you chase me away. . . . (*Perceiving* MASHA *and* VERSHININ; *joyfully*) Oh, it's you? Good
  evening!

IRINA: I'm finally back at home, too. (*To* MASHA) Just now,
  a woman came to send a telegram to her brother at Saratov,[16]
  to say that she had lost her son today, and she couldn't
  remember the address. She finally sent it without an address,
  simply to Saratov. She was crying. I was rude to her for
  no reason at all. I told her, "I don't have any time to
  waste." It was so stupid. Are the maskers coming tonight?

MASHA: Yes.

IRINA (*sits in an armchair*): A little rest. I'm tired.

TUSENBACH (*smiling*): When you return from work, you seem
  so young, a miserable little girl. . . .

  (*Pause.*)

IRINA: I'm tired. No, I don't like this telegraph office, I don't
  like it.

MASHA: You've gotten thinner. . . . (*She whistles.*) And you
  seem younger, you look like a little boy.

TUSENBACH: That's because of your hairdo.

IRINA: I've got to find another job, this doesn't suit me. What
  I wanted so much, what I hoped for . . . that's exactly
  what it wasn't. It's just work without anything poetic or
  spiritual about it.

  (*A knock on the floor.*)

IRINA: The doctor's knocking. (*To* TUSENBACH) My friend,
  will you knock. I can't . . . I'm tired. . . .

  (TUSENBACH *knocks on the floor.*)

IRINA: Now he'll be right up. We should do something about this whole thing. Yesterday the doctor and our Andrey went to the club again, and again they lost. They say Andrey lost two hundred rubles.

MASHA *(indifferently)*: What can we do about it!

IRINA: He lost two weeks ago, he lost in December. The sooner he loses everything, the sooner we leave this town. Lord God, I dream of Moscow every night, I'm like a madwoman. *(She laughs.)* We're moving to Moscow in the month of June, and until June there remains . . . February, March, April, May . . . almost half a year!

MASHA: Just so that Natasha doesn't find out he lost his money gambling.

IRINA: It's all the same to her, I suppose.

> (CHEBUTYKIN, *who has just had a snooze—he went to rest after dinner—enters the ballroom, combs his beard and then sits down at the table and takes a newspaper out of his pocket.*)

MASHA: Here he is. . . . Has he paid his rent?

IRINA *(laughs)*: No. In eight months, not a penny. Obviously he forgot.

MASHA *(laughs)*: Look how grand he is sitting there.

> *(Everybody laughs. Pause.)*

IRINA: You're not saying anything, Alexander Ignatyevich?

VERSHININ: No, not much. I'd like some tea. My kingdom for a glass of tea! I haven't eaten since this morning. . . .

CHEBUTYKIN: Irina Sergeyevna!

IRINA: What do you want?

CHEBUTYKIN: Will you please be so kind as to come nearer. *Venez ici.* (IRINA *approaches and sits down at the table.*) I can't do it without you.

> (IRINA *lays out cards for a game of patience.*) [27]

VERSHININ: Fine. Since the tea is not forthcoming, let's have a philosophical conversation.

TUSENBACH: All right. What subject?

VERSHININ: The subject? Suppose we dream? For example, of the life after us, in two or three hundred years.

TUSENBACH: Why not? After us people will fly around in balloons, jackets will change style, a sixth sense will perhaps be discovered and developed, but life will remain the same, a difficult life, full of mysteries and happiness. In a thousand years, man will be sighing just as he does now: "Ah, how hard life is!" and just like today, he'll be afraid and will not want to die.

VERSHININ (*after reflecting*): How shall I say it? It seems to me that little by little, everything on earth will be transformed, and is already being transformed under our very eyes. In two or three hundred years, or even a thousand years—the time is immaterial—there will be a new, happy life. We will have no part in this life, of course, but it is for it that we are living today, that we're working and, yes, suffering, for we are creating it; and that is the goal of our existence and, if you wish, of our happiness.

(MASHA *laughs softly.*)

TUSENBACH: What's the matter?

MASHA: I don't know. I've been laughing since this morning.

VERSHININ: I come from the same school as you, I didn't go on to the academy; I read a great deal, but I don't know how to choose my readings and it may be that I don't read what I should be reading, and yet, the longer I live, the more I desire to learn. My hair is getting gray, I am already an old man, but how little I know, oh, how little! Yet it seems to me that I know what is genuinely essential and that I know it all the way. And I wish I could prove to you that there is no happiness for us, that there mustn't be any and that there won't be any for us. . . . We must only work and work, but as for happiness, it belongs to our distant descendants. (*Pause*) It's not for me, but perhaps only for my descendants' descendants.

(FEDOTIK *and* RODĒ *appear in the room; they sit down and sing softly, accompanying themselves on a guitar.*)

TUSENBACH: In your opinion, one mustn't even dream of happiness! But I am happy!

VERSHININ: Oh, no, you're not.

TUSENBACH (*raising his arms in the air and laughing*): It's clear we don't understand one another. What must I do to convince you? (MASHA *laughs softly.* TUSENBACH *points his finger at her.*) Come on and laugh! (*To* VERSHININ) It's not just in two or three hundred years; even in a million years, life will remain as it has been; it doesn't vary, it remains constant, following its own laws, which do not concern us, or at least, which we will never understand. The migratory birds, the storks, for example, fly and fly and whatever their thoughts, large or small, which ramble around in their heads, they shall continue to fly without knowing why they do it or where they are going. The birds fly and will fly, whoever the philosophers may be who appear in their midst, and they can philosophize all they like, as long as they fly. . . .

MASHA: But all the same, what is the point of all of this?

TUSENBACH: The point . . . Look, it's snowing. What's the point of that?

(*Pause.*)

MASHA: It seems to me that a man must have a faith or he must be searching for a faith, otherwise his life is just empty, empty. . . . To live without knowing why the cranes fly, why children are born, why there are stars in the sky . . . Either you know why you are living or else everything is foolish, no point to it.

(*Pause.*)

VERSHININ: It's a pity all the same that my youth has passed.

MASHA: Gogol said it: "How boring it gets to live in this lowly world, gentlemen!" [18]

TUSENBACH: And I would say: How difficult it is to discuss things with you, gentlemen! So keep your ideas. . . .

CHEBUTYKIN (*reading his newspaper*): Balzac was married in Berdichev.[19] (IRINA *hums softly.*) I must write that down in my notebook. (*He notes it down.*) Balzac was married in Berdichev. (*He reads the newspaper.*)

IRINA (*continuing her game of patience; thoughtfully*): Balzac was married in Berdichev.

TUSENBACH: The die is cast. You know, Maria Sergeyevna, I've sent in my resignation.

MASHA: I've heard. I don't see any cause for rejoicing. I don't like civilians.

TUSENBACH: It's all the same. *(He gets up.)* I'm not handsome, why should I be a military man. After all, it's all the same. . . . I shall work. For once in my life, for one single day, to work to the point where I returned in the evening exhausted enough to fall into my bed and fall sound asleep immediately. *(He goes toward the room.)* Workers must sleep well!

FEDOTIK *(to* IRINA*)*: Just now, at Pizhikov's, on Moskovskaya Street, I bought you some colored crayons. And this new penknife . . .

IRINA: You've taken on the habit of treating me like a little girl, but I'm already a big girl. . . . *(She takes the crayons and the penknife, joyously.)* How lovely!

FEDOTIK: And for myself I bought a knife. Look . . . a blade, another blade, a third one, that's to scratch the inside of your ears, these are little scissors, this is for cleaning your nails. . . .

RODÉ *(in a strong voice)*: Doctor, how old are you?

CHEBUTYKIN: Me? Thirty-two.

(Laughter.)

FEDOTIK: I'll teach you another game of patience. . . .

> *(He lays out the cards. They bring the samovar;* ANFISA *stands next to the samovar: a moment after, enter* NATASHA, *who busies herself, she, too, around the table; enter* SOLYONY, *who sits down at the table after having greeted everyone.)*

VERSHININ: That's some wind!

MASHA: Yes. I've had enough of the winter. I've already forgotten what summer is like.

IRINA: The patience is going to work out. I can see it already. We shall go to Moscow.

FEDOTIK: No, it will not. See, the eight comes on the two of spades. *(He laughs.)* So you will not go to Moscow.

CHEBUTYKIN (*reads the newspaper*): Tsitsihar.[20] Smallpox is raging there.

ANFISA (*approaching* MASHA): Masha, come and take your tea, my little one. (*To* VERSHININ) It is served, your honor ... excuse me, my good fellow, I have forgotten your name.

MASHA: Nurse, bring it to me. I don't want to go over there.

IRINA: Nurse!

ANFISA: In a moment!

NATASHA (*to* SOLYONY): Infants understand marvelously. I tell him, "Good morning, Bobik. Good morning, my darling." He looks at me in such a way. You think it's my imagination because I'm a mother, but no, no, I assure you! He is an exceptional child.

SOLYONY: If that child were mine, I would throw him in the frying pan and eat him. (*He takes his glass to the drawing room and sits in a corner.*)

NATASHA (*covering her face with her hands*): What a rude, uncivilized man!

MASHA: The ones who don't notice whether it's summer or winter are happy. It seems to me that if I were in Moscow, I'd be completely indifferent about the weather.

VERSHININ: These last days I have been reading the journal of a French minister, written in prison. This minister had been sentenced for the Panama business.[21] With what ecstasy and exaltation he spoke of the birds he saw from the prison window which, in former days, when he was a minister, he never noticed. Now that he is once again free, just as before, he does not notice the birds. That is exactly how you will not notice Moscow when you live there. We are not happy and happiness doesn't exist, we can only desire it.

TUSENBACH (*takes a box from the table*): But where are the candies?

IRINA: Solyony ate them.

TUSENBACH: All of them?

ANFISA (*serving the tea*): A letter for you, my good man.

VERSHININ: For me? (*He takes the letter.*) From my daughter. (*He reads it.*) Yes, evidently ... I must go. .... I'm sorry, Maria Sergeyevna, I'll just slip out. I shan't have my tea. (*He gets up, agitated.*) Same old story ...

MASHA: What's the matter? If it isn't indiscreet?

VERSHININ (*in a low voice*): My wife has poisoned herself again. I must go to her. I shall go without disturbing anyone. It's awfully painful, all this. My dear, my lovely, my wonderful woman . . . I'll just slip out quietly here. . . . (*He goes.*)

ANFISA: Where is he going? And I just poured some tea for him. . . . That's not nice.

MASHA: That's enough! You're always on my back, leave me alone, will you. (*She goes with her cup toward the table.*) I've had enough of you, old lady. . . .

ANFISA: But what have I done to you! My dear!

ANDREY'S VOICE: Anfisa!

ANFISA (*imitating him*): Anfisa! He doesn't put himself out, that one. . . . (*She goes out.*)

MASHA (*in the ballroom, by the table, annoyed*): Allow me to sit down! (*She mixes up the cards on the table.*) With your cards, there's only room for you. Drink your tea!

IRINA: Masha, you're nasty.

MASHA: If I'm so nasty, don't talk to me. Don't touch me!

CHEBUTYKIN (*laughing*): Don't touch her, don't touch her. . . .

MASHA: You're sixty years old, but you're like a little schoolgirl, always making a fuss about who the hell knows what.

NATASHA (*sighs*): Dear Masha, why use such expressions in the conversation? With your nice appearance, you could be in the best civilized society; I tell you, you're simply charming, if it weren't for those words you use. *Je vous prie pardonnez-moi, Marie, mais vous avez des manières un peu grossières.*[22]

TUSENBACH (*trying not to laugh*): Will you . . . will you pass me . . . I think there's some cognac there. . . .

NATASHA: *Il paraît que mon Bobik déjà ne dort pas,* he has wakened. He is a little sick today. I am going to him, excuse me. . . . (*She goes out.*)

IRINA: And where did Alexander Ignatyevich disappear to?

MASHA: He went home. There's something extraordinary with his wife.

TUSENBACH (*goes to* SOLYONY *with a flask of cognac in his hand*): You always sit by yourself, there you are ruminating, one wonders about what. Let's make peace. Let's drink a glass of cognac.

(*They drink.*)

I shall be obliged to stay at the piano all night and play all sorts of silly things, I suppose. . . . Well, so what!

SOLYONY: And why make peace? I have not had a quarrel with you.

TUSENBACH: You always give the impression that there has been something between us. You have a strange character, one must admit.

SOLYONY (*reciting*): "I am strange, who isn't!" [23] Don't be angry, Aleko!" [24]

TUSENBACH: Aleko has nothing to do with it. . . .

(*Pause.*)

SOLYONY: When I am with someone, face to face, that's fine, I'm like everyone else, but in society I get morose and shy . . . and I say the most absurd things. But I am still more honest and decent than many, many other people. And I can prove it.

TUSENBACH: I am often furious with you when we are among people, you never cease to provoke me, and despite that, in some way, I like you. So what, I shall get drunk today. Here's to you!

SOLYONY: Here's to you. (*They drink.*) I have never had anything against you, baron. But I have the character of a Lermontov. . . . [25] (*In a lower voice*) I even resemble him a bit, they say. . . . (*He takes a flask of perfume out and douses his hands.*)

TUSENBACH: I'm resigning. *Basta!* I have thought about it for five years, and now I'm finally decided. I am going to work.

SOLYONY (*reciting*): "Don't be angry, Aleko . . . Forget, forget your dreams."

(*As they speak,* ANDREY *enters with a book and sits down noiselessly next to a candle.*)

TUSENBACH: I shall work.

CHEBUTYKIN (*entering the drawing room with* IRINA): And the dishes were also authentically Caucasian: onion soup and a roast meat, a *chekhartmá.* [26]

SOLYONY: A *cheremchá* was never meat, but a plant that resembles our onion.

CHEBUTYKIN: No, my angel. The *chekhartmá* is not an onion, but a roast of mutton.

SOLYONY: And I say to you, the *cheremchá* is an onion.

CHEBUTYKIN: Why do you want me to discuss it with you? You have never been in the Caucasus and you have never eaten *chekhartmá*.

SOLYONY: I haven't eaten it, because I couldn't stand it. *Cheremchá* has the same odor as garlic.

ANDREY *(begging)*: That's enough, people! Please!

TUSENBACH: When are the maskers arriving?

IRINA: About nine o'clock. Just about now.

TUSENBACH *(puts his arms around* ANDREY *and sings)*: "Oh my porch, my porch, my nice new brand-new porch . . ." [27]

ANDREY *(dances and sings)*: "New porch, made of maple wood."

CHEBUTYKIN *(dancing)*: "With latticework in the maple wood!"

(Laughter.)

TUSENBACH *(embraces* ANDREY*)*: The hell with it, let's drink another. Andriucha, let's drink to you and me. I, too, Andriucha, am going to Moscow, to the university, with you.

SOLYONY: Which one? There are two universities in Moscow.

ANDREY: There is only one university in Moscow.

SOLYONY: And I tell you there are two.

ANDREY: Three if you wish. So much the better.

SOLYONY: There are two universities in Moscow. *(Muttering and grumbling)* There are two universities in Moscow, the old and the new. But if it is disagreeable to hear me say it, if what I say irritates you, I can also keep quiet. And I can even go into another room. . . . *(He goes out by one of the doors.)*

TUSENBACH: Bravo, bravo! *(He laughs.)* Ladies, gentlemen, choose your partners, I shall sit down at the piano! He is strange, that Solyony. . . . *(He sits down at the piano and plays a waltz.)*

MASHA *(waltzes by herself)*: The baron is drunk, the baron is drunk, the baron is drunk.

(Enter NATASHA.)

NATASHA *(to Chebutykin)*: Ivan Romanich!

> *(She says something to CHEBUTYKIN, then goes out quietly. CHEBUTYKIN touches TUSENBACH on the shoulder and whispers something in his ear.)*

IRINA: What is it?

CHEBUTYKIN: It's time to go. Good night.

TUSENBACH: Good night. It's time to go.

IRINA: But wait. What about the maskers?

ANDREY *(confused)*: There will be no maskers. You understand, my dear, Natasha says that Bobik is not well, and so . . . in short, I don't know any more, myself, it's all the same to me.

IRINA *(shrugging her shoulders)*: Bobik isn't well!

MASHA: Well, what the hell! We're being chased. Let's go. *(to IRINA)* It's not Bobik who's sick, it's she . . . here! *(She knocks with a finger on her forehead.)* Petty bourgeoise!

> *(ANDREY goes out by the right stage door, which leads to his room. CHEBUTYKIN follows him; in the ballroom, good-byes are being said.)*

FEDOTIK: What a pity! I thought I'd spend a nice evening, but obviously if the little child is sick, well, then . . . Tomorrow I'll bring him some toys. . . .

RODÉ *(in a loud voice)*: I purposely had a little snooze after dinner, I expected to be dancing all night. It's only nine o'clock now!

MASHA: Let's go outside in the fresh air. We can decide outside what to do.

> *(You hear: "Good-bye! Be well!" TUSENBACH's merry laugh is heard. Everybody goes out. ANFISA and the maid clear the table, extinguish the lights. The nurse is heard singing. ANDREY, in his hat and overcoat, and CHEBUTYKIN enter noiselessly.)*

CHEBUTYKIN: I didn't have time to get married because life

passed by with the rapidity of a flash of lightning and because I loved your mother madly and she was married.

ANDREY: One is wrong to marry. It's wrong because one gets bored.

CHEBUTYKIN: Of course, yes, but there is solitude. You can philosophize about it all you like, solitude is a frightful thing, my boy . . . although, essentially, it positively comes right down to the same thing!

ANDREY: Let's hurry up.

CHEBUTYKIN: Why hurry? We have time.

ANDREY: I'm afraid my wife may prevent me from going out.

CHEBUTYKIN: Oh!

ANDREY: Today I don't have any intention of playing, I'm just going for a moment. . . . I don't feel well. . . . What do you do when you're short of breath, Ivan Romanich?

CHEBUTYKIN: What a question! I don't remember, my boy, I don't know.

ANDREY: Let's go through the kitchen.

(They go out. The doorbell rings, then it rings again; voices and laughter are heard.)

IRINA *(enters)*: What's that?

ANFISA *(whispering)*: The maskers!

(The bell rings.)

IRINA: Nurse, tell them there's no one here. They'll have to excuse us.

(ANFISA goes out. IRINA, meditating, walks up and down; she is agitated. Enter SOLYONY.)

SOLYONY *(perplexed)*: Nobody . . . Where have they all gone?

IRINA: They've all gone home.

SOLYONY: That's strange. You're alone here?

IRINA: Yes. *(Pause)* Good evening.

SOLYONY: A while ago I behaved badly and was tactless. But you're not like the others, you're lofty and pure, you see things clearly . . . only you could understand me. I love you, profoundly, infinitely. . . .

IRINA: Good night! Please leave.

SOLYONY: I cannot live without you. *(Following her)* Oh, my happiness! *(Through tears)* Oh, happiness! Oh, my magnificent, marvelous, astonishing eyes, I have never seen the like in any other woman. . . .

IRINA *(coldly)*: Please finish, Vassili Vassilievich!

SOLYONY: It's the first time that I speak of my love for you, and it is as if I was not upon this earth, but on another planet. *(He scratches his forehead.)* Well, so what. One cannot make oneself loved by force, of course . . . but if I had a fortunate rival, I wouldn't allow it . . . certainly not. I swear to you on all I hold sacred, a rival, I would kill him. . . . Oh, my marvelous one!

(Enter NATASHA, carrying a taper.)

NATASHA *(glances at one door, then another, and passes in front of the one that leads to her husband's room)*: Andrey is there. I'll let him read. Excuse me, Vassili Vassilich, I didn't know you were there, I'm in my negligee. . . .

SOLYONY: It's all the same to me. Farewell! *(He goes out.)*

NATASHA: You are tired, my dear, poor little girl! *(She kisses IRINA.)* You ought to go to bed early.

IRINA: Is Bobik sleeping?

NATASHA: Yes, but it's a fitful sleep. By the way, my dear, I wanted to tell you, but you're never there and I'm busy. . . . It seems to me that Bobik is cold in his room and it's damp. While your room is completely what a child would need. My dear, nice girl, move for a while into Olga's room!

IRINA *(not understanding)*: Where?

(The bells of a troika are heard stopping in front of the house.)

NATASHA: You would, while waiting, be with Olya, in the same room, and Bobik would take yours. He is so cute; today I said to him, "My Bobik! You're all mine! Mine!" And he looked at me with his sweet little eyes. *(The bell rings.)* That must be Olga. She's back so late!

(The maid comes to NATASHA and whispers something in her ear.)

NATASHA: Protopopov? What a silly fool! It's Protopopov, he wants to take me for a ride in his troika. *(She laughs.)* Men are so funny. . . . *(The bell rings.)* There's someone there. . . . If I went for a quarter of an hour . . . *(To the maid)* Tell him I'll be right there. *(The bell rings.)* They're ringing. It must be Olga.

(She goes out. The maid goes out, running; IRINA is seated, lost in her thoughts. Enter KULYGIN, OLGA, followed by VERSHININ.)

KULYGIN: What's happening? Didn't they tell me there would be a gathering?

VERSHININ: It's strange, I left just a while ago, hardly a half hour ago, and they were waiting for the maskers.

IRINA: Everybody left.

KULYGIN: Masha, too? Where did she go? And why is Protopopov waiting down there in a troika? Who is he waiting for?

IRINA: Don't ask me any questions. . . . I'm tired.

KULYGIN: Come, my capricious little girl. . . .

OLGA: The council meeting just ended. I'm exhausted. Our director is sick, I'm replacing her. Oh, my head, my poor head, it hurts so. *(She sits down.)* Yesterday, Andrey lost two hundred rubles at cards. . . . The whole town is talking about it.

KULYGIN: Yes, and the council meetings tired me out, too. *(He sits down.)*

VERSHININ: Today my wife tried to frighten me, she tried to poison herself. It's all right now, and I'm content, I can rest. . . . If I understand rightly, we must go. Then allow me to wish you good night. Fyodor Ilyich, let's go somewhere! I cannot remain at home, totally impossible. . . . Come!

KULYGIN: I'm tired. I won't go anywhere. *(He gets up.)* I'm tired. My wife has returned home?

IRINA: I suppose.

KULYGIN *(kisses IRINA's hand)*: Farewell. Tomorrow and the next day I've got completely free. All the best! *(About to leave)* I wanted some tea! I thought I would spend the evening in agreeable company and . . . *O fallacem hominem spem!* . . .[28] The exclamation requires the accusative.

VERSHININ: I'll go alone then. *(He goes out with* KULYGIN, *whistling.)*

OLGA: I've got a headache, I have a headache. . . . Andrey lost. . . . The whole town is talking. . . . I'm going to lie down. *(Going off)* Tomorrow I'm free. . . . My God, what happiness. I'm free tomorrow, free after tomorrow. . . . I have a headache, such a headache. . . . *(She goes out.)*

IRINA *(alone)*: Everybody's gone. Nobody's left.

(In the street, the sound of an accordion; the nurse sings.)

NATASHA *(wearing a fur-lined cloak and a fur bonnet, she crosses the room; the maid follows her)*: I'll be back in half an hour. I'm just going for a ride. *(She goes out.)*

IRINA *(remaining alone, full of nostalgia)*: Moscow! Moscow! Moscow!

CURTAIN

ACT THREE

> *The room that* OLGA *and* IRINA *share.
> There are beds behind the screens both
> at the left and at the right. It is after two
> in the morning. The fire alarm is heard
> repeatedly; there is a fire somewhere
> and the alarm has been ringing for some
> time. Evidently nobody in the house has
> gone to bed yet.*

> MASHA, *dressed as usual in black, is
> stretched out on the divan. Enter* OLGA
> *and* ANFISA.

ANFISA: Now they're sitting downstairs under the staircase.
. . . I told them, "Please come up, don't stay here, that's
not the thing to do"—that's what I said to them, and they
just sit there crying, "We don't know where our papa is.
God forbid, he may be burned." Imagine! And there are
others in the courtyard . . . and they're all undressed.

OLGA (*taking dresses from the wardrobe*): Take the little gray
one there . . . and this one. . . . And the blouse, too . . . and
this skirt, nurse dear. . . . My God, how awful! It seems that
Kirsanov Street has burned to the ground. . . . Take this . . .
and this. . . . (*She piles the dresses over her arm.*) The poor
Vershinins had a great scare. . . . Their house very nearly
burned down. They'd better spend the night here. . . . We
mustn't let them go home. . . . Poor Fedotik has lost everything, everything was completely burned. . . .

ANFISA: Call Ferapont, Olyushka, it's too heavy for me. . . .

OLGA (*rings*): We can ring all we like—there's no answer. . . .
(*Shouting through the door*) Will somebody please come up
here! (*Through the open door one can see a window pro-*

171

jecting a red glow because of the fire; we hear the firemen passing in front of the house.) How horrible! I've had enough of it!

(Enter FERAPONT.*)*

OLGA: Take this and carry it all downstairs. . . . You'll find the Kolitiline girls under the staircase—it's for them. And give them these, too. . . .

FERAPONT: Very well. In the year 1812 Moscow burned down, too.[29] Lord God in Heaven! The French couldn't get over it.

OLGA: Go ahead, now. . . .

FERAPONT: Very well. *(He goes out.)*

OLGA: Nurse dear, you can give them everything we have. We don't need anything, you can give it all, dear. . . . I'm tired, I can't stand up any more. . . . We mustn't let the Vershinins go. . . . The children can sleep in the drawing room, and Alexander Ignatyevich downstairs with the baron. . . . We'll put Fedotik in with the baron, too, or else in our dining room. . . . The doctor is drunk, he's done it on purpose, frightfully drunk, and nobody can go in with him. We'll put Vershinin's wife in the drawing room, too.

ANFISA *(very weary)*: Olyushka, my dear, don't throw me out! Don't throw me out!

OLGA: You're talking nonsense, nurse dear. Nobody's throwing you out!

ANFISA *(places her head on* OLGA's *bosom)*: My darling, my treasure, I work, I do my best. . . . When I haven't any strength left, they'll tell me, "Get out!" And where will I go? Where? I'm over eighty years old. I'm in my eighty-second year. . . .

OLGA: Sit down there, nurse dear. . . . You're tired, my poor dear. . . . *(She sits her down.)* Rest yourself, my dear. How pale you are!

(Enter NATASHA.*)*

NATASHA: They say we must organize a committee as quickly as possible to help the fire victims. Well? It's an excellent idea. One should above all help the poor, that is the duty of the rich. Bobik and Sophochka are asleep, sound asleep as if nothing had happened. We have so many people in every little corner, wherever you look, the house is overrun. The flu is breaking out now, I'm afraid the children may catch it.

OLGA *(not listening)*: One can't see the fire from this room. It's peaceful here. . . .

NATASHA: That's right. . . . My hair must have come undone. *(In front of the mirror)* They say I'm gaining weight . . . it's not true! Not at all! Masha is sleeping, she's tired, poor thing. . . . *(To* ANFISA, *without feeling)* I forbid you to be seated in my presence! Get up! Out of here! *(*ANFISA *goes. Pause.)* Why you keep that old woman, I don't understand!

OLGA *(amazed)*: Excuse me, but . . . I don't understand, either.

NATASHA: She has nothing to do here. She's a peasant, she should be living in a village. . . . This is overindulgence! I like a house to be in order! No use having useless people. *(She caresses* OLGA's *cheek.)* You're tired, poor dear! Our headmistress is tired! When my Sophie will be a big girl and go to school, I'll be afraid of you. . . .

OLGA: I will not be headmistress.

NATASHA: You'll be picked, Olyechka. That's for sure.

OLGA: I shall refuse. I wouldn't know how . . . it's more than I could face. . . . *(She drinks some water.)* Just now, you were so cruel with Anfisa. . . . You must pardon me, I cannot bear it. . . . It made me feel faint. . . .

NATASHA *(agitated)*: Pardon me, Olya, pardon me . . . I didn't wish to hurt you. . . .

*(*MASHA *gets up, takes her pillow and goes off, furious.)*

OLGA: Will you understand, my dear . . . the education we received is perhaps peculiar, but I cannot bear this. . . . This way of behaving is too much for me, it makes me sick. . . . I get despondent!

NATASHA: Forgive me, forgive me. . . . *(She kisses* OLGA.)

OLGA: The slightest rudeness, a lack of tact and delicacy, and I'm so upset. . . .

NATASHA: Sometimes I say things I shouldn't, it's true, but you can't deny, my dear, that she could be living in the village.

OLGA: She's been with us for thirty years.

NATASHA: But since she can't work now any more! Perhaps I

don't understand anything, or else it is you who will not understand. She is incapable of working, all she does is sleep or sit around.

OLGA: Then let her sit.

NATASHA (*astonished*): What do you mean, let her sit? She's only a servant! (*Through tears*) I don't understand you, Olya. I have a governess for the children and a wet nurse, we have a maid, a cook . . . what need is there for this old lady? Whatever for?

(*The fire alarm is heard offstage.*)

OLGA: I've aged ten years this night.

NATASHA: We must come to an understanding about certain things, Olga. You're at school, I'm in the house; you do the teaching, I run the household. And when I say something about the servants, I know what I'm talking about, I know of what I speak. . . . And from tomorrow on, let me not see that old thief here any more, that old shrew. . . . (*She stamps her feet.*) That witch! . . . How dare you infuriate me! How dare you! (*Pulling herself together*) Really, if you don't move downstairs, we're going to fight all the time. It's terrible.

(*Enter* KULYGIN.)

KULYGIN: Where is Masha? It's about time we went home. They say the fire has died down. (*Stretching*) Only one section of the town burned down, despite the wind, and in the beginning they thought the whole town was on fire. (*He sits down.*) I'm exhausted. . . . My dear Olyechka . . . Often I think if it hadn't been for Masha, I would have married you, Olyechka. You're a very nice person. . . . I'm exhausted. (*He listens intently.*)

OLGA: What is it?

KULYGIN: It's as if he did it on purpose, the doctor is on a binge, he's dead drunk, as if he did it on purpose! (*He gets up.*) I think he's coming up here. . . . Do you hear him? Yes, he's coming. . . . (*He laughs.*) I wonder what's got into him, really. . . . I think I'll hide. (*He goes over to the wardrobe and hides in a corner.*) Troublemaker!

OLGA: He stopped drinking for two years, and then, suddenly, he goes and gets drunk.

(She goes with NATASHA *to the back of the room. Enter* CHEBUTYKIN; *without staggering, as if he hadn't been drinking, he crosses the room, stops, looks about, goes to the washbasin and begins washing his hands.)*

CHEBUTYKIN *(sullen):* To hell with them all, damn them. They think I'm a doctor, that I can treat all kinds of diseases, and I know absolutely nothing, I've forgotten everything I once knew, I remember nothing, absolutely nothing. *(OLGA and* NATASHA *go out without being noticed.)* To hell with them. Last Wednesday I treated a woman, she died, and it's my fault she died. Yes . . . Twenty-five years ago I knew a thing or two, but now I remember nothing. Nothing. It may very well be that I'm not even a man, that I only look as if I have arms and legs and a head. Maybe I don't even exist, and it only seems that I walk, that I eat and that I sleep. *(He cries.)* Oh, if only we could stop existing! *(He stops crying, sullen.)* What the hell . . . Day before yesterday they were talking at the club . . . about Shakespeare, Voltaire. I've never read them, not a word, but I tried to give the impression I had read them. And the others did the same. How vulgar! How low! And again I saw the woman I killed on Wednesday, again I saw her. . . . I saw everything again, and I was heartsick, heavy with disgust, vile . . . and so I went out and got drunk.

(IRINA, VERSHININ and TUSENBACH enter; TUSENBACH is in civilian dress, his clothes are new and fashionable.)

IRINA: Let's stay here. Nobody will come in here.
VERSHININ: If it weren't for the soldiers, the entire town would have been burned down. More power to them! *(He rubs his hands together with relish.)* They're as good as gold! More power to them!
KULYGIN *(coming to them):* What time is it, people?
TUSENBACH: Almost four in the morning. It's getting light.
IRINA: Everybody's staying in the ballroom, nobody wants to leave. Your Solyony's there, too. . . . *(To* CHEBUTYKIN*)* You might as well go to bed, doctor.

CHEBUTYKIN: Very well . . . thanks. (*He combs his beard.*)

KULYGIN (*laughs*): You've had it, Ivan Romanich! (*He pats him on the shoulder.*) Bravo! *In vino veritas,* as the ancients put it.

TUSENBACH: They've asked me to organize a concert for the benefit of the fire victims.

IRINA: And who are they?

TUSENBACH: If we wanted to, it could be done. In my opinion, Masha plays the piano splendidly.

KULYGIN: Splendidly.

IRINA: She's forgotten how to play. She hasn't played for three or four years.

TUSENBACH: In this town nobody understands music, not a single soul, except me; I understand it and I give you my word of honor that Masha is an excellent pianist, and she's almost professional.

KULYGIN: You're right, baron. I love Masha so much. She's so nice.

TUSENBACH: Imagine playing the piano with such extraordinary talent and realizing that nobody, just nobody understands!

KULYGIN (*sighing*): Yes . . . But would it be the thing for her to take part in a concert? (*Pause*) I don't know about such things, people. Perhaps it's perfectly all right. I must admit that our director is a very fine fellow, yes, very, very fine, he has a superior intelligence, but he has such opinions. It doesn't concern him, of course, but all the same, if you wish me to, I could talk to him about it.

(CHEBUTYKIN *takes a porcelain clock into his hands and examines it.*)

VERSHININ: I got all dirtied up in the fire, what I must look like . . . (*Pause*) I overheard in passing yesterday that our brigade was going to be sent somewhere far away. Some say it will be to Poland, others think it will be to Chita.[30]

TUSENBACH: I heard about it, too. Well! Then the town will be completely deserted.

IRINA: We'll go away, too!

CHEBUTYKIN (*lets the clock fall and break*): To smithereens!

(*Pause; everybody is annoyed and embarrassed.*)

KULYGIN (*picking up the pieces*): To break an object of such value, oh, Ivan Romanich, Ivan Romanich, I'm going to give you zero in conduct!

IRINA: It was Mother's clock.

CHEBUTYKIN: It's quite possible. . . . It was Mother's clock if you say it was Mother's clock. Besides, it may be I didn't break it, perhaps it only looks as if I broke it. Perhaps we only look as if we exist, when in reality we don't at all. I know nothing, and nobody knows anything. (*He stands at the door.*) Why are you looking at me? Natasha is having a little affair with Protopopov, and you don't see it. . . . You sit there and you see nothing, and all this time Natasha is having a little affair with Protopopov. . . . (*He sings.*) "A cup of coffee, a sandwich, and you . . ." [31] (*He goes out.*)

VERSHININ: Yes . . . (*He laughs.*) When you think of it, how strange all this is! (*Pause*) When the fire started, I ran home as fast as I could; I arrive, I see that the house is intact and not threatened, but my two little girls are on the doorstep, in their nighties, their mother isn't there, everybody around is terribly distressed, horses and dogs running about, and on the faces of the little girls such an expression of distress, terror, supplication, I can't tell you; when I saw those faces, it broke my heart. My Lord, I thought to myself, what those two little girls will have to live through yet in their long lives! I grabbed them up, I ran off with them and I could think of only one thing: of what they would yet have to live through in this dreadful world! (*The alarm is heard, then a silence.*) I arrive here and I find their mother shouting, furious. . . .

(MASHA *returns with her pillow and sits down on the divan.*)

VERSHININ: And when I saw my two little girls in their nighties, standing at the doorstep, and the street red with the flames, the terrible din, I thought it must all resemble what happened years and years ago, when the enemy suddenly appeared, pillaging, burning. . . . And meanwhile, as a matter of fact, what difference is there between then and now! And a little more time will pass, scarcely more than two or three hundred years, and our present life will seem a little frightening and they will mock us, and our present existence will seem awkward, heavy and very inappropriate and strange. Ah, and what a life it will be, what a life! *(He laughs.)* Pardon me, I'm philosophizing again. Let me continue, people, I'm terribly much in need of philosophizing, that's my mood right now. *(Pause)* It's as if everyone were asleep. I was saying: what a life it will be! Only think of it. . . . Women like you . . . there are only three in this whole town now, but in the generations to come there will be others, and still others and others, and a time will come when everything will have changed to the way in which you see life, when people will live like you, and after that you too shall be out of date, and people better than you will be born. . . . *(He laughs.)* I'm in a strange mood today. I want to live devilishly. . . . *(He sings.)* "Man's love just never fails him. /It's good for all that ails him." [32] *(He laughs.)*

MASHA: Tram-tam-tam . . . [33]
VERSHININ: Tam-tam . . .
MASHA: Tra-ra-ra?
VERSHININ: Tra-ta-ta. *(He laughs.)*

(Enter FEDOTIK.*)*

FEDOTIK *(dancing)*: I was burned out! I was burned out! Wiped out!

(Laughter.)

IRINA: That's not a laughing matter. Did everything burn?
FEDOTIK *(laughing)*: Everything burned up, wiped out. My guitar burned, and my photographic equipment burned, and all my letters. . . . And I wanted to make you a present of a little notebook, and it burned, too.

(Enter SOLYONY.*)*

IRINA: No, please, Solyony, go away. You're not allowed to come in here.
SOLYONY: Why is the baron allowed, and I am forbidden?
VERSHININ: We really must go. How's the fire?
SOLYONY: It seems to be dying down. No, I find it positively

strange . . . why is the baron allowed and not me? (*He takes out a perfume bottle and sprinkles himself.*)

VERSHININ: Tram-tam-tam . . .

MASHA: Tram-tam . . .

VERSHININ (*to* SOLYONY, *laughing*): Let's go down to the ballroom.

SOLYONY: Very well, I shall remember that. "These thoughts might be further clarified,/But I fear the geese might get rather rarefied." [34] (*Looking at* TUSENBACH) Tsip, tsip, tsip . . . (*He goes out with* VERSHININ *and* FEDOTIK.)

IRINA: He smoked us out, that Solyony. (*Astonished*) The baron is sleeping. Baron! Baron!

TUSENBACH (*coming to*): I'm so tired. . . . The brickyard . . . No, I'm not delirious, it's really happening. I'll be going to the brickyard soon. I'm going to start working. . . . I've already talked it over with them. (*To* IRINA, *tenderly*) You're so pale, so beautiful, so fascinating. . . . It's as if your pallor made the darkness a little lighter, like a light. . . . You're sad, you're dissatisfied with life. . . . Then come with me, we'll work together!

MASHA: Nikolai Lvovich, will you please go.

TUSENBACH (*laughing*): Are you there? I can't see. (*He kisses* IRINA's *hand.*) Farewell, I'm going. . . . . Now that I look at you, I think how once, long ago, on your birthday, you were joyous and enthusiastic, you spoke of the joys of work. . . . The happy life I dreamed of at the time . . . where is it? (*He kisses her hand.*) You have tears in your eyes. Go to bed, it's getting light out. . . . If only I could give my life for you!

MASHA: Nikolai, go away! Now really . . .

TUSENBACH: I'm going. . . . (*He goes out.*)

MASHA (*lying down*): Are you sleeping, Fyodor?

KULYGIN: What?

MASHA: Why don't you go home.

KULYGIN: My dear Masha, my darling Masha . . .

IRINA: She's tired. Let her rest, Fedya.

KULYGIN: I'm going. . . . My wife, my good, sweet wife . . . I love you, my incomprehensible one. . . .

MASHA (*with annoyance*): *Amo, amas, amat, amamus, amatis, amant.* [35]

KULYGIN (*laughs*): No, really, she's astonishing. We've been married for seven years and it seems as if I married you yesterday. My word of honor. No, really, you're an astonishing woman. I'm content, I'm content, I'm content.

MASHA: I've had enough, enough, enough. . . . *(She gets up, sits down and continues speaking where she sits.)* I can't think of anything else. . . . It's simply revolting. I can't get it out of my head, I cannot keep quiet about it. I'm talking about Andrey. . . . He's mortgaged the house and all the money went to his wife, yet the house belongs not to him alone, but to all four of us! He must know that if he's a decent human being.

KULYGIN: That's enough, Masha! No need for that. Andriucha is in debt up to his ears, so leave him alone.

MASHA: At any rate, it's revolting. *(She lies down.)*

KULYGIN: We're not poor, you and I. I work at the high school, afterward I give lessons. . . . I'm an honest fellow . . . simple. . . . *Omnia mea mecum porto,*[36] as they say.

MASHA: I don't need anything, what disgusts me is the unfairness of it all. *(Pause)* Go on, Fyodor.

KULYGIN *(he kisses her)*: You're tired, rest here for a half hour or so, and I'll sit here and I'll wait for you. Sleep. . . . *(Leaving)* I am content, I am content, I am content. *(He goes out.)*

IRINA: If the truth be known . . . how petty our Andrey has become, how faded and old beside that woman! There was a time when he was working for his professorship, and yesterday he boasted of having finally become a member of the county council. He is a member of the council and Protopopov is the president. . . . The whole town is talking and everybody makes fun of him, and only he knows nothing and sees nothing. . . . And when everybody ran off to the fire, he alone remained here in his room, without taking any notice. All he does is play the violin. *(Nervously)* Oh, it's awful, awful, awful! *(She cries.)* I cannot stand it, I cannot bear it any more! . . . I cannot, I cannot! . . . *(OLGA enters and arranges her little table.)*

IRINA *(noisily weeping)*: Throw me out, throw me out, I can't stand it any more.

OLGA *(frightened)*: What's the matter, what's the matter, darling?

IRINA *(sobbing)*: Where? Where did it go? Where is it? Oh, my God, my God! I've forgotten everything, everything. . . . It's all mixed up in my head. . . . I don't remember

how to say "window" in Italian, or "ceiling," either. I forget everything, every day I forget things, and all this time
life slips away and it will never come back, never, and
we'll never go to Moscow. . . . I tell you we'll never go. . . .

OLGA: My dear, my dear . . .

IRINA (*getting hold of herself*): Oh, how unhappy I am. . . . I
cannot work, I will not work. . . . I've had enough, enough!
I worked for the telegraph office, now I work for the
county council, and I hate it, I despise everything they've
given me to do. . . . I'm going to be twenty-four years old,
I've been working for a long time, my brain is dried up,
I've lost weight, I've gotten ugly, old and there is nothing,
nothing, no satisfaction in life, and time passes, and it
seems always that we go farther and farther away from
the true, beautiful life, farther and farther away, down into
some terrible abyss. I'm desperate, I don't know how I
stay alive, I don't understand how it is I haven't yet killed
myself. . . .

OLGA: Don't cry, my little girl, don't cry. It hurts me so.

IRINA: No, I'm not crying . . . that's over with. . . . You see,
I'm not crying any more. Enough . . . enough!

OLGA: Darling, I'm telling this to you as a sister, as a friend;
if you want my advice, marry the baron.

(IRINA *cries softly.*)

OLGA: You have a great deal of respect for him, you think
highly of him. . . . He's not handsome, it's true, but he is so
decent, such a good man. . . . One doesn't marry for love,
don't you see, but to do one's duty. At least that's what I
think, and I would have married without being in love. I
would have taken anybody, as long as he was a decent man.
Even if he were old . . .

IRINA: I was always waiting. We would go to Moscow, there
I would meet my true love, I dreamed of him, I was in
love with him. . . . But that turned out to be so much nonsense, nonsense. . . .

OLGA (*puts her arms around her sister*): My dear, wonderful
sister, I understand it all; when the baron left the army
and came to see us in an everyday coat, he seemed so
ugly to me that I couldn't stop myself from crying. He
asked me, "Why are you crying?" What should I have told

him! But if it is God's will that you should marry him, I would be happy because that's something else again, something else again.

(NATASHA, a candle in her hand, crosses the stage without saying anything, going from the door at the right to the door at the left.)

MASHA *(sitting down)*: She walks around as if it were she who had started the fire.

OLGA: You're silly, Masha. You're the silliest one in the family. Pardon me for saying that.

(Pause.)

MASHA: I need to confess, my dear sisters. My heart is heavy. I shall confess before you, and then never again, to anyone. I will tell you right now. *(In a low voice)* It's my secret, but you must all know it. I can't keep quiet about it. . . . *(Pause)* I'm in love . . . in love. . . . I love that man . . . you just saw him. . . . Very well, I'll come right to the point . . . In a word, I love Vershinin. . . .

OLGA *(going behind the screen)*: That's enough. Anyway, I can't hear you.

MASHA: What shall I do! *(She takes her head in her hands.)* First, he seemed strange to me, then I pitied him . . . then I began to love him. . . . I loved him with his voice, his talking and his unhappiness, his two little girls. . . .

OLGA *(behind the screen)*: All the same, I don't hear anything. You may say all the silly things you like, I don't hear anything anyway.

MASHA: Oh, Olya, you're foolish. I love and that's my destiny. It was meant to be. . . . And he, too, loves me . . . and that's frightening, isn't it? Don't you approve? *(She pulls IRINA by the hand and draws her over.)* Oh, my darling . . . If only we knew how we were going to live out our lives, what will become of us. . . . When one reads a novel, it all seems so old-hat and so obvious, but all one needs is to fall in love oneself in order to see that nobody knows anything and that everyone must decide for himself. . . . My darlings, my sisters . . . I confessed it to you, and now I

shall keep silent. . . . I shall be now like Gogol's madman [37] . . . silence . . . silence. . . .

(Enter ANDREY *and, after him,* FERAPONT.)

ANDREY *(annoyed)*: What do you want? I don't understand.
FERAPONT *(in the doorway, impatiently)*: I've already told
you a dozen times, Andrey Sergeyevich.
ANDREY: And, in the first place, I'm not Andrey Sergeyevich
to you, but your honor.
FERAPONT: Your honor, the firemen would like to be allowed
to go through your garden to go to the river. Otherwise
they have to go around the old way, that's such a nuisance.
ANDREY: Good, tell them it's perfectly all right. (FERAPONT
goes out.) They give me a pain. Where is Olga? (OLGA
comes out from behind the screen.) It's you I've come to
see; give me the key to the cupboard. I've lost mine. You
have that little one, I think. . . .

*(*OLGA *gives him the key without saying anything.* IRINA
disappears behind her screen. Pause.)

ANDREY: What a terrible fire it's been! It's just beginning to
die down. Damn Ferapont, he made me so furious, I behaved like an idiot. . . . Your honor . . . *(Pause)* Why don't
you say anything, Olya? *(Pause)* It's about time we stopped
all this foolishness and pouting for no reason whatsoever.
. . . Masha is there, Irina is there, very well then, let's go
to the heart of the matter, once and for all. What have you
got against me? Hmm?
OLGA: That's enough, Andriucha. We'll talk about it tomorrow. *(Agitated)* What a terrible night!
ANDREY *(very embarrassed)*: Calm yourself. You see, I am
perfectly calm and I am asking you: what have you got
against me? Tell it to me straight out.
THE VOICE OF VERSHININ: Tram-tam-tam!
MASHA *(gets up; in a loud voice)*: Tra-ta-ta! *(To* OLGA*)* Good
night, Olga, God be with you. *(She goes behind the screen
and kisses* IRINA.) Sleep well. . . . Good night, Andrey.
Go away, they're tired, you'll have it out with them tomorrow. . . . *(She goes out.)*

OLGA: Really, Andriucha, let's put it off till tomorrow. . . .
(She goes behind the screen.) It's time to go to bed.

ANDREY: I will say what I have to say and I will go. First,
you have something against Natasha, my wife, I was aware
of it from the first day of our marriage. Natasha is a fine
human being, honest and decent, that is my belief. I love
and I respect my wife and I insist, do you understand, I
respect her and I insist that others respect her as well. I
repeat, she is a fine and noble human being, and all of
your displeasure is, if you will pardon me, just a whim.
(Pause) Secondly, it would seem that you have a grudge
against me for not having become a professor, for not busy-
ing myself with my studies. But I am in the county council,
I am a member of the county council, and I consider that I
am fulfilling a sacred and elevated duty, as if I were a
scholar. . . . I am a member of the county council, and I
am proud of it, if that interests you. . . . *(Pause)* Thirdly
—I still have more to say—I have mortgaged the house
without asking for your permission. . . . I am guilty of
that, I admit it, and I wish to apologize. I was forced to
it by debts . . . thirty-five thousand. I no longer gamble, I
gave up playing cards long ago, but my main excuse is that
you, the girls of the family, live off your pension, and I
didn't have the wherewithal, so to speak. . . .

(Pause.)

KULYGIN *(in the doorway)*: Masha isn't here? *(Uneasy)* But
where is she? That's strange. . . . *(He goes out.)*

ANDREY: They're not listening to me. Natasha is a fine, decent human being. *(He paces across the room without a
word, then stops.)* When we were married, I believed we
were all of us going to be happy . . . all of us. But, my
God . . . *(He weeps.)* My dear sisters, my poor darlings,
don't believe me, don't believe any of it.

(He goes out. The fire signal sounds, the stage is empty.)

IRINA *(behind the screen)*: Olya! Who's knocking on the
floor?

OLGA: It's Ivan Romanich. He's drunk.

IRINA: What a disturbing night! *(Pause)* Olya! *(She sticks her head out from behind the screen.)* Did you hear? The brigade is going to be sent somewhere else, far away from here.

OLGA: Those are only rumors.

IRINA: Then we'll be all alone. . . . Olya!

OLGA: Yes?

IRINA: My sweet, darling sister, I respect and admire the baron, he's a very good man, I'll marry him, I'll do it, only let's go to Moscow! I beg of you, let's go there! Moscow, there's no better place in all the world! Let's go there, Olya! Let's go there!

CURTAIN

ACT
FOUR

The old garden encircling the PROZOROV *house. A long alleyway of fir trees, at the end of which is a view of the river. On the other side of the river, the forest. At the right, the veranda of the house; there, on the table, bottles and glasses: someone has been drinking champagne. It is noon. From time to time, one sees passersby who go through the garden to the river; a group of soldiers, five perhaps, descend the alleyway rapidly.*

CHEBUTYKIN, *in a good humor that will not desert him for the rest of the act, sits in a garden chair, waiting to be called; he has his peaked cap on and holds a cane.* IRINA, KULYGIN (*with a decoration around his neck and his moustache shaved*) *and* TUSENBACH *stand on the veranda saying farewell to* FEDOTIK *and* RODÉ, *who come down the steps; the two officers are in field dress.*

TUSENBACH (*embraces* FEDOTIK): You are a nice fellow. We've always gotten on well together. (*He embraces* RODÉ) Once again . . . farewell, old fellow!

IRINA: *Au revoir!*

FEDOTIK: No, not *au revoir,* but farewell . . . we shall never see one another again!

186

KULYGIN: Who knows! (*He wipes his eyes and smiles.*) There, I'm crying.

IRINA: One day or another, we'll meet again.

FEDOTIK: In ten years, or in fifteen? But then, we'll hardly know one another, we'll say hello coldly. . . . (*He takes a photo.*) Don't move. Just once more.

RODÉ (*passes his arm around* TUSENBACH): We shall not see each other again. . . . (*He kisses* IRINA's *hand.*) Thanks for everything, for everything!

FEDOTIK (*irritated*): Please, let's stand still!

TUSENBACH: If God keeps us alive, we'll see each other again. Write to us. Without fail.

RODÉ (*embraces the garden with a glance*) Farewell, trees! (*He shouts.*) Yahooooo! (*Pause*) Farewell, echo!

KULYGIN: If it happens that you go and get married in Poland, your Polish wife will embrace you and say: "Kochanny!" [38] (*He laughs.*)

FEDOTIK (*after a glance at his watch*): We have less than an hour. From our battery, there is only Solyony who'll take the barge; we'll leave with our unit. Three divisions are going today, tomorrow three more will leave . . . and peace and quiet will descend on the town.

TUSENBACH: And also a terrible boredom.

RODÉ: And Maria Sergeyevna, where is she?

KULYGIN: Masha is in the garden.

FEDOTIK: We'd like to say farewell to her.

RODÉ: Farewell, we must go, or I'll begin to cry. . . . (*He embraces* TUSENBACH *and* KULYGIN *rapidly and kisses* IRINA's *hand.*) We have spent good moments here. . . .

FEDOTIK (*to* KULYGIN): This is for you . . . a little remembrance, a notebook with a pencil. . . . We're going down this way to the river.

(*They go off, turning to glance back.*)

RODÉ (*shouting*): Yahooooo!

KULYGIN (*shouting*): Good-bye!

(*Way upstage,* FEDOTIK *and* RODÉ *meet* MASHA *and say their farewells; she goes out with them.*)

IRINA: There, they've gone. . . . *(She sits down on the last step of the veranda.)*

CHEBUTYKIN: And they forgot to say good-bye to me.

IRINA: Well, what about you?

CHEBUTYKIN: I forgot, too, I don't know how. Well, I'll see them again, I'm leaving tomorrow. Yes . . . I'll stay yet another day. In a year they will give me my retirement, I'll come back here, and I'll finish my days by your side. . . . I only have one little year to wait for my pension. . . . *(He puts a newspaper in his pocket and takes out another.)* I shall return to you, and I will change my way of living, radically. . . . I shall become a good little boy . . . so well behaved, so proper. . . .

IRINA: It wouldn't do any harm to change your way of life, dear friend. It would be a good idea. . . .

CHEBUTYKIN: Yes. I understand. *(He hums.)* "Ta-ra-ra boom-di-é . . . I'm sitting on a tomb-di-é . . ." [39]

KULYGIN: Incorrigible! You're incorrigible, Ivan Romanich!

CHEBUTYKIN: You should have been in charge of me, you'd fix me up.

IRINA: Fyodor shaved off his moustache. I can't look at him!

KULYGIN: And why?

CHEBUTYKIN: I could say what your face reminds me of, but I wouldn't dare.

KULYGIN: What shall I do! It's the custom, the *modus vivendi*. Our director is shaved, and since I have become inspector, I shaved my moustache, too. It pleases no one, it's all the same to me. I'm satisfied. Moustache, or no moustache, I am equally satisfied. . . . *(He sits down.)*

(At the back of the stage, ANDREY can be seen passing, pushing a baby carriage with a sleeping baby in it.)

IRINA: Ivan Romanich, my dear, my good Ivan Romanich, I am terribly upset. You were on the boulevard last night, tell me, what went on?

CHEBUTYKIN: What went on? Nothing. Of no interest. *(He reads his paper.)* Of what importance is it?

KULYGIN: But they say that Solyony and the baron met on the boulevard yesterday near the theater. . . .

TUSENBACH: Will you please stop! Really . . . *(He makes a gesture and enters the house.)*

KULYGIN: Near the theater . . . Solyony began to provoke him, and the baron lost his temper and said something offensive to him.

CHEBUTYKIN: I don't know. It's all nonsense.

KULYGIN: A high school teacher wrote "nonsense" on a composition, and the student read *"reniksa"*—he thought he was writing in Latin. . . .[40] *(He laughs.)* It's really astonishing! They say that Solyony is in love with Irina and that he has got it in for the baron. . . . I can understand that. Irina is a charming young lady. I would even say she resembles Masha a bit, she's so pensive. Only, you're sweeter, Irina. However, Masha also has a good character. I love my Masha.

(In the depths of the garden, backstage: "Yahooooo!")

IRINA *(shudders)*: Everything frightens me today. *(Pause)* I've packed everything, they're coming for the baggage after dinner. The baron and I, we'll be married tomorrow, and immediately after, we'll leave for the brickworks and the day after tomorrow I'll already be in school; the new life is beginning. By the grace of God! While I was passing my teaching exam, I was even crying for joy and contentment. *(Pause)* At any moment the wagon will be here for my things. . . .

KULYGIN: That's all very well, but it doesn't sound very serious to me. A lot of ideas, but not much seriousness. Nevertheless, I wish you all the best. . . .

CHEBUTYKIN *(moved)*: My adorable, sweet girl . . . my little golden child . . . You've gone so far, we can no longer even catch up with you. I have been left behind like a migratory bird who has gotten old and can no longer fly. Fly, my children, fly and God keep you! *(Pause)* You were wrong to shave your moustache, Fyodor Ilyich.

KULYGIN: That's enough! *(He sighs.)* Today the military are leaving, and everything will begin again as before. You may say what you like, Masha is an excellent, decent woman, I love her a great deal and I am thankful for my fate. . . . People's fate varies greatly. . . . In the tax office there is a certain Kozyrev. We were at school together; he was kicked out of the fifth grade because he was unable to understand the *ut consecutivum*.[41] Now he is terribly poor and sick, and when I meet him, I say to him, "Hello, *ut* plus the subjunctive!" "Yes," he says, "exactly, *ut* plus the subjunctive . . ." and then he starts coughing. . . . While I, I've been lucky all my life, I'm happy, I've even gotten the Order of Stanislas,[42] second class, and I teach *ut* plus the subjunctive to others. It's because, of course, I am an intelligent man, more intelligent than many others, but that doesn't make for happiness. . . .

(*In the house, one hears the piano being played: it is "The Maiden's Prayer."*)[43]

IRINA: Tomorrow evening I won't be listening to this "Maiden's Prayer"; I won't be meeting up with Protopopov. . . . (*Pause*) Protopopov's sitting there in the drawing room; he's there again today. . . .

KULYGIN: Hasn't the headmistress returned yet?

IRINA: No. They've gone for her. If only you knew how difficult my life is here alone without Olya. . . . She lives at the school; she's the headmistress, she has her entire day taken up, and I am lonely, I'm bored, I have nothing to do and I detest the room I live in. . . . I said to myself, If it is not given to me to go to Moscow, then it is because it must not be. That is my destiny. Nothing to do about that . . . Everything is in God's hands, it's true. Nikolai Lvovich has asked for my hand in marriage. . . . Well, I reflected and I have decided to do it. He is a very fine man, it's extraordinary how nice he is. . . . Suddenly, it's as if my soul had wings, and I've become happier, as if a terrible weight had been taken from me and I wanted to work once again, to work. . . . Only yesterday, something happened, I feel as if something mysterious is hanging over me. . . .

CHEBUTYKIN: Foolishness.

NATASHA (*through the window*): The headmistress!

KULYGIN: The headmistress is here. Come in. (*He returns with* IRINA *into the house.*)

CHEBUTYKIN (*reads the newspaper and hums softly*): "Ta-ra-ra boom-di-é . . . I'm sitting on a tomb-di-é . . ."

(MASHA *approaches; in the background,* ANDREY *passes by with the baby carriage.*)

MASHA: There he is sitting, living it up.

CHEBUTYKIN: What's wrong with that?

MASHA (*sits down*): Oh, nothing . . . (*Pause*) You loved my mother?

CHEBUTYKIN: A great deal.

MASHA: And did she love you?

CHEBUTYKIN (*after a pause*): That I don't remember.

MASHA: Is my man here? Our cook, Marfa, spoke that way in the old days, about her policeman: my man. Is my man here?

CHEBUTYKIN: Not yet.

MASHA: When you seize happiness in bits and pieces, and then you lose it, as I have, little by little you get hard, you get malicious. . . . (*She points to her chest.*) It's at the boiling point in there. . . . (*She looks at her brother,* ANDREY, *who passes with the baby carriage.*) There's our Andrey, our brother. . . . All hopes lost. Thousands of people were raising a big bell, they put in a great deal of time and money, and all of a sudden, it fell and got smashed. All of a sudden, for no apparent reason. That's what's happened to Andrey. . . .

ANDREY: When will this house calm down? There's such an uproar. . . .

CHEBUTYKIN: Soon. (*He looks at his watch.*) I have an old watch, which strikes the hours. . . . (*He winds his watch and it strikes.*) The first, second and fifth batteries will go off in exactly one hour. (*Pause*) I'm going tomorrow.

ANDREY: Forever?

CHEBUTYKIN: I don't know. Perhaps in a year I shall return. Although, who the devil knows . . . or cares.

(*They hear the sounds of a harp and a violin, coming from far away.*)

ANDREY: The town will be deserted, it's as if they put a lid over it. (*Pause*) Something happened yesterday in front of the theater, everybody is talking about it and I don't know what it's all about.

CHEBUTYKIN: Nothing. Idiotic behavior. Solyony got the baron all excited, the baron lost his temper and insulted him, and the upshot is that it led to Solyony having to challenge him to a duel. (*He looks at his watch.*) It's time,

I think . . . At twelve-thirty, in the small wood, the one you see from here, on the other side of the river . . . Ta-tum! *(He laughs.)* Solyony imagines he is Lermontov, and he even writes verses. But, joking aside, that make his third duel.

MASHA: Whose?

CHEBUTYKIN: Solyony's.

MASHA: And the baron's?

CHEBUTYKIN: The baron's what?

(Pause.)

MASHA: Everything's all mixed up in my head. . . . All the same, I say we shouldn't allow it. He could wound the baron or even kill him.

CHEBUTYKIN: The baron is a brave fellow, but one baron more or less . . . what can that mean? So let them! It's all the same! *(Behind the garden someone shouts, "Yoohooooo! Yoohooooo!")* You can wait. It's Skvortsov, the second, who's shouting. He's sitting in his boat.

(Pause.)

ANDREY: In my opinion, to participate in a duel, even to be present at it, if one is not there in the capacity of a doctor, is simply immoral.

CHEBUTYKIN: It only seems so. . . . We're not here, nothing's here in this world, we do not exist, it is only an illusion. . . . Besides, it's all the same!

MASHA: That's how it is all day long—talk, talk, talk. . . . *(Going off)* It's not enough to live in this climate—the snow may fall at any moment—we have to have all this talk as well. . . . *(Stopping)* I will not enter this house, I cannot bear to enter it. . . . When Vershinin is here, let me know. . . . *(She walks in the alleyway.)* There are two birds of passage flying off. . . . *(She raises her head.)* Swans or geese . . . My dear ones, my happy ones . . . *(She goes out.)*

ANDREY: The house is deserted. Once the officers have left, and you, too, and sister's getting married, I shall remain alone in the house.

CHEBUTYKIN: And your wife?

(Enter FERAPONT with some papers.)

ANDREY: A wife is a wife. She is honest, decent and even a good woman, but with all of that there is something debased about her, something small, blind, which reduces her to the level of an animal, a sort of wild beast. . . . In any case, she's not a human being. . . . I tell it to you as a friend, the only man I may open myself up to. I love Natasha, it's true, but sometimes she seems to me to be extraordinarily vulgar, and then I am mortified, I don't understand any more why it happened that I love her so, or, at least, why I loved her. . . .

CHEBUTYKIN *(getting up)*: I'm leaving tomorrow, old fellow, we may never see each other again, but here is the advice I give you: put your hat on, put a walking stick in your hand, and leave . . . leave and walk, walk without ever turning back. And the farther away you go, the better it will be.

(SOLYONY, with two officers, crosses upstage; seeing CHEBUTYKIN, he goes toward him; the officers continue on their way.)

SOLYONY: Doctor, it's time! Twelve-thirty already. *(He greets ANDREY.)*

CHEBUTYKIN: I'm coming. I have had enough of you all. *(To ANDREY)* If someone asks for me, Andriucha, you will say that I'll be back. . . . *(He sighs.)* Oh my, oh me.

SOLYONY: "Before he'd time to cry out, the bear had sought him out." *(He leaves with the doctor.)* Why are you sighing, old fellow?

CHEBUTYKIN: Go on!

SOLYONY: How are you feeling?

CHEBUTYKIN *(annoyed)*: Most appealing.[44]

SOLYONY: The old man's upset for no good reason. I shan't go too far. I shall only wing him like a woodcock. *(He takes the perfume out and douses his hands.)* I emptied an entire flask today, and they still have this smell. Always the smell of a corpse. *(Pause)* Yes . . . You remember these lines? "Rebellious, he seeks the storm,/As if the storm could give him peace." [45]

CHEBUTYKIN: Yes. "Before he'd time to cry out, the bear had sought him out."

(He goes out with SOLYONY. *They hear cries of: "Yoo-hooooo! Yoohooooo!" Enter* ANDREY *and* FERAPONT.)

FERAPONT: Some papers to sign . . .

ANDREY *(nervous)*: Leave me alone! Please! I beg of you! *(He goes out with the baby carriage.)*

FERAPONT: That's what papers are for, to be signed.

(He goes toward the back of the stage. Enter IRINA *and* TUSENBACH, *who wears a straw hat.* KULYGIN *crosses the stage, shouting: "Masha! Hey, Masha!")*

TUSENBACH: I think he is the only man in town who is glad the military are leaving.

IRINA: That's understandable. *(Pause)* Our town shall be deserted now.

TUSENBACH *(looking at his watch)*: My dear, I am going and I'll be right back.

IRINA: Where are you going?

TUSENBACH: I must go to town, and then . . . see some of my comrades off.

IRINA: That's not true. . . . Nikolai, why are you so distracted today? *(Pause)* What happened yesterday in front of the theater?

TUSENBACH *(with a gesture of impatience)*: In an hour I shall be back, and again with you. *(He kisses her hands.)* My dearest . . . *(He gazes at her in rapt attention.)* It's five years now that I love you, and I cannot get used to it, you seem to me always more beautiful. This splendid, marvelous hair! Such eyes! I'll take you away tomorrow. We shall work, we shall be rich, my dreams will become realities. You shall be happy. There is only one thing, only one thing: you don't love me!

IRINA: It's not in my power! I shall be your wife, faithful and submissive, but I'm not in love, what can I do! *(She cries.)* I have never loved in my life. Oh, I thought about it day and night, but my soul is like a precious piano, locked up and the key lost. *(Pause)* You look anxious.

TUSENBACH: I didn't sleep all night. In my life, there is nothing terrible, nothing which could frighten me, only that precious key which tears at my heart and prevents me from sleeping. . . . Say something to me. *(Pause)* Tell me something. . . .

IRINA: What? Say what? What?

TUSENBACH: Something.

IRINA: Come now! Come on!

(Pause.)

TUSENBACH: Sometimes idiotic, minimal details take on importance in life, one wonders why. One continues to laugh about them, they are only trivial, and despite all that, one is launched, and one feels one hasn't the strength to stop. Oh, let's not talk about it! I feel wonderful. You might say it's the first time in my life that I see these fir trees, these maples, these birch trees, and everything that surrounds me looks at me with curiosity and waits. How beautiful these trees are, and how life among them ought to be, in truth, beautiful! *(A cry: "Yoohooooo!")* I must leave, it's time. . . . See this tree, it's dried up, but when a bit of wind comes up, it sways with the others. That's how, it seems to me, when I shall be dead, I shall participate in life in one way or another. Good-bye, my darling . . . *(He kisses her hands.)* The papers that you gave me are on the table, under the calendar.

IRINA: I'm coming with you.

TUSENBACH *(alarmed)*: No, no! *(He goes off rapidly, stops in the alleyway.)* Irina!

IRINA: Yes?

TUSENBACH *(not knowing what to say)*: I didn't have any coffee today. Tell them to prepare some for me. . . .

(He goes out rapidly. IRINA remains standing, deep in thought, then goes toward the back of the garden and sits on the swing. Enter ANDREY with the baby carriage; FERAPONT appears.)

FERAPONT: Andrey Sergeyich, these papers, they're not mine, they're official papers. I didn't invent them.

ANDREY: Oh, where are you, where did you go, my past . . . when I was young and intelligent, when I had dreams and

I thought of beautiful things and my past and future were illumined with hope? Why, when we have hardly begun to live, are we dull, gloomy, uninteresting, lazy, complacent, useless, unhappy? . . . Our town exists for two hundred years now, it has a hundred thousand inhabitants, and not a single one of them is any different from all the others, not one ascetic, neither in the past nor the present, not one scholar, not one painter, not one man who contains something remarkable, which could excite our envy, or the passionate desire to imitate him. . . . All they do is eat, drink, sleep and then die; others are born and they too eat, drink, sleep, and so that the boredom doesn't stupefy them completely, they put diversity into their lives with infamous gossip, vodka, card playing, litigation . . . and the women deceive their husbands, and the husbands lie and behave as if they notice nothing, understand nothing, and this irresistibly vulgar influence weighs on the children, snuffs out the divine spark that lived in them, and they become miserable living corpses like their fathers and mothers. . . . *(To* FERAPONT, *with annoyance)* What do you want of me?

FERAPONT: What? Papers to sign.

ANDREY: I've seen enough of you.

FERAPONT *(giving him the papers)*: The porter of the tax office has just said that this winter in Petersburg it's two hundred degrees below zero.

ANDREY: The present is disgusting, but when I think of the future, how marvelous everything becomes! One feels so light, as if one had plenty of room and one sees a light shining in the distance. . . . I see liberty, I see us, my children and I, liberated from the sloth, the drinking kvass, the eating goose and cabbage, the falling asleep after dinner, all this parasitical living. . . .

FERAPONT: He said that some two thousand people froze to death. Everybody was, as he said, frightened silly. It was either in Petersburg or in Moscow, I don't remember any more.

ANDREY *(allowing himself to have tender feelings)*: My dear sisters, my wonderful sisters! *(Through his tears)* Masha, my dear sister . . .

NATASHA *(through the window)*: Who is speaking so loudly? Is it you, Andriucha? You'll wake Sophochka. *Il ne faut*

*pas faire de bruit. La Sophie est dormée déjà. Vous êtes
un ours.*[46]

NATASHA *(angrily)*: If you wish to make conversation, give
the carriage to somebody else. Ferapont, take the carriage
from him.

FERAPONT: Yes, madame. *(He takes the carriage.)*

ANDREY *(confused)*: I wasn't talking loud.

NATASHA *(behind the window, cajoling her little one)*: Bobik,
have pity, Bobik! Bad little Bobik!

ANDREY *(examining papers)*: That's fine, I'll look through
them, sign what has to be signed, and you'll take it to the
council. . . . *(He enters the house, reading the papers, while
FERAPONT pushes the carriage, directing himself toward
the back of the garden.)*

NATASHA *(behind the window)*: Bobik, what's Mama's name?
My dear little darling! And who is that? It's Aunt Olya,
tell her, to Auntie, hello, Olya!

*(Traveling musicians appear, a man and a girl, they play
the violin and the harp; from the house come VERSHI-
NIN, OLGA, and ANFISA, and for a moment they listen in silence; IRINA approaches.)*

OLGA: Our garden is like a public throughfare, they come
by foot and on horseback. Nurse, something to these musicians!

ANFISA *(gives money to the musicians)*: Go along. God be
with you, dear people. *(The musicians greet them and go.)*
Poor people. Those who eat their fill don't make music. *(To
IRINA)* Good day, Irina. *(She embraces her.)* Ah, my little
one! It's a good life. The good, good life! In the school,
with Olyushka, in the apartment paid for by the state, as
good as gold . . . in my old age, the good God has taken
pity on me. In all my life, I've never lived this way . . . a
great apartment paid for by the state, and in it a little room
for me all alone, and a little bed. It's all free. I wake up
at night, and oh, my God, sainted Virgin, there is no one
in the world happier than I!

VERSHININ *(with a look at his watch)*: We shall be going,
Olga Sergeyevna. I must go. *(Pause)* I wish you all the
best. . . . Where is Maria Sergeyevna?

IRINA: She is somewhere in the garden. . . . I'll go get her.

VERSHININ: I would be much obliged to you. I'm in a hurry.

ANFISA: I'll go get her, too. *(She shouts.)* Mashenka, yoo-hoo! *(She goes off into the garden with* IRINA.)

VERSHININ: Everything comes to an end. Now we are leaving here, too. *(He looks at his watch.)* The town gave a sort of luncheon in our honor. I ate, I listened, but in spirit I was here, in your home. . . . *(He looks at the garden.)* I was so accustomed to it here with you.

OLGA: We will see each other again one day or another?

VERSHININ: Probably never. *(Pause)* My wife and the two little ones will remain here for about two months; I beg of you, if ever something were to happen, or if they needed . . .

OLGA: Of course, of course. You can rest assured. *(Pause)* Tomorrow, already, there will not be one single military man in town, all will only be a memory, and, of course, a completely different life will begin for us. . . . *(Pause)* Everything happens contrary to the way we thought it would. I never wanted to become a headmistress but I did. Of course, I shall not go to Moscow. . . .

VERSHININ: Ah . . . thank you for everything. . . . Forgive me if everything hasn't been just right. . . . I have talked too much—excuse me for that, too, don't think ill of me.

OLGA *(wiping her eyes)*: Why doesn't Masha come. . . .

VERSHININ: What else can I tell you before leaving? On what theme to philosophize one last time? . . . *(He laughs.)* Life is heavy to bear. Many of us consider that it is a blind alley, hollow and hopeless, and yet, we must admit that it becomes each day more luminous, easier, and everything leads us to believe that the time will not be far off when it will be entirely enlightened. *(He looks at his watch.)* I must leave, really I must leave! Formerly humanity was occupied with wars, invasions, victories; now all that has been lived, leaving behind an enormous void that one doesn't, evidently, know how to fill; humanity is seeking passionately, and will find, it is certain. Oh, if it could only be soon! *(Pause)* If we could only have the capacity for hard work, education and culture, the capacity for hard work . . . *(Looks at his watch.)* But I must, absolutely, go. . . .

OLGA: She's coming.

(Enter MASHA.)

VERSHININ: I've come to say my good-byes. . . .

*(*OLGA *goes off so as not to embarrass them.)*

MASHA *(looking at him)*: Farewell . . .

(A long kiss.)

OLGA: Enough, enough . . .

*(*MASHA *sobs heavily.)*

VERSHININ: Write to me. Don't forget me! Let me go . . .
it's time. . . . Olga Sergeyevna, take her, it's time. . . . I'm
late. . . . *(Deeply moved, he kisses* OLGA's *hands, then, yet
again, he takes* MASHA *in his arms and goes out rapidly.)*
OLGA: Enough, Masha! Stop, my darling. . . .

(Enter KULYGIN.)

KULYGIN *(confused)*: Never mind, let her cry, let her. . . .
My good Masha, my sweet Masha . . . you are my wife,
and I am happy, despite everything. . . . I don't complain,
and I don't make a single reproach. . . . Olga will be my
witness . . . we shall take up our old life again, as before,
and on my part not a word, not an allusion. . . .
MASHA *(continuing her sobs)*: "On the curved shore, a green
oak stands, around the oak, golden strands . . . Around
the oak, golden strands . . ." I'm going mad. . . .[47] "On the
curved shore . . . a green oak . . ."
OLGA: Calm yourself, Masha . . . calm yourself. . . . Get her
some water.
MASHA: I'm not crying any more.
KULYGIN: She's not crying any more . . . she's a good girl.

(We hear a muffled shot in the distance.)

MASHA: "On the curved shore, a green oak stands, around
the oak, golden strands . . . a green cat . . . a green oak . . ."
I'm mixing everything up. . . . *(She drinks some water.)* A

wasted life . . . I don't need anything any more. . . . I shall
be calm in a moment. It doesn't matter. . . . What does it
mean: "On a curved shore?" Why do I have these words
in my head? Everything is all mixed up inside.

(Enter IRINA.*)*

OLGA: Calm yourself, Masha. There, you're a good girl. . . .
Let's go back in.
MASHA *(angrily)*: I will not go in there. *(She begins to sob and
stops right away.)* I no longer go into that house, and I shall
not enter now. . . .
IRINA: Let's stay together for a little moment, without saying
anything. Think, tomorrow, I'm leaving. . . .

(Pause.)

KULYGIN: Yesterday I took some mustachios and a beard
away from a kid in the third grade. . . . *(He puts them on.)*
Exactly like the German professor . . . *(He laughs.)* Isn't
it? They are funny, these kids.
MASHA: It's true, it's exactly like your German teacher.
OLGA *(laughs)*: Yes.

*(*MASHA *weeps.)*

IRINA: Enough, Masha!
KULYGIN: A very good likeness . . .

(Enter NATASHA.*)*

NATASHA *(to the maid)*: What? Protopopov—Mikhail Ivanich
—will keep an eye on Sophochka, and Andrey Sergeyich
can walk Bobik. What trouble these children . . . *(To* IRINA*)*
Irina, you'll be going tomorrow, it's such a shame. Stay a
little while longer, if only for a week. *(Seeing* KULYGIN, *she
cries out in fright; the latter laughs and takes off his mustachios and beard.)* Are you satisfied, you frightened me!
(To IRINA*)* I have gotten accustomed to you, and you think
the separation will be easy for me? I shall make Andrey
move with his violin into your room—let him scratch away
in there!—and in his room we shall install Sophochka. She

is an admirable child, divine. What a cute little girl! Today she looked at me with such eyes and said, "Mama!"

KULYGIN: The child is beautiful, it's true.

NATASHA: Well, tomorrow I shall already be on my own here. *(She sighs.)* I shall begin by having this alley way of fir trees cut down, then this maple . . . it is so ugly in the nighttime. . . . *(To* IRINA*)* Darling, this belt doesn't go with you at all . . . it's a lack of good taste. You must wear light, pleasant things. And here I'll have some flowers planted, flowers, and it will smell good. . . . *(Severely)* Why is this fork lying on the bench out here? *(Entering the house, to the maid)* Why is this fork lying on the bench out here, I ask you? *(She shouts.)* Shut up!

KULYGIN: It's starting!

(Behind the stage, military music; everybody listens.)

OLGA: It's the departure.

(Enter CHEBUTYKIN*.)*

MASHA: It's the departure of our men. Well, let them go. . . . Let them be happy! *(To her husband)* We must go back. . . . Where is my hat, my cape?

KULYGIN: I put them in the house. . . . I'll bring them to you.

OLGA: Yes, now each can go back to his own home. It is time.

CHEBUTYKIN: Olga Sergeyevna!

OLGA: Yes? *(Pause)* What is it?

CHEBUTYKIN: Nothing . . . I don't know how to tell you. . . . *(He whispers something in her ear.)*

OLGA *(frightened)*: It's not possible!

CHEBUTYKIN: Yes . . . What a business . . . I'm exhausted, I can't stand it any more, I have nothing more to say. . . . *(Irritatedly)* Anyway, it's all the same!

MASHA: What happened?

OLGA *(taking* IRINA *in her arms)*: What a terrible day . . . I don't know how to tell you, my darling. . . .

IRINA: What? Tell me quickly: what? For the love of Heaven! *(She cries.)*

CHEBUTYKIN: The baron has just been killed in a duel.

IRINA (*crying softly*): I knew it, I knew it. . . .

CHEBUTYKIN (*At the back of the stage, seated on a bench*): I'm tired. . . . (*He takes a newspaper out of his pocket.*) Let them cry. . . . (*He hums softly.*) Ta-ra-ra boom-di-é . . . I'm sitting on a tomb-di-é . . ." What difference could it make?

(*The three sisters are standing, huddled close together.*)

MASHA: Oh, this music! They're leaving us, one of them has left us for good, forever, we are remaining alone, to begin our life all over again. . . . One must live. . . . One must live.

IRINA (*putting her head on* OLGA's *chest*): A day will come when the world will know why these things have happened, why all this suffering; there will be no more mysteries . . . but life must go on. . . . While we wait, we must try to live . . . we must work, only work! Tomorrow I shall leave here alone, I shall teach in a school and I will give my life to those who have need of it, perhaps. It's autumn, soon it will be winter, the snow will bury everything, and I shall work, I shall work. . . .

OLGA (*putting her arms around her two sisters*): The music plays so gaily, it's so full of abandon, and we want so much to live! Oh, my God! The time will pass and we shall leave forever, they will forget us, our faces will be forgotten, our voices, they will no longer know whether we were many, but, for those who shall live on after us, our suffering will be transformed into joy, happiness and peace will reign on the earth, and for those who live now, they will have a good word and blessings. Oh, dear sisters, our life has not yet been ended. We shall live! The music plays so gaily, so joyously, and one would almost believe we were on the point of knowing why we live, why we suffer. . . . If only we could know, if only we could know!

(*The music gets quieter and quieter.* KULYGIN *cheerfully brings* MASHA's *hat and cape.* ANDREY *pushes the carriage in which* BOBIK *is seated.*)

CHEBUTYKIN (*hums softly*): Ta-ra-ra boom-di-é . . . I'm

sitting on a tomb-di-é . . ." *(He reads the newspaper.)* What difference does it make! What difference!

OLGA: If we could only know, if we could only know!

CURTAIN

AFTERWORD

In an age of apparently formless plays, we are beginning to understand that the form of a play depends on an inner secret development and proliferation and not on a series of "necessary scenes." The nineteenth-century "well-made play" (Scribe or, later, Ibsen) still flourishes, but it has become a less and less satisfactory peg on which to hang an evening in the theater. However, in the history of drama, only a very few masters have given their plays coherent form. Sophocles, Racine, Ibsen, Lorca, Chekhov and Beckett evolved certain inherent laws for their own theater. "All works of art conform to certain laws," Chekhov wrote to his friend Suvorin on November 3, 1888. These laws are discoverable and must be revealed skillfully if the play's architecture is to catch the conscience of an audience. In this sense a play is like a blueprint or a piece of music, whose form must be rediscovered before it can be brought to fullest life.

The penultimate Chekhovian work, *The Three Sisters,* is perhaps the best play to choose if one seeks to demonstrate the workability of the mechanism set up by Chekhov. It is his most "difficult" work. As intricate as a timepiece, its perfectly constructed apparatus reveals, upon examination, a consistently sound architecture. One need only follow the plot from moment to moment to be struck by the beauty and the subtlety of the construction. Time in the most literal sense is the key to its architecture.

General Prozorov, the father of the three sisters and their brother, Andrey, died exactly one year before the beginning of the play. The characters are gathered together in the drawing room of his house. It is the fifth of May, Irina's saint's day as well as the anniversary of their father's death. In the midst of Olga's remembrance of the past, the clock strikes twelve. She recalls that the clock struck twelve when their father died. The characters in *The Three Sisters* are poised at a moment of their history that is a reflection of a tragic moment in the near past. But how joyous they are now! In this first act of the play, they have come together to celebrate Irina's day, and while they do so, as they eat and make merry, the beginning of the end is already occurring. Chekhov once said that a man's destiny is worked out, unknown to him, as he sits at table. In this play he dramatizes this truth subtly as time ticks away.

Against a background of passing time, Chekhov unfolds a panorama of disappointed people. Olga is dissatisfied with her life as a schoolteacher; Masha is unhappy in her marriage to the pedant Kulygin; Irina yearns for a life of work, which she cannot fathom; Baron Tusenbach yearns to share with her a kind of life he has never yet experienced: Solyony would be a poet like Lermontov and his irritation with people makes him dangerous; Chebutykin adores Irina as he once adored her mother, without hope; Andrey loves Natasha and he hopes to become a professor; Kulygin lives a smug existence and pontificates to everyone; Vershinin suffers from an impossible marriage to a harridan. Each aspires to something he cannot quite reach, and those who do act—Andrey marries Natasha and Masha falls in love with Vershinin—live to regret their choice. The Prozorov girls look back to a childhood of contentment in Moscow and forward to the regaining of that happiness in only six months. They live most meaningfully in the past and future. Their present is undetermined. Chekhov fixes the portrait in time. Two of the military wags, Fedotik and Rodé, photograph the others at a specific moment of the present, as they are eating at table. The climax of Act One is the "photographing" of a moment fixed in present time. Chekhov introduces four children of a general, who yearn for a better life and are about to commit or have just committed the errors that will render that life impossible to attain.

Act Two occurs in the same milieu. It is eight in the evening on a night in February during carnival week. About two years have passed. Andrey and Natasha have married and produced a child called Bobik. It is significant that the first act ended with the appearance of Natasha. The second begins with Natasha and demonstrates how, in a short time, she has become mistress of the Prozorov house. This act bristles with small actions; most of them appear irrelevant but all are significant. The act is clocked as it might be in real life, taking place from eight till shortly after nine P.M. It is the detailed chronicling of what has happened to the Prozorov household since Natasha entered it.

Natasha and Andrey's marriage is a disappointment. Andrey has relinquished his dream of becoming a professor and is now secretary to Protopopov, president of the county council and also Natasha's lover. The act begins with Natasha asking her husband to get Irina's room for little Bobik and it ends with Natasha asking Irina directly for the room. Andrey is gambling away the money that was needed to get to Moscow. Irina's fond hopes are being ruined by the forces surrounding her. The baron loves her and gives her his life unconditionally. The important revelation of Act Two is that Solyony is also in love with Irina. The longer this love remains a mystery, the more Solyony's petulance seems grotesque and gratuitous. Once his feeling for her is revealed, his cruelty to the baron becomes plausible. Irina, Tusenbach and Solyony are one triangle in a series, and the one most important to the developing plot of the play. Masha, Kulygin and Vershinin are the second triangle. The third, consisting of Natasha, Andrey and Protopopov, remains shadowy and out of focus, as the third character is never introduced into the play. In Chekhov's characteristically subtle development, the characters of any triangle never confront one another all together. But each moment of the play enhances the development of the triangles. The slow process of ruin is already festering. Solyony and Tusenbach put pressure on Irina. Vershinin's wife tries suicide yet again, and he finds Masha an irresistible consolation. Andrey resorts to gambling and Natasha sublimates her disappointments by having an affair with his superior.

The second act of *The Three Sisters* is rooted in metaphysical discussions and the growing realization of the passing of time. Irina wants everyone to realize she is no longer a child. Vershinin realizes he is no longer young. Dr. Chebutykin lies about his age. (He keeps repeating that the writer Balzac was married in Berdichev, a small town in Russia. Balzac married the rich Polish lady Mme Hanska three months before his death. Ironically enough, Chekhov himself made a very late marriage, which he was unable, for reasons of illness and his wife's profession as traveling actress, to enjoy sufficiently. *The Three Sisters* is full of such subtle, ironic allusions.) Little irrelevancies and ironies throughout the act point out symbolically the true nature of the events being acted out. Chekhov thus shows that everyday life is tremendously momentous even though it may seem inconsequential. Beneath each trivial moment lies a profound truth. Irina plays patience and hopes to find in the cards an answer that she hasn't the will to produce herself. Tusenbach is hungry for chocolates and Solyony has eaten them all. From there to Solyony's total destruction of the baron we need wait only two acts. Each of the major actions of the play is thus foreshadowed and suggested much before. Vershinin's desire for tea is frustrated as he receives a letter telling him that his wife has again tried to commit suicide. His wife is potentially destructive to even his simplest needs. She comes between him and his slightest happiness. Solyony's preposterous outbursts against Bobik prepare us for his delight in gratuitous violence.

At the end of the act, Natasha asks Irina to give up her room. The second act is thus the history of a completed action. In the inner coherence and logic of Chekhov's plays, the end occurs when all of the given facts have been resolved. The second act ends ideally when Natasha has suggested to Irina what she earlier proposed to Andrey. Just so, the end of the play will bring all three sisters back to one another, huddled close, their destinies worked out.

There is no single hero or heroine in *The Three Sisters*. It is an entire way of life that is being undermined, a *modus vivendi,* as Kulygin would put it. The second act has been a spoiled evening. Act One was a spoiled birthday party. The characters are eroded by the doubts that devastate them all—a sense of their age, their insurmountable problems and their mortality. They are also blind to the enemies within their walls. At the end of Act One, Irina yearned for Moscow and Moscow was imminent. The forces that made the dream untenable were unleashed. At the end of Act Two, Irina's yearning already seems futile. The apparent irrelevancies of everyday life have been shaped into a meaningfully timed pattern. The setting is working.

Act Three begins with another spoiling event—the fire. The scene is the very bedroom now shared by Olga and Irina. The room is a logical choice for the setting as the action of the play progresses. It coincides with the movement of the plot. It is now three in the morning. The first act took place at noon, the second between eight and nine in the evening, now we are in the middle of the night, the unfolding time is also a cyclical progression. A few months have elapsed since Act Two. A fire has been raging for some time. No one in the house has been to bed.

Act Three reveals the dissolution that one sensed beginning in Act Two. All of the troubles have materialized. The act is slow-paced, from two in the morning until early dawn. At the end of it, hope springs eternal and desperate in Irina's heart once again. As in Greek and French tragedy, the light appears to be dawning just before the final darkness: the peripeteia of apparent joy before the final deluge.

There are meaningful juxtapositions during this long night's journey into day. The catastrophe of the fire is only an outward reflection of the inner turmoil in the Prozorov household. The fire did not destroy their home but it is damaged nevertheless. Throughout the act, the characters realize that time has inevitably passed them by. The threat to the elderly Anfisa when Natasha expresses her wish to get rid of her is one symbol of the ending of a way of life. An alarm bell is sounded offstage. Olga says she feels ten years older. Chebutykin confesses the reason for his drunken stupor—he has caused the death of a woman. He examines a clock that once belonged to the mother of the three sisters. The next moment, Vershinin announces that the army will be leaving the town. This triggers the end of the play. Once the military have left the town, all hope is over for the sisters' happiness. At that precise moment of realization, Chebutykin drops the clock, intensifying the sense of doom. Kulygin chides Chebutykin for dropping the clock as he would one of his bad schoolboys for a prank. Chebutykin retaliates by revealing that Natasha is having an affair with Protopopov. This kind announcement (Andrey is not there to hear it) is only a substitute for the revelation he might have made: that Masha is having an affair with Vershinin. He gives Kulygin a very broad hint. From this point on, the men exit slowly. Chebutykin, Solyony,

Vershinin, Fedotik, Tusenbach and Kulygin are all prevailed upon to leave. Each leaves with a sense of loss: Chebutykin has lost his self-respect, Solyony now knows he can never have Irina, Vershinin must leave Masha, Fedotik has lost his possessions. Tusenbach does not know he will never possess Irina; Kulygin still has his empty prize—an unfaithful wife. Natasha passes through the scene like a modern Lady Macbeth, casting a shadow on everyone's happiness. Three years have passed and the third act, in subtle gradations, reveals the dissolution that has taken place. The act ends on an optimistic note, a pathetic and vain hope for a better future. All has imperceptibly been lost and yet no real tragedy has occurred. It has all happened inevitably in time, given these characters and their motivations. A way of life has begun to end. The last act will end it.

Act Four of *The Three Sisters* is enacted, ironically enough, outdoors, in the old garden surrounding the house. As in the first act, it is midday. The passage of time has come full circle: early afternoon, evening, late night and dawn, early afternoon. And as they stand huddled together at the end of the play, listening to the music of the military band, we know that each character has come full circle, too, though each has been changed irrevocably. Olga is now headmistress and Irina will soon follow in her footsteps. Masha returns to her husband without ever having left him. Andrey has lost everything to Natasha without gaining her. Even Protopopov, her lover, is now her servant as he takes care of the child they have had out of wedlock.

The restless and fitful last act of the play is a fine edifice constructed in time. With echoes of the past and intimations of the future, it breathes the formless present as it moves to its impending conclusion. The entire act is a long and carefully orchestrated leave-taking. The time element generates suspense. The duel between Solyony and Tusenbach is to occur at twelve-thirty. The soldiers are due to leave at one. The act, which takes as long as it would in real life, pivots neatly around the two events. People are constantly watching their timepieces. Fedotik, Chebutykin, Kulygin and Vershinin all tick time off. Kulygin even mentions the Latin locution *ut consecutivum*—the consecutive-time-oriented grammatical construction.

Once more the subtle juxtapositions ironically reveal the meaning of the play. Andrey mentions that the town will soon be deserted. After a pause, he adds that Tusenbach and Solyony had words outside the theater. The life that will be snuffed out like a candle is actually the baron's. The underlying impending tragedy is sensed by all the characters even as they attempt to deny it. Andrey's emotions suddenly overwhelm him and he cries out for his sisters. The very next moment, Natasha leans her head out the window and shuts him up. This small action signifies to what extent Natasha has taken over his life. At the end of the act, a series of these juxtapositions are ingeniously woven into the fabric of the play. As Vershinin bids farewell to Masha, Kulygin enters. As she grieves for the loss of her lover and is simultaneously forgiven by her husband, the sound of the shot that kills the baron echoes far in the distance. It is ironic that the shot should come in the midst of another sister's grief. It is ironic that Kulygin, of all people, should be consoling his own wife for the loss of her lover. It is ironic that Vershinin's long farewell to Masha should have to be conducted for the most part to his watch. He constantly stares at it while waiting for her. Because Masha arrives late, Kulygin arrives early. Chekhov makes use here of a rubato time rhythm. Each event occurs at the wrong moment to the wrong person. Irina comes in, sensing that something terrible has happened. She sits there and wonders while Masha is comforted. Natasha is mean to Irina about the color of her belt, avenging Olga's treatment of her when she paid her first visit to them. Natasha's last action is to requite her early humiliation; but she has chosen the wrong victim. At the end of the play the three sisters stand huddled together as they did at the very beginning. We know that they will soon be separated. The joyous final music is completely out of keeping with the mood of the play. It is as offkey as the time juxtapositions.

One theme of *The Three Sisters* is man's vision of himself as he is, as he was and as he thinks he will be in the far distant future: a constantly clocked metaphysical excursion. The characters are plagued and harrassed by time, and time also reflects their deepest hopes and fears. The consciousness of time is communicated directly—timepieces are watched, worn, broken. Chekhov was a skillful imitator of everyday reality. The sense of passing time is the base of the metaphysical yearning in *The Three Sisters*. By giving the play a time-oriented architecture, Chekhov also quite possibly achieved a true timelessness—the play is valid for any culture at any time. Its construction admirably suits its premise. Its architecture suits its meaning. That is the most that can ever be said for a play: that it is built to reveal itself and that its parts fit together meaningfully and essentially.

NOTES

First performance: January 31, 1901, Moscow Art Theatre.

First published in two editions: Volume 2 of Russian Thought, *1901; and in May, 1901, in a volume of Chekhov's* Collected Works, *published by Marks.*

1. The day of the saint after whom a person is named, sometimes known as the name day; also, the day on which a person is christened. In Catholic countries, this day is celebrated much more than the actual date of birth.

2. One and a half poods. The pood equals 36.113 pounds. Thus, it is 54.1 pounds. Six poods would be more than 216 pounds.

3. St. Petersburg was founded in 1703 and was the capital of the Russian Empire until 1917. It was renamed Petrograd in 1914 and Leningrad in 1924.

4. Nikolai Alexandrovich Dobrolyubov (1836–1861), a Russian literary critic, was one of the most influential figures in nineteenth-century Russian criticism of the "socioutilitarian" school.

5. Masha quotes the opening lines of Alexander Sergeyevich Pushkin's (1799–1837) romantic and mock-heroic poem "Ruslan and Lyudmila" (1820). In an earlier version of *The Three Sisters*, Chekhov had given Masha a rather crude dispatch sent by the celebrated Russian general Suvorov to remember and quote. It may have been more appropriate, since it was a remark by a general and could have been recited by her father. This more "poetic" quote may have been one of a few attempts on Chekhov's part to subdue the natural vulgarity of Masha's character. Even so, her dialogue is the most "liberated" of the three sisters.

6. Solyony's fondness for puns and plays on words and embroiderings is part of his extravagant and resentful nature.

7. This excerpt from a fable by Ivan Andreyevich Krylov (1768–1844), "The Peasant and the Workman" (1815), has become proverbial.

8. Chebutykin's extravagant present of a samovar was totally inappropriate for a girl of her age; such a gift would ordinarily be given to a married lady.

9. A verst equals .66 miles; 20 versts would be 13.2 miles.

10. Chekhov himself was buried in the Novo-Devichy convent in Moscow.

11. Kulygin's Latin quotations are always rich in humorous overtone. This one is as humble as he generally is: "He can only do the little he can and others stronger than he may accomplish more." The history of the school is a characteristic "modest" effort.

12. The traditional meat pie, *pirog*, was specially prepared on the *Emyaninny,* or name day. Before the Revolution this day was far more important than the birthday. The special *pirog* served on that day was a delicious concoction of rice, onions, eggs, white fish, butter and seasonings in layers as a filling for a flaky dough. Meat *pirog* are even more popular.

13. During *Maslenitsa,* or carnival time, the last week before Lent, one eats heartily and celebrates before the austere time beginning with Ash Wednesday.

14. Some people customarily dressed in costumes and masks during carnival week and went visiting and making merry.

15. Tiestov's was one of the great restaurants of Moscow. The *Bolshaya Moskovskaya* were a group of Russian restaurants, which occasionally had rooms to let upstairs.

16. Saratov is a Volga River port and railway junction.

17. We call the game solitaire. The name "patience" seems particularly appropriate for the waiting game that Irina is playing in all areas of her life.

18. The last words of Gogol's story "How Ivan Ivanovich Quarreled with Ivan Nikiforovich" (1835).

19. Berdichev, a Ukrainian town near Kiev, was where Honoré de Balzac married the Polish lady Mme Hanska, three months before he died, in 1850.

20. Tsitsihar is the capital of Heilungkiang province in Manchuria. It is now known as Lungkiang.

21. A reference to an event in 1888, in which a scandal broke out because of fraudulent activities of a French company that had been set up to help build the Panama Canal.

22. Natasha's use of the French language is relentless and stilted. She seems to be parroting phrases she once learned and Chekhov's subtly attuned ear reproduces them with cruel accuracy. Amusingly, some French editions of the play correct her mistakes. It is quite certain that the errors, as the Latin errors in *The Sea Gull,* were made for the sake of humor and as a commentary on Natasha's lack of sensibility: she would speak French and she would speak it incorrectly.

23. A quote from Alexander Sergeyevich Griboyedov's (1795–1827) play of 1824, *Gore ot Uma* (sometimes translated *Woe from Wit*), which in rhymed iambics satirized Moscow society of the time.

24. Aleko is the hero of Pushkin's poem "The Gypsies" (1824).

25. Mikhail Yurevich Lermontov (1814–1841) was born in Moscow, of Scottish extraction. His fame was posthumous, for he was killed in a duel at an early age. He had been banished for an earlier duel with the son of the French ambassador. Lermontov was known for his poetry and a novel, *A Hero of Our Time.* His moody personality was the subject of Chekhov's ironic pastiche. When *The Three Sisters* was produced, Chekhov suggested that Solyony be made up to look like Lermontov though, of course, the resemblance was mostly in his mind.

26. The *chekhartmá* is a traditional Caucasian dish of meat in soup and the *cheremchá* is a member of the onion family, somewhat like a scallion.

27. This is a traditional peasant's song. The "porch" was more of a "vestibule" or "antechamber," which one entered before going into the main part of the home.

28. This would correspond to our expression: "The best-laid plans . . ."

29. Ferapont is alluding to Napoleon's invasion of Russia in 1812.

30. Chita is an industrial city in a coal-mining region of Russia, close to the Mongolian border.

31. Actually, literally: "Would you be so kind as to accept one of these dates . . ." (i.e., the fruit of the date palm). This is a quote from an operetta at the Hermitage Theater that

Chekhov recalled though he didn't remember which operetta it was. It was one of those silly moments that stick unspecifically in the mind.

32. This is a well-known quote from Pushkin's verse novel *Yevgeny Onegin* (1828). Tchaikovski turned it into an aria for Prince Gremin, in his opera based on the novel.

33. This passage, in which Vershinin and Masha communicate by means of a series of drum rolls in the voice, has been called the tersest declaration of love ever heard on a stage. Every one of the "tram-tam-tams" has a specific subtext, as do most of Chekhov's speeches. They are simply substitutes for communication, as effective as any secret language used by children or lovers. They are like question and answer, a stroke of genius on Chekhov's part to show the degree of intimacy between Masha and Vershinin most subtly. When the time came to act the play, Chekhov had to explain the meaning of these expressions to his wife, Olga Knipper Chekhova, who was playing the part of Masha. He didn't tell her what to do specifically, however, for he felt she was a good enough actress to find the proper intonations herself.

34. A quote from Krylov's fable "The Geese." Solyony's ominous quotes invariably refer to some menacing allusion—mystery for mystery's sake.

35. Masha's Latin declension is pure malice, indicating that she believes he loves her as passionlessly as someone conjugating a Latin verb.

36. A well-known Latin expression, which refers to the philosopher's scorn for external goods and possessions: "I carry all my possessions with me." This is yet another example of Kulygin's humble pie.

37. Poprishchin, in Gogol's *Diary of a Madman* (1835).

38. The Polish word for "darling."

39. Chebutykin's ominous use of this old-fashioned song underscores the suspense of the last act. It becomes a Cassandra-like refrain, pointing to the imminence of an explosive situation.

40. In Russian script, the word *chepuha* ("nonsense") looks like "renyxa," which appears as if it might be a Latin word. One of those farfetched amusing experiences that happen to teachers and that would titillate Kulygin.

41. *Ut* plus the subjunctive. Europeans have special names for the Latin grammatical points.

42. The Order of Stanislas is one of the most distinguished medals and, as an order of merit for distinguished cultural services, has a superficial resemblance to the Légion d'honneur. Kulygin's decoration was, however, not the most distinguished, but second class.

43. "The Maiden's Prayer" is one of those old pianistic war-horses played by generations of amateur pianists.

44. Chebutykin's "ridiculous" and "sarcastic" answer is a punning one. In Russian the two expressions rhyme. "How are you?" *("Kak zdorovie?")* says Solyony. "Like cow's butter" *("Kak maslo korovie"),* answers Chebutykin. Rather than translate the expression literally, which would make less sense, one is left to invent a plausible alternative in English. It is for the actor to project Chebutykin's annoyance.

45. The last lines of Lermontov's poem "The Sail." This was also quoted in Chekhov's one-act play "The Wedding." It has somewhat the cultural cliché value of "Invictus."

46. Natasha's French leaves much to be desired. It is, however, more delightful than if it were correct, or proper.

47. See Note 5.

The Cherry Orchard

A Drama in Four Acts

CHARACTERS

RANEVSKAYA, LYUBOV ANDREYEVNA,
  lady of the manor

ANYA,
  her daughter, seventeen years old

VARYA,
  her adopted daughter, twenty-four years old

GAYEV, LEONID ANDREYEVICH,
  her brother

LOPAHIN, YERMOLAI ALEXEYEVICH,
  a merchant

TROFIMOV, PYOTR SERGEYEVICH,
  a student

SIMEONOV-PISHCHIK, BORIS BORISOVICH,
  a landowner

CHARLOTTA IVANOVNA,
  a governess

YEPIHODOV, SEMYON PANTELEYEVICH,
  a clerk

DUNYASHA,
  a chambermaid

FIRS,
  a manservant, an old man of eighty-seven years of age

YASHA,
  a young manservant

A PASSERBY
A STATIONMASTER
A POST OFFICE CLERK
GUESTS, SERVANTS

The action takes place on MME RANEVSKAYA's *estate.*

ACT ONE

A room that is still called the children's room. One of the doors leads to ANYA's room. It is dawn, the sun is about to rise. It is already the month of May, the cherry trees are in bloom, but in the early morning it is still cold. The windows are shut.

Enter DUNYASHA, with a candle, and LOPAHIN, a book in hand.

LOPAHIN: The train has arrived, thank God. What time is it?

DUNYASHA: Almost two o'clock. *(She blows the candle out.)* It is already daylight.

LOPAHIN: How late was the train? Two hours, at least. *(He yawns and stretches.)* I take the cake, what an idiot! I came specially to go and get them at the station, and I woke up all of a sudden . . . I fell asleep sitting down. How annoying! You could at least have awakened me.

DUNYASHA: I thought you had gone. *(She listens intently.)* I think they're here now.

LOPAHIN *(listening intently)*: No . . . it takes time to get the baggage and everything. . . . *(Pause)* Lyubov Andreyevna has been living abroad for five years now; I wonder what she's like. . . . She was always so nice! No fuss, no bother. I remember when I was a boy, fifteen, my poor father, he owned a store here in the village at that time, hit me right in the face and made my nose bleed . . . we'd come over here together to this very courtyard, he had been drinking. Lyubov Andreyevna, I remember it as if it had

219

just happened, she was quite young and slender, she took me to the washroom, in this very room, the children's room, and she said to me, "Don't cry, little muzhik,[1] it will be all right for the day of your wedding. . . ." *(Pause)* Little muzhik . . . It's true, my father was a peasant, and I, here I am with a white vest and yellow shoes on. In short, like a pig in a parlor. Only now, I'm rich, I have a great deal of money, but all you have to do is to scratch away a little and you'll find the same muzhik. . . . *(He leafs through the book.)* I was trying to read this book, I couldn't make head or tail of it, I fell asleep reading.

(Pause.)

DUNYASHA: The dogs didn't sleep all night long, they can tell the masters are coming.

LOPAHIN: What's the matter with you, Dunyasha?

DUNYASHA: My hands are trembling. I'm going to faint.

LOPAHIN: You're really too delicate, Dunyasha. You dress like a lady, and look at this hairdo, will you? That's not right. One must know one's place.

(Enter YEPIHODOV, a bouquet in hand; he is wearing a jacket and his well-shined boots are squeaking; on entering, he drops the bouquet.)

YEPIHODOV *(picking up the bouquet)*: Here, it's the gardener who sent it. He says they're for the dining room. *(He gives the bouquet to DUNYASHA.)*

LOPAHIN: You will bring me some kvass.[2]

DUNYASHA: Very well, sir. *(She goes out.)*

YEPIHODOV: It's three below this morning and the cherry blossoms are in bloom. I cannot approve of our climate. *(He sighs.)* No, I cannot. Our climate is not a cooperative climate, you know. And if you will permit me, Yermolai Alexeyevich, I shall add just this: the day before yesterday I bought myself a pair of boots and I'm telling you that they squeak like nothing you've ever heard. What should I grease them with?

LOPAHIN: Get out of here. You annoy me.

YEPIHODOV: Every day something terrible happens to me. And

I don't complain about it, I am resigned to it, and it even makes me smile.

(DUNYASHA *enters and pours the kvass for* LOPAHIN.)

YEPIHODOV: I'm going. (*He knocks into a chair and turns it over.*) There . . . (*A triumphant air*) You can see for yourself, if you'll pardon the expression, what vicissitudes, really . . . it's just remarkable! (*He goes out.*)

DUNYASHA: To tell you the truth, Yermolai Alexeyevich, Yepihodov asked me to marry him.

LOPAHIN: Oh, is that so?

DUNYASHA: I don't know what I should do. He's a quiet fellow, but when he starts talking sometimes, you can't understand a word of what he's saying. It's nice and sincere, but you can't make head or tail of it. He doesn't exactly displease me. And he loves me madly. He's just an unlucky man, every day something happens to him. Everybody here calls him "Twenty-two Troubles," just to annoy him.

LOPAHIN (*listening intently*): I think they're coming. . . .

DUNYASHA: They're coming! What's the matter with me . . . I'm freezing all over.

LOPAHIN: It's them, they've arrived. Let's go meet them. Will she recognize me? We haven't seen each other for five years.

DUNYASHA (*nervous*): I shall faint. . . . Oh, I'm going to faint!

(*Two carriages are heard arriving in front of the house.* LOPAHIN *and* DUNYASHA *hurry out. The stage is empty. From the neighboring rooms, noise filters in.* FIRS, *who has been to the station, crosses the room hurriedly, leaning on his cane; he wears livery and a top hat; he talks to himself, but one cannot understand a word of what he says. The noise backstage gets louder. A voice is heard: "Let's go this way. . . ."* LYUBOV ANDREYEVNA, ANYA *and* CHARLOTTA IVANOVNA, *holding a little dog on a leash, all three in traveling clothes, enter.* VARYA, *a kerchief round her head and wearing an overcoat;* GAYEV, SIMEONOV-PISHCHIK, LOPAHIN, DUNYASHA, *carrying a package and an umbrella; servants with luggage go back and forth in the room.*)

ANYA: Let's go this way. Mama, do you remember this room?

LYUBOV ANDREYEVNA *(happily, through her tears)*: It's the children's room!

VARYA: It's so cold, my hands are like ice. *(To* LYUBOV ANDREYEVNA*)* Your rooms, the white one and the mauve one, have stayed just as you left them, little Mother.

LYUBOV ANDREYEVNA: The children's room, my dear, my lovely room . . . I slept here when I was a child. . . . *(She cries.)* I feel again just as I did when I was little. . . . *(She embraces her brother, then* VARYA, *then, once again, her brother.)* Varya is still the same, just like a nun. And I recognized Dunyasha. . . . *(She embraces* DUNYASHA.*)*

GAYEV: The train was two hours late. How do you like that? How's that for organization?

CHARLOTTA *(to* PISHCHIK*)*: My dog also eats hazel nuts.

PISHCHIK *(astonished)*: Imagine that!

(Everybody goes out, except ANYA *and* DUNYASHA.*)*

DUNYASHA: We couldn't stand it any longer waiting for you. . . . *(She helps* ANYA *take her coat and hat off.)*

ANYA: I haven't slept for four nights on the trip. . . . Now I'm chilled through and through.

DUNYASHA: You left during Lent, it snowed and it froze, and look at it now. . . . My dear! *(She laughs and embraces her.)* I was longing to see you, my sweetness and light. . . . I've just got to tell you something, I can't hold it in another moment. . . .

ANYA *(in a languid voice)*: What is it now?

DUNYASHA: The bookkeeper Yepihodov asked me to marry him after Holy Week.

ANYA: That's all you talk about. . . . *(Arranging her hairdo)* I lost all my hairpins. . . . *(She is very tired and reels on her feet.)*

DUNYASHA: I don't know what to think. He loves me so, he loves me so!

ANYA *(she looks at her bedchamber lovingly)*: My room, my windows, as if I had never left them. I'm home! Tomorrow morning I'm going to get up and run into the orchard. . . . Oh, if only I could sleep! I didn't shut my eyes once during the whole trip, I was in an agony of anticipation.

DUNYASHA: Pyotr Sergeyevich has been here since the day before yesterday.

ANYA (*joyous*): Petya!

DUNYASHA: He's asleep in the bathhouse, he moved in there.
. . . He says he's afraid of disturbing us. (*She looks at her
pocket watch.*) We should wake him, but Varvara Mikhailovna forbade me to. Don't you wake him up, she said
to me.

(*Enter* VARYA; *she has a bunch of keys hanging from
her belt.*)

VARYA: Dunyasha, hurry with the coffee . . . Mama is asking
for coffee.

DUNYASHA: Right away. (*She goes out.*)

VARYA: Thank God you're here. You're home again. (*In a
caressing tone*) My little girl is back again! My pretty one
is at home!

ANYA: What an ordeal!

VARYA: I can imagine.

ANYA: We left during Holy Week, it was cold, Charlotta never
stopped talking all the way and doing tricks. Why did you
ever saddle me with her?

VARYA: You couldn't very well travel alone, my dear. At
seventeen!

ANYA: When we arrived in Paris, it was cold there, it was
snowing. My French is terrible. Mother lived on the sixth
floor, I arrived, it was full of Frenchmen, ladies, an old
priest with a book . . . it reeked of stale tobacco, I didn't
feel at home there. . . . I all of a sudden felt so sorry for
Mama, so sorry, I took her head in my arms, I couldn't let
go. Later, Mama was so sweet to me and she cried. . . .

VARYA (*through her tears*): Don't say anything more, nothing
more. . . .

ANYA: The villa she had near Menton[3] is already sold, she had
nothing left, absolutely nothing. I hadn't either, not a
kopeck, just enough to get here. And Mama just doesn't understand. When we eat in the station restaurants, she orders
the most expensive dishes and she gives the waiters ruble
tips. And so does Charlotta. Yasha ordered a portion for
himself alone. It was simply awful. For Mama has a servant, Yasha, whom we brought home with us here. . . .

VARYA: I saw him, the worthless creature.

ANYA: Well? Have you paid the interest?

VARYA: That would be the day.

ANYA: My God, my God . . .

VARYA: The estate will be sold in the month of August.

ANYA: My God.

LOPAHIN (*glances in through the door and moos*): Mooooo. . . .
(*He goes out.*)

VARYA (*through her tears*): I'd like to beat that one up. (*She
shakes her fist in the direction of the door.*)

ANYA (*takes* VARYA *in her arms, quietly*): Varya, has he asked
you to marry him? (VARYA *shakes her head no.*) But since
he loves you . . . why don't you have it out, what are you
waiting for?

VARYA: I don't think anything will ever come of it. He's a very
busy man, he hasn't any time for me . . . he doesn't even
notice me. Let him go then, it's painful for me to see him.
. . . Everybody talks of our marriage and everybody con-
gratulates me, when there's really nothing to it, it's all like
a dream. . . . (*Changing tone*) You have a little brooch like
a sort of bee.

ANYA (*sadly*): Mama bought it. (*She goes toward her room and
says, gaily, like a child*) And in Paris I went up in a balloon!

VARYA: My little one has returned! My pretty one is home!

(DUNYASHA, *having returned with the coffeepot, prepares
the coffee.*)

VARYA (*standing at the door*): All day long, my darling, while
I'm busy with the house, I still have my dreams. I'd marry
you off to a rich man, then I would be content and would
go off to a convent, and then to Kiev,[4] Moscow, from holy
place to holy place . . . one place to another . . . such
bliss. . . .

ANYA: The birds are singing in the garden. What time is it?

VARYA: It must be almost three. It's time to go to bed, my
dear. (*Passing into* ANYA's *room*) Such bliss . . .

(*Enter* YASHA, *carrying a traveling rug and a traveling
bag.*)

YASHA (*crossing the room mincingly*): Is it allowed to come
through here?

DUNYASHA: One would never recognize you, Yasha. Travel abroad has changed you.

YASHA: Hmm . . . and who are you?

DUNYASHA: When you left here, I was as tall as this. . . . *(She shows him her height, pointing from the floor up.)* Dunyasha, the daughter of Fyodor Kozoyedov. You won't remember!

YASHA: Hmm . . . Little cucumber! *(He looks around and takes her by the waist; she screams and lets a saucer fall. YASHA goes out quickly.)*

VARYA *(in the doorway, distressed)*: And now what?

DUNYASHA *(through tears)*: I broke a saucer. . . .

VARYA: That's for good luck.

ANYA *(comes out of her room)*: We should tell Mama: Petya is here. . . .

VARYA: I told them not to wake him.

ANYA *(lost in her thoughts)*: Six years ago Father died, a month later brother Grisha drowned in the river, he was such a sweet seven-year-old. Mama couldn't stand the pain, she left, left without looking back. . . . *(She shudders.)* How I understand her, if she only knew! *(Pause)* Petya Trofimov, Grisha's tutor, he might bring it all back. . . .

(Enter FIRS in his jacket and white waistcoat.)

FIRS *(aproaching the coffeepot, preoccupied)*: Madame will take her coffee here. *(He puts on white gloves.)* Is the coffee ready? *(To DUNYASHA, sternly)* You there! Where is the cream?

DUNYASHA: Oh, my God! *(She goes out, running.)*

FIRS *(busy round the coffeepot)*: Clumsy . . . *(He murmurs something unintelligible.)* They're back from Paris. . . . At one time, the master went to Paris also . . . in a carriage. . . . *(He laughs.)*

VARYA: What is it, Firs?

FIRS: What do you wish? *(Joyous)* My mistress is home again! At last! Now I can die quietly. . . . *(He cries with joy.)*

(Enter LYUBOV ANDREYEVNA, GAYEV, LOPAHIN and SIMEONOV-PISHCHIK; SIMEONOV-PISHCHIK is dressed in a peasant costume made of fine material and a pair of large Oriental pants.[5] As GAYEV enters, he makes ges-

tures with his body and arms as if he were playing billiards.)

LYUBOV ANDREYEVNA: How was it already? Let me remember . . . Pocket the red in the corner! Bank shot in the side pocket! [6]

GAYEV: I cut into the corner! There was a time, my sister, when we slept in this room, and now I am fifty-one years old, strange as that may sound. . . .

LOPAHIN: Yes, time marches on.

GAYEV: What?

LOPAHIN: Time, I said, marches on.

GAYEV: There's an odor of patchouli here. [7]

ANYA: I'm going to bed. Good night, Mama. *(She embraces her mother.)*

LYUBOV ANDREYEVNA: My adorable little girl. *(She kisses her hands.)* Are you glad to be home? I can't get over it.

ANYA: Good night, Uncle.

GAYEV *(kisses her face and her hands)*: God keep you. How you resemble your mother! *(To his sister)* At her age, Lyuba, you were exactly like her.

(ANYA holds her hand out to LONAHIN and PISHCHIK and shuts the door behind her.)

LYUBOV ANDREYEVNA: She's all worn out.

PISHCHIK: It must have been a long journey.

VARYA *(to LOPAHIN and PISHCHIK)*: Well, gentlemen? It's going on three o'clock. One shouldn't abuse hospitality.

LYUBOV ANDREYEVNA *(laughing)*: You haven't changed, Varya. *(She draws her to her and embraces her.)* When I've had my coffee, we shall retire. *(FIRS puts a cushion under her feet.)* Thank you, my dear one. I've gotten used to my coffee. I take it night and day. Thank you, my dear old fellow. *(She embraces FIRS.)*

VARYA: I'll go see if all the baggage has arrived. *(She goes out.)*

LYUBOV ANDREYEVNA: Is it really me who's here? *(She laughs.)* I have a desire to jump about, to wave my arms about. *(She hides her face in her hands.)* I must be dreaming! As God is my witness, I love my country, I love it fondly. I couldn't see anything out of the train, I was crying so hard. *(Through her tears)* But I must have my coffee. Thank you, my Firs, thank you, my dear good old fellow. I'm so glad you're still alive.

FIRS: The day before yesterday.

GAYEV: He's hard of hearing.

LOPAHIN: I must leave for Kharkov at five o'clock. No luck! I'd so much like to have gotten a better look at you and had a talk. . . . you're still just as splendid as ever.

PISHCHIK (*his breath comes heavily*): And even more beautiful . . . Dressed in Parisian style . . . You bowled me over completely!

LOPAHIN: Your brother, Leonid Andreyevich, says I'm only a boor, a kulak, but that's no concern of mine. Let him talk. All that I ask is that you have confidence in me as you did in the old days, that your astonishing, touching eyes look upon me as they once did. Merciful Heaven! My father was a serf of your grandfather and of your father, but you, you personally, did so much for me in the past that I have forgotten everything and I love you as if you were my family . . . and even more than that.

LYUBOV ANDREYEVNA: I can't sit still . . . I can't sit still. (*She gets up rapidly and begins to walk about agitatedly.*) I won't survive this joy. . . . Make fun of me, I'm an idiot. . . . My dear little bookcase . . . (*She embraces the bookcase.*) My little table . . .

GAYEV: Nanny died without you.

LYUBOV ANDREYEVNA (*sits down and drinks her coffee*): God rest her soul. They wrote me.

GAYEV: Anastassi also died. Petruchka Kossoi left me and now he works for the commissioner, in town. (*He takes a package of fruit drops from his pocket and sucks on one.*)

PISHCHIK: My daughter Dashenka sends you her best regards.

LOPAHIN: I'd like to say something nice and cheerful. (*He looks at his watch.*) I'm going, there is no more time to talk. . . . Well, a few words, all the same. You already know that your cherry orchard is being sold for your debts; the auction is fixed for the twenty-second of August, but don't get upset, dear friend, rest easy, there is a way out. . . . Here is my plan. A little attention, please. Your estate is only twelve miles or so from the town, not far from the new railroad line. If you divided the cherry orchard and the land by the river into summer plots and then leased them for the construction of summer villas, you would, at the least, have twenty-five thousand rubles income every year.

GAYEV: Excuse me, what nonsense!

LYUBOV ANDREYEVNA: I don't understand your meaning, Yermolai Alexeyevich.

LOPAHIN: You would obtain tenants for at least twenty-five thousand rubles a year per acre,[8] and if you advertise right now, I guarantee you that before autumn, you will not have a bit of land left, they'll be fighting to grab it up! In short, I congratulate you, you are saved. The site is marvelous, the river is deep. All you have to do is put it into some order, clean it up a bit . . . for example, demolish the old buildings, this house which is no longer worth anything, cut down the old cherry orchard. . . .

LYUBOV ANDREYEVNA: Cut down? Excuse me, my dear, but you don't quite understand. If there is anything interesting, even remarkable, in the environs, it is certainly our cherry orchard.

LOPAHIN: The only remarkable thing about this cherry orchard is its size. It only yields cherries every two years and nobody knows what to do with them, nobody buys any.

GAYEV: Even the encyclopedia mentions this cherry orchard.

LOPAHIN (*looks at his watch*): If we don't think anything up, if we don't make a decision, then on the twenty-second of August, the cherry orchard, and with it the entire estate, will be sold at auction, you can make up your mind to that! There is no other solution, I swear to you. There is none, and that's final.

FIRS: Formerly, forty or fifty years ago, they dried the cherries, they dipped them, they marinated them and they made preserves, in those days. . . .

GAYEV: Firs, shut up.

FIRS: And in those days they sent the dry cherries in open wagons to Moscow and to Kharkov. And did that bring in the money! And the dry cherries were soft and juicy, sweet smelling. . . . They knew how to do it in those days. . . .

LYUBOV ANDREYEVNA: And what happened to the recipe?

FIRS: It has been forgotten. No one remembers it.

PISHCHIK (*to* LYUBOV ANDREYEVNA): And Paris? How was it? Did you eat frogs?

LYUBOV ANDREYEVNA: I ate crocodiles!

PISHCHIK: Imagine that!

LOPAHIN: Until now, in the country there were only the masters and the muzhiks; now the summer people have come. All the towns, even the smallest ones, are surrounded now with summerhouses. And it looks as if in about twenty years the summer people will multiply extraordinarily. Today all he does is take his tea on the terrace, but he may perhaps begin to cultivate his little bit of land and then your cherry orchard will become rich, magnificent, luxurious . . .

GAYEV *(indignant)*: Such nonsense!

(Enter VARYA *and* YASHA.)

VARYA: Mother, there are two telegrams for you. *(She takes a key and noisily unlocks the old-fashioned bookcase.)* Here they are.

LYUBOV ANDREYEVNA: These are from Paris. *(She tears up the telegrams without reading them.)* I'm finished with Paris.

GAYEV: Do you know, Lyuba, how old this bookcase is. Last week, I pulled out the bottom drawer and I noticed some figures burned in the wood. This bookcase was made exactly one hundred years ago! How's that! Hmm! We could celebrate its jubilee. It's only an inanimate object, but all the same, after all, it's a bookcase.

PISHCHIK *(astonished)*: A hundred years . . . Imagine that!

GAYEV: Yes . . . That's something. . . . *(Touching the bookcase)* Dear, honored bookcase! I salute your existence, which for more than a hundred years has aspired to the glorious ideals of goodness and justice: your silent appeal to productive travail has not faltered in the course of a century, sustaining . . . *(through tears)* in the generations of our lineage the fervent faith in a better future, cultivating in us the ideals of goodness and social conscience.

(Pause.)

LOPAHIN: Yes . . .

LYUBOV ANDREYEVNA: You haven't changed, Lenya.

GAYEV *(a little embarrassed)*: Bank it off the right into the pocket! Cut it into the side pocket!

LOPAHIN: Well, I must go.

YASHA *(brings* LYUBOV ANDREYEVNA *some medicine)*: It's perhaps time for you to take your pills, madame. . . .

PISHCHIK: Mustn't ever take medicine, dear friend . . . Doesn't do any harm or any good. . . . Give them here, my dear. *(He takes the box of pills, empties it in his hands, breathes on them, puts the pills in his mouth and drinks them down with some kvass.)* There!

LYUBOV ANDREYEVNA *(frightened)*: You're out of your mind!

PISHCHIK: I have swallowed them all.

LOPAHIN: What a devil!

(Everybody laughs.)

FIRS: When the gentleman came to see us at Easter time, he ate a half barrel of salted cucumbers all by himself. . . . *(He murmurs something.)*

LYUBOV ANDREYEVNA: What is he mumbling about?

VARYA: He's been mumbling like that for three years. We're used to it.

YASHA: Old age.

(CHARLOTTA IVANOVNA, in a white dress, very thin and tightly corseted, a lorgnette hanging from her belt, crosses the stage.)

LOPAHIN: Excuse me, Charlotta Ivanovna, I haven't greeted you yet.

(LOPAHIN prepares to kiss her hand.)

CHARLOTTA *(taking her hand away)*: If one allowed you a kiss on the hand, you should allow yourself as far as the elbow, then to the shoulder . . .

LOPAHIN: I'm not lucky today. *(Everybody laughs.)* Charlotta Ivanovna, show us one of your tricks.

LYUBOV ANDREYEVNA: A trick, Charlotta!

CHARLOTTA: No. I want to go to sleep.

LOPAHIN: In three weeks we'll see each other again. *(He kisses LYUBOV ANDREYEVNA's hand.)* Good-bye, till then. I must leave. *(To GAYEV)* Farewell. *(He embraces PISHCHIK.)* Farewell. *(He squeezes VARYA's hand, then FIRS's and YASHA's.)* I don't feel like leaving. *(To LYUBOV ANDREYEVNA)* If you decide on the villas, let me know, I'll find you fifty thousand rubles to borrow. Think about it, seriously.

VARYA (*angrily*): Will you please get going!

LOPAHIN: I'm going, I'm going. . . . (*He goes.*)

GAYEV: He's a brute. That is to say, pardon me. . . . Varya is going to marry him, he's Varya's little fiancé.

VARYA: Don't talk too much, uncle.

LYUBOV ANDREYEVNA: Well, Varya, it would make me very happy. He's a very nice man.

PISHCHIK: What a fellow! To tell the truth . . . a very worthy fellow and my Dashenka . . . she also says so . . . she says lots of things. (*He begins to snore, then he gets up right away.*) However that may be, my dear lady, would you . . . lend me two hundred and forty rubles. . . . I must pay the interest on the mortgage tomorrow.

VARYA (*frightened*): Oh, no, not that!

LYUBOV ANDREYEVNA: I really haven't any.

PISHCHIK: It'll turn up. (*He laughs.*) I never lose hope. Just when I tell myself that the jig is up, finished, right then and there they build a railway over my land and . . . they give me money. So you see, something, at any moment; if not today, tomorrow. . . . Dashenka could win two hundred thousand rubles . . . she has a lottery ticket.

LYUBOV ANDREYEVNA: Now that we've drunk our coffee, we might as well get some rest.

FIRS (*brushing Gayev and remonstrating with him*): You put the wrong trousers on again. I don't know what to do with you any more!

VARYA (*softly*): Anya is sleeping. (*She opens the window without making any noise.*) The sun has already risen, it's not cold. Look, little Mother, how beautiful the trees are! And the air, my Lord! And the starlings are singing!

GAYEV (*opening another window*): The orchard is all white. You haven't forgotten, Lyuba? That long path goes straight down like a tight strap, it shines on moonlit nights. You do remember? You haven't forgotten?

LYUBOV ANDREYEVNA (*looks at the garden out the window*): Oh, my childhood, my innocence. I slept in this children's room, from here I could see the orchard, happiness awoke with me each morning, and the orchard was as it is now, nothing has changed. (*She laughs joyfully.*) It is quite, quite white! Oh, my orchard! After a somber, rainy autumn, a cold winter, there you are again, young, full of happiness, the angels of heaven have not abandoned you. . . . If I could take this heavy burden off my chest, from my shoulders, if I could forget my past!

GAYEV: Yes, the orchard shall be sold for debts, as strange as that may sound.

LYUBOV ANDREYEVNA: Look, poor Mama is walking in the orchard. . . . She's wearing a white dress! *(She laughs joyously.)* It's she.

GAYEV: Where?

VARYA: God keep you, little Mother.

LYUBOV ANDREYEVNA: There's no one, I was dreaming. At the right, where the path turns toward the summerhouse, there is this little white tree that stoops over, it resembles a woman. . . .

(Enter TROFIMOV; *he wears an old student's uniform, glasses.)*

LYUBOV ANDREYEVNA: This orchard is astonishing! The masses of white flowers, the blue sky . . .

TROFIMOV: Lyubov Andreyevna! *(She turns toward him.)* I have only to greet you and then go. *(He kisses her hand warmly.)* I was told to wait until morning, but I didn't have the patience. . . .

*(*LYUBOV ANDREYEVNA *looks at him, perplexed.)*

VARYA *(tears in her eyes)*: It's Petya Trofimov. . . .

TROFIMOV: Petya Trofimov, the former tutor of your Grisha . . . Have I really changed so much?

*(*LYUBOV ANDREYEVNA *puts her arms around him and cries softly.)*

GAYEV *(embarrassed)*: Come, come, Lyuba.

VARYA *(weeps)*: Didn't I tell you, Petya, to wait until tomorrow.

LYUBOV ANDREYEVNA: My Grisha . . . my little . . . Grisha . . . my son . . .

VARYA: We can't help that, Mama. It was God's will.

TROFIMOV *(gently, tears in his eyes)*: There, there . . .

LYUBOV ANDREYEVNA *(crying softly)*: My little boy died, he drowned. . . . Why? Why, my friend? *(In a lower voice)*

Anya is sleeping, and here I am talking loud . . . making
noise. . . . Well, Petya? How is it that you have become so
ugly? Why so old?

TROFIMOV: A lady in the train called me "the shabby gentleman."

LYUBOV ANDREYEVNA: You were quite young then, a nice
little student, and now your hair is thinning, you have
glasses. Is it possible you're still a student? (*She goes toward
the door.*)

TROFIMOV: I'll probably remain the eternal student.

LYUBOV ANDREYEVNA (*kisses her brother, then Varya*): Now
go to bed. . . . You look older, too, Leonid.

PISHCHIK (*following her*): So now we must go to bed. . . . Oh,
this gout of mine! I shall stay and sleep here. . . . If you
were able, Lyubov Andreyevna, my dear lady, tomorrow
morning . . . two hundred and forty rubles . . .

GAYEV: That one certainly never lets up.

PISHCHIK: Two hundred and forty rubles . . . the interest on
the mortgage.

LYUBOV ANDREYEVNA: I haven't any money, my dear fellow. . . .

PISHCHIK: I'll return them to you, my friend . . . it's a mere
bagatelle.

LYUBOV ANDREYEVNA: Well, all right, Leonid will give it to
you. . . . You give it, Leonid.

GAYEV: I give it to him! Nothing doing!

LYUBOV ANDREYEVNA: What shall we do . . . give it . . . he
needs it. . . . He'll give it back.

(LYUBOV ANDREYEVNA, TROFIMOV, PISHCHIK *and* FIRS *go
out.* GAYEV, VARYA *and* YASHA *remain.*)

GAYEV: My sister has not yet lost the habit of wasting money.
(*To* YASHA) Stand a little farther off, my man, you smell like
the henhouse.

YASHA (*smiling mockingly*): And you, Leonid Andreyevich,
you're the same as ever.

GAYEV: What? (*To* VARYA) What is he saying?

VARYA (*To* YASHA): Your mother came from the village, she
has been here since yesterday at the servants' quarters. She
wants to see you. . . .

YASHA: She gives me a pain.

VARYA: Oh, shame on you!

YASHA: Who needs her! She could have waited until tomorrow. (*He goes out.*)

VARYA: Mama is still the same, she hasn't changed at all. If you'd let her do it, she'd give away everything she has.

GAYEV: Yes. (*Pause*) If a quantity of remedies are prescribed for an illness, that means that the illness is incurable. I've been thinking and racking my brains, I have many remedies, a great many, which means, practically speaking, that I don't really have any. It would be nice to have an inheritance come from out of nowhere, it would be nice if we could marry our Anya off to a very rich man, it would be nice to go to Yaroslavl[9] and try our luck with our aunt the countess, since Auntie is very, very rich.

VARYA (*crying*): If God would only help us.

GAYEV: Don't snivel. Auntie is very rich but she doesn't love us. Because—first of all—my sister married a lawyer, not a nobleman. . . . (ANYA *appears at the doorway.*) She married a man who didn't belong to the nobility, and she behaved . . . we really couldn't say it was very virtuously. She is nice, good, brave, and I love her very much, but it's no use thinking up attenuating circumstances, one must admit that she's a depraved woman. One may sense it in her slightest gesture.

VARYA (*whispers*): Anya's there in the doorway.

GAYEV: What? (*Pause*) It's extraordinary, I have some dust in my right eye. . . . I can hardly see out of it. And Thursday, when I went to the county court . . .

(ANYA *enters.*)

VARYA: How is it you're not sleeping, Anya?

ANYA: I can't fall asleep, I just can't.

GAYEV: My little darling! (*He kisses* ANYA's *face and hands.*) My child . . . (*Tears in his eyes*) You're not my little niece, you are my angel, you are everything to me. You must believe me, you must. . . .

ANYA: I believe you, Uncle. Everybody loves you and esteems you. . . . But, Uncle darling, you mustn't talk so much, you must keep quiet. What were you just saying about my mother, your own sister? Why were you saying that?

GAYEV: Yes, yes . . . *(He covers his face with her hand.)* It's true, it's terrible! My God! My God! Help me! And the speech in front of the bookcase I made a little while ago . . . it's idiotic! Had I only understood after I had finished that it was idiotic!

VARYA: It's true, little Uncle, that you ought never to talk. Keep quiet, that's all.

ANYA: If you didn't talk, you'd be a lot better off.

GAYEV: I'll keep quiet. *(He kisses ANYA's and VARYA's hands.)* I'll keep quiet. Just this, about our business. Thursday I was at the county court and there was a whole crowd of people there, they got to talking about this and that, in snatches, and it seems as if it might be possible to get a loan by signing a promissory note and paying the interest to the bank.

VARYA: With the help of God.

GAYEV: I shall return Tuesday to talk about it again. *(To VARYA)* Stop sniveling! *(To ANYA)* Your mother will talk to Lopahin; he will certainly not refuse her. . . . And you, as soon as you are rested, you will go to Yaroslavl . . . to the countess, your great-aunt. That is how we'll be making three different tries—and it will be in the bag. *(He puts a piece of fruit candy in his mouth.)* I swear on my honor, on anything you like, that the estate will not be sold! *(Excited)* I swear it on my happiness! Here is my hand, you can call me good for nothing, tell me I'm dishonest, if I let it go so far as the auction! I swear on my life!

ANYA *(once again calm and happy)*: How good you are, my Uncle, how clever. *(She puts her arms around him.)* Now I am content! I am content! I'm happy!

(Enter FIRS.)

FIRS *(reproachfully)*: Leonid Andreyevich, aren't you ashamed! When are you going to bed?

GAYEV: Right away, right away. Go away, Firs, I shall undress by myself, quite well for once. Well, my children, beddy bye . . . We'll look into the details tomorrow; now go to bed. *(He kisses ANYA and VARYA.)* I am a man of the eighties. . . .[10] People hardly have anything good to say about those days, but I certainly can say that I have suffered not a little in my life for my convictions. It is not for nothing that the muzhik loves me. One must know the muzhik! One must know how to . . .

ANYA: You're starting again, Uncle!

VARYA: Don't say anything, my dear Uncle.

FIRS (*angrily*): Leonid Andreyevich!

GAYEV: I'm coming, I'm coming. . . . Go to bed. Double bank into the side pocket! I hit it right on! Right into it . . . (*He goes out; behind him,* FIRS *trots along.*)

ANYA: Now I am content. I don't want to go to Yaroslavl, I don't love my great-aunt, but I am content all the same. Thanks to Uncle. (*She sits down.*)

VARYA: We must go to bed. I'm going. While you were away, we had plenty of trouble here. The old servants' quarters, you know, is only lived in by some of the old servants: Yefimuchka, Polya, Yevstigney, and even Karp. They got it into their heads to put up some low life for the night. I didn't make any remarks about it, only I heard them say I said to feed them peas and nothing else. Out of stinginess, it would seem . . . And all that comes from Yevstigney. . . . I said to myself, if that's the way things are, just you wait. . . . I called for Yevstigney . . . (*She yawns.*) He comes to me . . . I say to him, "What's got into you, Yevstigney . . . you idiot, really . . . (*She looks at* ANYA.) Anichka! (*Pause*) She's sleeping. . . . (*She takes* ANYA *by the arm.*) Come into your little bed. . . . Come! (*She leads her.*) My little darling has fallen asleep! Come. . . .

(*They go out. Far off, beyond the garden, a shepherd plays his pipe.* TROFIMOV *crosses the stage, sees* VARYA *and* ANYA, *and stops.*)

VARYA: Shh . . . she's sleeping . . . she's sleeping. . . . Come, darling.

ANYA (*softly, half asleep*): I'm so tired . . . so many bells . . . Uncle . . . darling, and Mama and Uncle . . .

VARYA: Come, my darling, come. . . .

(*They go out by the door that leads to* ANYA'S *bedchamber.*)

TROFIMOV (*touched*): Light of my life! My spring!

CURTAIN

ACT TWO

A meadow. A little old chapel, long since abandoned; near the chapel, a well, large stones that look like old tombstones, and an old bench. One sees the road that leads to GAYEV's country estate. On one side, the dark shadows of the large poplar trees, and here begins the cherry orchard. In the distance, a line of telegraph poles, and all the way to the horizon, the vague outlines of a large city, which is visible only on a fine clear day. The sun will soon be setting.

CHARLOTTA, YASHA and DUNYASHA are seated on the bench; near them YEPIHODOV stands playing his guitar; each is lost in his own thoughts. CHARLOTTA, wearing an old cap, has taken her gun from her shoulder and is arranging the strap buckle.

CHARLOTTA *(dreamily)*: I do not have a real passport, I don't know my age, it seems to me all the time that I am a young lady. When I was very young, my father and my mother worked at fairs, they gave performances, very good ones. I did the *salto mortale* [11] and other tricks. And when Mama and Papa died, a German lady took me and she raised me. Very well. I grew up and then I became a governess. But where I come from and who I am . . . I don't know at all. Who my parents were, whether they were even married . . . I know nothing of that. *(She takes*

237

a cucumber from her pocket and bites into it.) I know nothing. *(Pause)* I have such a desire to confide in someone . . . but there's nobody . . . I have no one.

YEPIHODOV *(plays the guitar and sings)*: "What do I care for this noisy world, What are friends or foes to me? . . ." [12] How nice it is to play the mandolin!

DUNYASHA: It's not a mandolin, it's a guitar. *(She looks into a pocket mirror and puts powder on.)*

YEPIHODOV: For the madman in love, it is a mandolin. . . . *(He hums.)* "If only my heart were warmed by the heat of requited love . . ."

(YASHA sings with him.)

CHARLOTTA: These people sing so badly . . . phooey! Veritable jackals.

DUNYASHA *(to YASHA)*: How lucky all the same to travel abroad . . .

YASHA: That's true. I cannot but agree with you on that. *(He yawns, then lights a cigar.)*

YEPIHODOV: It's obvious. Abroad everything has been pretty much built up.

YASHA: To be sure.

YEPIHODOV: I am a well developed man. I read the most remarkable books, but I can't really find what direction I'm going in. Strictly speaking, what I want is to live or to shoot myself; strictly speaking, the truth is nevertheless, I always have a revolver on me. Here it is. . . . *(He shows his revolver.)*

CHARLOTTA: I'm finished. Now I'm going. *(She slings the gun over her shoulder.)* Yepihodov, you are a very clever man and very frightening; women must be mad about you. Brrr! *(Departing)* These clever men are all so stupid, nobody to talk to. . . . I am alone, always alone, I have nobody, and neither who I am, nor why I exist, is known. . . . *(She goes out slowly.)*

YEPIHODOV: Strictly speaking, and passing over other subjects, I must talk about myself, by the way; fate is pitiless to me, like a tempest tossing a small boat. If, supposing, I am in error, then why this morning, when I got up, first thing, did I see on my chest a spider of immense proportions . . . as big as this. *(He shows how big it is with his two hands.)*

Besides, all I have to do is pour out a glass of kvass, and what do I see there? The worst form of obscenity in the form of a cockroach. *(Pause)* Have you read Buckle? [13] *(Pause)* May I disturb you, Avdotya Fyodorovna, just a few words.

DUNYASHA: Speak.

YEPIHODOV: I would rather it were private. . . . *(He sighs.)*

DUNYASHA *(confused)*: Well . . . but first bring me my cape . . . it's next to the cupboard. It's a little damp out here. . . .

YEPIHODOV: Very well . . . I shall bring it to you. . . . Now I know what I must do with my revolver. . . . *(He takes the guitar, goes off strumming the strings lightly.)*

YASHA: Twenty-two Troubles! He's an idiot, let it be said *entre nous.* . . . *(He yawns.)*

DUNYASHA: As long as he doesn't kill himself. *(Pause)* I'm always upset, always anxious these days. The masters took me in when I was still quite a little girl, I have lost touch with ordinary, everyday living, I have such white hands, white as white can be, like a lady's. I have become so delicate, so fine, so noble. . . . I'm afraid of everything. . . . It's terrible. And if you deceive me, Yasha, I don't know how it will affect my nerves.

YASHA *(kisses her)*: Little chickadee! A young lady must know how to behave properly, that's quite clear, and there's nothing I dislike more in a young lady than when she misbehaves.

DUNYASHA: I love you passionately, you're so educated, you can discuss anything. . . .

(Pause.)

YASHA *(yawning)*: Yes . . . I see things this way: if a young lady is in love, then she is immoral. *(Pause)* It is pleasant to smoke a cigar in the pure air. . . . *(He listens intently.)* They're coming. . . . It's the masters. . . .

(DUNYASHA throws herself in his arms, impulsively.)

YASHA: Return to the house, as if you had been bathing in the river, take this path so you won't meet them. They might think we had an appointment. I couldn't stand that.

DUNYASHA *(coughing)*: The cigar has given me a headache. . . .

(She goes off. YASHA remains seated near the chapel. Enter LYUBOV ANDREYEVNA, GAYEV and LOPAHIN.)

LOPAHIN: You must decide once and for all, there's no time left. It's a simple matter all around. Do you or do you not wish to rent out the land for summer houses? Answer yes or no. One word only . . .

LYUBOV ANDREYEVNA: Who is it who's smoking such a disgusting cigar? *(She sits down.)*

GAYEV: This newly constructed railroad is quite convenient. *(He sits down.)* We've made a little jaunt into town, we've had lunch there. . . . I put the red into the side pocket. I must go by the house first and play one round. . . .

LYUBOV ANDREYEVNA: There's time.

LOPAHIN: One word only! *(Begging)* Give me an answer!

GAYEV *(yawning)*: What?

LYUBOV ANDREYEVNA *(looking in her purse)*: Yesterday it was filled with money, and today it is almost empty. For economy's sake, my poor Varya makes us eat milk soup, in the kitchen they feed the old people on peas, and I . . . money falls through my fingers senselessly. . . . *(She lets the purse fall, the gold pieces scatter.)* There they go rolling. . . . *(She is angry.)*

YASHA: Allow me, I'll gather them up. *(He picks the pieces up.)*

LYUBOV ANDREYEVNA: Be so good, Yasha. Why did I need to go have lunch? . . . Your filthy restaurant with its music, and the tablecloths that smelled of soap . . . Why drink so much, Lenya? Why eat so much? Why talk so much? You talked too much again at the restaurant, and always out of place. Sometimes about the seventies, sometimes about the Decadents.[14] And to whom? Talk about the decadents to the waiters in the restaurant!

LOPAHIN: Yes.

GAYEV *(with a gesture)*: I'm incorrigible, that's true. . . . *(To YASHA, irritated)* Why are you always pestering us?

YASHA *(laughs)*: I cannot hear your voice without laughing.

GAYEV *(to his sister)*: You get rid of him or me. . . .

LYUBOV ANDREYEVNA: Go away, Yasha, leave us. . . .

YASHA *(gives LYUBOV ANDREYEVNA her purse)*: I'm going now. *(Trying not to laugh)* Right away . . . *(He goes out.)*

LOPAHIN: Your estate is all set to be bought by that rich man

Deriganov. They say he'll be there at the auction, in person.

LYUBOV ANDREYEVNA: And where did you hear that?

LOPAHIN: They're talking about it in town.

GAYEV: Our Yaroslavl aunt has promised to send the money, but when and how much, nobody knows.

LOPAHIN: How much will she send? A hundred thousand? Two hundred?

LYUBOV ANDREYEVNA: Well . . . if she sends ten or fifteen thousand, we should be thankful.

LOPAHIN: You will pardon me, but such frivolous people as you, so incapable of doing business, so strange as you are, I've never seen before. I tell you in simple language, your estate has been put up for sale, and you do not seem to comprehend.

LYUBOV ANDREYEVNA: But what must we do? Tell us, what?

LOPAHIN: I tell it to you every day. Every day I tell you the same thing. You must rent out the cherry orchard and the rest of the land. You must lease it out for summer cottages and do it immediately, as soon as possible—the auction is upon us! Will you get that into your heads! When you've finally made the decision on the cottages, you will receive all the money you want, and you will be saved.

LYUBOV ANDREYEVNA: Villas, summer people . . . it's so vulgar . . . if you will excuse me.

GAYEV: I'm in complete agreement with you.

LOPAHIN: I shall begin to sob or to cry out, or go into a dead faint. I cannot bear it any longer! You exhaust me! *(To* GAYEV) You old woman!

GAYEV: What?

LOPAHIN: Old woman! *(He gets ready to go.)*

LYUBOV ANDREYEVNA *(frightened)*: No, don't go, stay, my friend. I beg of you. Perhaps we can think of something!

LOPAHIN: What do you want to think of!

LYUBOV ANDREYEVNA: Don't go, I beg of you. When you're here, it's somehow more enjoyable. *(Pause)* I'm always waiting for something to happen, for the house to collapse over us. . . .

GAYEV *(plunged in his reveries)*: Double bank into the corner . . . Bank into the side pocket . . .

LYUBOV ANDREYEVNA: We've committed so many sins. . . .

LOPAHIN: What sins could you have committed? . . .

GAYEV *(puts a fruit candy in his mouth)*: They say I've eaten up my fortune in candies. . . . *(He laughs.)*

LYUBOV ANDREYEVNA: Oh, my sins . . . I've always squandered money uncontrollably like a madwoman, and I married a man who never had anything but debts. My husband died of champagne—he drank terribly—and I, for my sins, I began to love another man, had an affair with him and just then—it was the first punishment; what a cruel blow—here at the river, my little one drowned, and I went abroad forever, never to return, never to see this river again. . . . I fled, I shut my eyes and fled, I had lost my senses, and *he*, he followed me . . . pitiless, brutal. . . . I had bought a villa near Menton because he fell ill there; and for three years I knew no rest, day or night; his illness exhausted me, I'm bone dry. And last year, when the villa was sold for its debts, I left for Paris, and there, after having robbed me, he left me and took up with another. . . . I tried to poison myself . . . so shameful, so stupid. . . . And suddenly, I began to long for Russia, my homeland, my little daughter. . . . *(She wipes her tears.)* My God, my God, be merciful, pardon my sins! Don't punish me any more! *(She takes a telegram out of her pocket.)* I received this from Paris today. . . . He begs my pardon, he begs me to return. . . . *(She tears up the telegram.)* I think I hear music. . . . *(She strains to hear.)*

GAYEV: It's our famous Jewish orchestra. You remember: four fiddles, a flute and a double bass.

LYUBOV ANDREYEVNA: Is it still in existence? We must bring them over here, organize an evening.

LOPAHIN *(listening intently)*: I don't hear it any more. . . . *(He hums softly.)* "For money, our Germans would Frenchify a Russian. . . ." [15] *(He laughs.)* What a play I saw yesterday, at the theater, it was so funny. . . .

LYUBOV ANDREYEVNA: I am sure there was nothing funny about it. You shouldn't go and see plays, rather you'd do better to look at yourselves a little more often. How dull your lives are, how you do talk on and say nothing.

LOPAHIN: It's true. We must admit it, our life is idiotic. . . . *(Pause)* My father was a muzhik, an idiot who understood nothing, and who taught me nothing. All he could do was to beat me, and always with a stick. As a matter of fact, I'm as much of a fool and an idiot as he was. I haven't learned anything, I have an impossible handwriting. I write so badly that I am ashamed in front of people, a real pig.

LYUBOV ANDREYEVNA: You should get married, my friend.

LOPAHIN: Yes, that's true.

LYUBOV ANDREYEVNA: To our Varya. She's a good girl.

LOPAHIN: Yes.

LYUBOV ANDREYEVNA: She's from a very simple family, she works all day, and the main thing is, she loves you. And you, too, you find her to your taste, and you have for a long time now.

LOPAHIN: Well, why not? I've nothing against it. . . . She's a good girl.

(Pause.)

GAYEV: I've been offered a position in a bank. Six thousand a year . . . Did you know that?

LYUBOV ANDREYEVNA: Come on! That's not for you. . . .

(Enter FIRS; he carries an overcoat.)

FIRS *(to GAYEV)*: Put this on, sir; it's getting damp.

GAYEV *(putting the overcoat on)*: I'm sick and tired of you, old man.

FIRS: That's not right. . . . Already in the morning he left without telling me. *(He examines him on all sides.)*

LYUBOV ANDREYEVNA: How you've aged, Firs!

FIRS: Madame wishes?

LOPAHIN: They say you've gotten old!

FIRS: It's because I've been living for a long time, they tried to marry me off when your father wasn't even on this earth. . . . *(He laughs.)* And when we were freed, I was already the head valet. Then I refused to be freed, I stayed with the masters. . . . *(Pause)* I remember, everybody was happy, and about what, they didn't even know themselves.

LOPAHIN: You were well off in those days, at least there were beatings.

FIRS *(who doesn't hear)*: We sure were. The muzhiks had masters, the masters had muzhiks, while now it's a big confusion, not to be understood.

GAYEV: Will you please shut up, Firs. I must go to town tomorrow. I've been promised to meet a general who would cosign my loan.

LOPAHIN: Nothing will come of it. You will not succeed in paying the interest, you can be sure of that.

LYUBOV ANDREYEVNA: He's delirious. Such a general has never existed.

(Enter TROFIMOV, ANYA and VARYA.)

GAYEV: All our group is arriving.

ANYA: Mama's there.

LYUBOV ANDREYEVNA *(tenderly)*: Come, come . . . my darlings. . . . *(She puts her arm around ANYA and VARYA.)* If you knew how much I love you. Sit down next to me, like this.

(Everybody sits down.)

LOPAHIN: Our eternal student is always with the ladies.

TROFIMOV: That's none of your business.

LOPAHIN: He'll soon be fifty and he's still a student.

TROFIMOV: Stop these idiotic jokes.

LOPAHIN: Why are you getting angry, you queer fellow?

TROFIMOV: Then leave me alone.

LOPAHIN *(laughing)*: Let me ask you, what's your opinion of me?

TROFIMOV: My opinion, Yermolai Alexeyevich, is as follows: you are rich, soon you will be a millionaire. And since, in relation to the metamorphosis of matter, we need birds of prey who devour everything in their path, you're needed, too.

(Everybody laughs.)

VARYA: Petya, wouldn't it be better if you talked to us about the planets.

LYUBOV ANDREYEVNA: No, let's go on with yesterday's conversation.

TROFIMOV: What was that all about?

GAYEV: We were talking about man's pride.

TROFIMOV: Yesterday we talked for a long time, without getting anywhere. In matters of man's pride, as you see it, there is something mystical. It may be that you are right, but if one looks at it quite simply, without getting too clever about it, what kind of pride is this, does it make any sense, since man is physiologically a bad arrangement, since in the great majority of cases he is crude, unintelligent and profoundly miserable. We must stop admiring ourselves. All we need is to work.

GAYEV: At any rate, we shall die.

TROFIMOV: Who knows? And what do you mean by "we shall die"? Perhaps man has a hundred senses and, with death, only the five senses known to us perish, while the other ninety-five will remain.

LYUBOV ANDREYEVNA: How intelligent you are, Petya!

LOPAHIN (*ironically*): Frightfully!

TROFIMOV: Humanity is progressing and perfecting its forces. All that is inaccessible to it today will one day become familiar, comprehensible; only we must, in order for that to happen, work and help with all one's strength those who seek the truth. Here in Russia, those who work are still very few. The enormous majority of Russian intellectuals that I know seek nothing, do nothing, they have at the present time no capacity for work. They think they belong to the intelligentsia, but they treat their servants like inferiors, they treat the muzhiks like beasts, they can hardly study, they read nothing seriously, in fact they do absolutely nothing; sciences are only a subject of conversation and they understand very little about art. All these intellectuals are very serious, they make serious faces, they only talk about significant things, and they philosophize . . . while all during this time, under everyone's eyes, workers are fed abominably, they sleep without pillows, thirty to forty in a room, the bedbugs swarm all over the place, it stinks, it's damp and morally degrading. And it's clear that all our fine words serve only to fool ourselves, and others. Show me all those day camps they talk about all the time, and where are the reading rooms? They are just written about in novels, and if the truth be known, they're not there at all. What is there is just filth, vulgarity, Asiatic squalor. . . . I'm afraid I can't bear all these serious faces, and I fear serious conversations. Better to keep quiet!

LOPAHIN: You know, I get up before five in the morning, I work from morning till night, I'm always handling money, mine and others'. So that I see what makes the world go round. All you have to do is start something to see how rare it is to find honest, decent people. Sometimes, when I can't get to sleep, I think, "My God, you have given us immense forests, endless vistas, the farthest horizons; living among them we should, truly, be giants ourselves.

LYUBOV ANDREYEVNA: You need giants. . . . They're only good in fairy tales; elsewhere they're frightening.

(Upstage YEPIHODOV *passes by, playing his guitar.)*

LYUBOV ANDREYEVNA *(dreaming)*: There's Yepihodov passing by. . . .

ANYA *(dreaming)*: Yepihodov passing by . . .

GAYEV: The sun has set, my friends.

TROFIMOV: Yes.

GAYEV *(in a low voice, as if reciting)*: Oh Thou, Nature, divine one, Thou shinest with an eternal radiance, thou art beautiful and indifferent, Thou, whom we call Mother, thou unitest in thyself existence and death, thou giveth life and thou taketh it away. . . .

ANYA *(begging)*: Uncle dear!

VARYA: You're starting again, uncle!

TROFIMOV: You'd better carom off the red into the side pocket. . . .

GAYEV: I'll keep quiet, I'll keep quiet.

(Everybody stays there, seated, each plunged in his own thoughts. Calm. All one hears is FIRS *muttering to himself. Suddenly, far away, as if coming from the sky, the sound of a breaking string, which dies away little by little, sadly.)*

LYUBOV ANDREYEVNA: What's that?

LOPAHIN: I don't know. It comes from afar . . . a tub falling in a mine shaft. But it's very far away.

GAYEV: Or perhaps it's a bird . . . some sort of crane.

TROFIMOV: Or an owl.

LYUBOV ANDREYEVNA *(shuddering)*: There was something unpleasant about it.

(Pause.)

FIRS: It was the same before the misfortune: the screech owl cried out and the samovar didn't stop humming.

GAYEV: Before which misfortune?

FIRS: Before the emancipation.[16]

(Pause.)

LYUBOV ANDREYEVNA: Come, my friends, it's time to return. Night is coming on. *(To* ANYA*)* There are tears in your eyes. . . . What is it, my little girl? *(She takes her in her arms.)*

ANYA: It's all right, Mama. It's nothing.

TROFIMOV: Somebody is coming.

(A PASSERBY *comes on; he has an old worn white cap on, and an overcoat; he is slightly drunk.)*

THE PASSERBY: Excuse me, could you tell me if I go through here to go directly to the station?

GAYEV: Yes. Take this road.

THE PASSERBY: I am infinitely grateful to you. *(His voice clears.)* It is beautiful weather. . . . *(He recites.)* "My brother, my suffering brother . . ." "Come to the Volga, you whose groans . . ."[17] *(To* VARYA*)* Mademoiselle, allow a famished Russian fellow to ask for a few kopecks.

(VARYA takes fright and screams.)

LOPAHIN *(annoyed)*: There are some limits to indecent behavior!

LYUBOV ANDREYEVNA *(surprised)*: Here . . . take it. . . . *(She searches in her purse.)* I don't have any silver. . . . It doesn't make any difference, here's some gold. . . .

THE PASSERBY: I am infinitely grateful.

(He goes out. Laughter.)

VARYA *(frightened)*: I'm going . . . I'm going . . . Oh, little Mother, the people in the house have nothing to eat, and you give gold.

LYUBOV ANDREYEVNA: What is to be done with me, I'm such a fool! When we get back, I'll give you all the rest of the money I have. Yermolai Alexeyevich, you will lend me some more!

LOPAHIN: At your orders.

LYUBOV ANDREYEVNA: Come, my friends, it is time to return. Do you know, Varya, that we have quite decided on your marriage. My congratulations.

VARYA *(through tears)*: That's not a subject to joke about, Mama.

LOPAHIN: Achmelia, get thee to a nunnery. . . . [18]

GAYEV: My hands are trembling: it's a long time since I've played billiards.

LOPAHIN: Achmelia, O nymph, in thy orisons, be all my sins remembered.

LYUBOV ANDREYEVNA: Let's go. It will soon be suppertime.

VARYA: He frightened me. My heart is beating so . . . strong.

LOPAHIN: May I remind you again, people: the twenty-second of August, the cherry orchard will be put up for sale. Think about that . . . remember it!

(Everybody goes out except TROFIMOV *and* ANYA.*)*

ANYA *(laughing)*: Give thanks to that passerby who frightened Varya, now we're alone.

TROFIMOV: Varya is afraid that we're in love, that's why she's on our back from morning till night. With her narrow mind she can't understand that we are above love. To evade everything is petty and illusory, everything which prevents us from being free and happy, that is the goal and meaning of our lives! Let us go forward! We are irresistibly attracted to the brilliant stars shining there, far up there. Forward! And no lagging behind, my friends!

ANYA *(joining her hands)*: How well you speak! *(Pause)* It's divinely beautiful today!

TROFIMOV: Yes, marvelous weather.

ANYA: What have you done to me, Petya, why don't I love our cherry orchard any more as I once did? I loved it so tenderly, it seemed to me that in all the earth there was no more beautiful place than our cherry orchard.

TROFIMOV: All of Russia is our orchard. The land is vast and beautiful, and marvelous places are to be found on it. *(Pause)* Just think, Anya, your father, your grandfather and all of your ancestors possessed serfs, living souls; can't you see them, these human beings, looking out at you from every cherry in the orchard, from every tree trunk, you must hear their voices. . . . To possess living souls . . . but that is what changed you all, you who have lived and are living now, so that your mother and you, yourself, and your uncle, you do not even notice that you are living on credit, at the expense of others, those whom you do not even allow as far as your threshold. . . . We are at least two hundred years late, we do not yet possess anything, not even a definite attitude about the past; all that we know how to do is philosophize, complain about our boredom or drink vodka. It is, however, abundantly clear that in order to begin to live in the present, we must first discharge our debts to the past, to finish with it, and one can only redeem that by suffering, only by some really hard work for a change. You must understand this, Anya.

ANYA: The house that we inhabit has not really been our house for a long time now, and I shall leave it, I give you my word.

TROFIMOV: If you possess the mistress' keys to the house, throw them in the well and leave. Be as free as the wind.

ANYA (*with exaltation*): How well you said that!

TROFIMOV: Trust me, Anya, trust me. I am not yet thirty, I am still quite young, I am still a student, but I have already endured so much. . . . As soon as winter comes, I'm starving, I'm ill, anxious, poor as a beggar. . . . Where hasn't my fate driven me! What have I not seen! My soul, at every moment, night and day, is full of inexpressible presentiments. I have a presentiment of happiness, Anya, I see it already. . . .

ANYA (*dreaming*): The moon is rising.

(*They hear* YEPIHODOV *playing on his guitar, always the same sad song. The moon appears. Somewhere, near the poplars,* VARYA *searches for* ANYA, *calling her: "Anya, where are you?"*)

TROFIMOV: Yes, the moon is rising. (*Pause*) And there is happiness, coming there, coming toward us nearer and nearer. I hear its footsteps already. And if we do not hear it, if we do not know how to recognize it, what's the great misfortune? Others will see it!

THE VOICE OF VARYA: Anya! Where are you?

TROFIMOV: That Varya again. *(Furious)* It's revolting!

ANYA: What shall we do? Let's go down to the river, we'll be fine there.

TROFIMOV: Let's go down there. . . .

(They go off.)

THE VOICE OF VARYA: Anya! Anya!

CURTAIN

ACT
THREE

The drawing room, separated from the ballroom by an archway. A lighted chandelier. In the vestibule, the Jewish orchestra that was mentioned in the second act is heard. It is evening. In the ballroom, they are dancing the grand rond. The voice of Simeonov-Pishchik is heard: "Promenade à une paire." The first couple to appear in the drawing room is formed by PISHCHIK and CHARLOTTA IVANOVNA, the second by TROFIMOV and LYUBOV ANDREYEVNA, the third by ANYA and the post office clerk, the fourth by VARYA and the stationmaster, etc. VARYA cries softly and, while dancing, wipes away her tears.

DUNYASHA and her partner make up the last couple. The dancers cross the drawing room and PISHCHIK cries out, "Grand rond! Balancez!" then "Les cavaliers, à genoux et remerciez vos dames!" [19]

FIRS, in a frock coat, brings some soda water on a platter. In the drawing room, enter PISHCHIK and TROFIMOV.

PISHCHIK: I have high blood pressure, I've already had two strokes, it is hard for me to dance, but as they say, "He who falls into a pack, if he can't bark, let him wag his

251

tail." But I'm as strong as a horse. My poor father, may God bless him, was a joker; concerning our lineage he said that the Simeonov-Pishchiks were descended from the very horse that Caligula made a senator.[20] (*He sits down.*) There is only one misfortune: lack of money! A hungry dog only believes in meat. . . . (*He starts snoring, but awakens immediately.*) That's how I am, I cannot talk about anything else but money. . . .

TROFIMOV: That's quite true, you have something horselike about your figure.

PISHCHIK: Well, there's nothing wrong with that. The horse is a good beast . . . a horse can be sold. . . .

(*From the next room, one hears the billiard cues clicking.* VARYA *appears in the ballroom, under the archway.*)

TROFIMOV (*teasing her*): Madame Lopahin! Madame Lopahin!

VARYA (*surly*): Ah, if it isn't the shabby gentleman!

TROFIMOV: I am a shabby gentleman, and I am proud of it.

VARYA (*in a bitter mood*): The musicians were invited, and how will they be paid? (*She goes out.*)

TROFIMOV (*to* PISHCHIK): If the energy that you have spent during your lifetime looking for money to pay the interest on loans were to be applied to something else, you would have turned the world upside down.

PISHCHIK: Nietzsche—a philosopher . . . a very great, very illustrious fellow, with a big head on his shoulders—says in his writings that one should have the right to make counterfeit money.

TROFIMOV: You've read Nietzsche?

PISHCHIK: Well . . . Dashenka told me about it. And I am at this moment in such a situation that all I have left is to make counterfeit money. . . . The day after tomorrow, I must pay three hundred and ten rubles. . . . I have already found one hundred and thirty. (*He feels his pockets, uneasily.*) They're no longer there! I have lost them! (*Ready to weep*) Where is the money? (*Joyous*) There it is, in the lining . . . that made me sweat. . . .

(*Enter* LYUBOV ANDREYEVNA *and* CHARLOTTA IVANOVNA.)

LYUBOV ANDREYEVNA *(humming a* lezghinka.)[21] Why has
Leonid still not returned? What is he doing so late in town?
(To DUNYASHA*)* Dunyasha, take some tea to the musicians.

TROFIMOV: The auction most likely didn't take place.

LYUBOV ANDREYEVNA: To have the musicians at such a time,
and the ball at such a time . . . well, no matter . . . *(She
sits down and hums quietly.)*

CHARLOTTA *(holds out a deck of cards to* PISHCHIK*)*: Here,
here is a deck of cards. Think of a card.

PISHCHIK: There it is.

CHARLOTTA: Shuffle the cards. Very well. Give them to me;
oh, my dear Mr. Pishchik. *Eins, zwei, drei!* Now look, it
is in your pocket. . . .

PISHCHIK *(takes a card out of his pocket)*: The eight of
spades. Absolutely right. *(Amazed)* Imagine that!

CHARLOTTA *(holds out a deck of cards in her open hand to*
TROFIMOV*)*: Tell me quickly, what is the top card?

TROFIMOV: Well . . . the queen of spades.

CHARLOTTA: There it is! *(To* PISHCHIK*)* And you? What is the
top card?

PISHCHIK: The ace of hearts.

CHARLOTTA: There it is! *(She claps her hands, the deck of
cards disappears.)* How beautiful it is today! *(A mysterious
female voice answers her, coming from below the floor:
"Ah, yes, it is magnificent weather, madame.")* Youse is
my ideal. . . . *(The voice: "I likes you a lot, too, lady.")*

THE STATIONMASTER: Bravo, Mme Ventriloquist!

PISHCHIK *(amazed)*: Imagine that! Adorable Charlotta Ivanovna . . . I am simply in love with you. . . .

CHARLOTTA: In love? *(Shrugging her shoulders)*: As if you
could love? *Guter Mensch, aber schlechter Musikant.*[22]

TROFIMOV *(gives* PISHCHIK *a tap on his shoulder)*: Good for
the old horse . . .

CHARLOTTA: Attention! Another trick . . . *(She takes a foot
warmer off the chair.)* Here is an excellent foot warmer I
wish to sell. *(She shakes it.)* Nobody wishes to buy it?

PISHCHIK *(astonished)*: Imagine that!

CHARLOTTA: *Eins, zwei, drei! (Rapidly she shakes the foot
warmer, behind it is discovered* ANYA, *she curtsies, runs
toward her mother, kisses her and runs back to the ballroom
amid general enthusiasm.)*

LYUBOV ANDREYEVNA (*applauding*): Bravo, bravo!

CHARLOTTA: Once again! *Eins, zwei, drei! (She raises the foot warmer, behind which* VARYA *appears and greets everyone.)*

PISHCHIK (*astonished*): Imagine that!

CHARLOTTA: That is all! (*She throws the foot warmer on* PISHCHIK, *bows and runs out toward the drawing room.*)

PISHCHIK (*running after her*): Ah, the bad girl . . . What a woman! What a woman! (*He goes out.*)

LYUBOV ANDREYEVNA: Leonid is still not here. What he is doing so late in town, I do not understand! Everything must be over, the property sold. . . . Unless the auction did not take place . . . Why leave us so long in ignorance.

VARYA (*trying to console her*): Uncle bought it, I'm sure of it.

TROFIMOV (*mocking*): That's right.

VARYA: Great-aunt sent him the authority to buy it in her name, with a transfer of the mortgage. She is doing it for Anya. And I am sure, God willing, that Uncle bought it.

LYUBOV ANDREYEVNA: Your great-aunt from Yaroslavl has sent fifteen thousand rubles to buy back the property in her name. She doesn't have trust in us—that sum wouldn't even pay the interest. (*She hides her face in her hands.*) Today my fate is being decided, my fate. . . .

TROFIMOV (*teasing Varya*): Mme Lopahin!

VARYA (*angered*): Eternal student! Thrown out of the university twice already.

LYUBOV ANDREYEVNA: Why are you so angry, Varya? Because he teases you with Lopahin? Well, so what? If you so desired, why shouldn't you marry Lopahin; he's a splendid, intelligent fellow. If it doesn't please you, then don't marry him; nobody, darling, is forcing you to do it. . . .

VARYA: Let's look at this seriously, little Mama, I must tell you straight out. He is a good man and I like him.

LYUBOV ANDREYEVNA: Well, get married, then. What are you waiting for? I don't understand!

VARYA: But, little Mama, I can't propose to him myself. For two years everybody has been talking to me about him, everybody is talking and he, he keeps silent, or he makes jokes. . . . I understand him. He is getting richer and richer, he has his business, he doesn't have time for me. If I had money, a little money, even a hundred rubles, I would let everything go and go away, far away. To a convent I'd go.

TROFIMOV: What bliss!

VARYA: A student must show off his cleverness! *(Softly, on the verge of tears)* How ugly you've become, Petya, you've grown old. *(To* LYUBOV ANDREYEVNA*)* There is one thing I cannot stand, little Mama. Every minute I must be doing something.

(Enter YASHA.*)*

YASHA *(making an effort not to burst out laughing)*: Yepihodov broke a billiard cue! *(He goes out.)*

VARYA: Why is Yepihodov here? Who allowed him to play billiards? I don't understand these people. *(She goes out.)*

LYUBOV ANDREYEVNA: Don't tease her, Petya, you can see that she has enough trouble without that.

TROFIMOV: That girl is much too zealous, she butts in all the time. All summer long, she hasn't wanted to leave either of us in peace, Anya or myself, because she is afraid that we may be in love. What business is it of hers? All the more so since I gave her no cause. I'm beyond such trivialities. We are above love.

LYUBOV ANDREYEVNA: So I must be below love. *(In great anxiety)* Why doesn't Leonid return? If only I knew: was the orchard sold or not? Such a misfortune seems so incredible that I don't even know what to think. I'm at my wit's end. . . . I could begin shouting . . . or I could do something foolish. Help me, Petya. Say something, anything. . . .

TROFIMOV: What difference would it make if the property were sold today or not? At any rate, it's over and done with. No turning back, that road is closed. Calm yourself, stop deceiving yourself. For once in your life, look the truth in the face.

LYUBOV ANDREYEVNA: Which truth? You see the truth and what is not the truth, and I . . . one would say that I have lost my sight. I do not see anything. You find solutions to all the important questions, but tell me, my dear one, isn't that because you are young, and you have not yet had the time to suffer for any of these questions? If you look ahead with such bravery, isn't it perhaps because you don't expect to find anything frightening there, because life is still hidden from your young eyes? You are more courageous, more honest, more profound than we, but reflect a little, be generous, if only with tongue in cheek, have pity on me. You see, I was born here, here lived my father and mother, and my grandfather. . . . I love this house. Without the cherry orchard, I cease to comprehend anything about my life, and if it truly must be sold, then sell me right along with the orchard. . . . *(She puts her arms around* TROFIMOV *and kisses him on the forehead.)* Think, here is where my son drowned. . . . *(She cries.)* Have pity on me, you are a good, generous man. . . .

TROFIMOV: You know very well that I feel for you with all my heart.

LYUBOV ANDREYEVNA: But you must say it differently. *(She takes her handkerchief out; a telegram falls to the ground.)* My heart is so heavy today, you cannot imagine. There is too much noise here. Every noise makes me jump and I tremble at everything. And I cannot get myself to go alone to my room; when I am all alone, in the silence, I am afraid. Don't judge me too severely, Petya. I love you as if you were one of mine. It would give me great joy to see Anya marry you, but I appeal to you, you really must, my dear, finish your studies. Finish them up. You don't do anything, one might say that your fate throws you hither and yon, it's so strange. It's true, isn't it? And then you must do something with this beard so that it grows. I don't know, somehow . . . *(She laughs.)* You're funny!

TROFIMOV *(picking the telegram up)*: I don't have any desire to be a handsome fellow.

LYUBOV ANDREYEVNA: It's a telegram from Paris. I receive one every day. Yesterday and today as well. That madman is sick again, things are all wrong with him again. . . . He begs my pardon, he begs me to come, and to tell the truth, I ought to make a trip to Paris and stay with him. You look very strict, Petya, but what shall I do, my dear, he is sick, alone, unhappy, and with nobody to look after him, to prevent him from doing silly things, to give him his medicine at the proper time. And why hide it or keep quiet about it, it's evident. I love him, I love him. . . . He is a millstone around my neck, dragging me down with him, but I love this millstone, and I cannot live without it. *(She squeezes* TROFIMOV'S *hand.)* Do not think badly of me, Petya, don't say anything, don't say anything. . . .

TROFIMOV (*almost in tears*): Pardon my frankness, for heaven's sake, but he has robbed you!

LYUBOV ANDREYEVNA: No, no, no, you must not say such things! (*She puts her hands over her ears.*)

TROFIMOV: But he is a villain, only you do not seem to know that! A little villain and a nonentity! . . .

LYUBOV ANDREYEVNA (*angry, but controlling herself*): You're twenty-six or twenty-seven years old, and you're still a second-rate student.

TROFIMOV: So let me be!

LYUBOV ANDREYEVNA: You should be more manly. At your age, one must have understanding for those who love. You should be in love yourself . . . you should fall in love. (*Angrily*) Yes, yes! You're not all that pure, you're only a dissatisfied little fellow, a ridiculous freak, a monster. . . .

TROFIMOV (*horrified*): What is she saying!

LYUBOV ANDREYEVNA: "I am above love!" You are not above love, you're only, as Firs says, a clumsy fool. At your age, not to have a mistress! . . .

TROFIMOV (*horrified*): That's horrible! What is she saying! (*His head between his hands, he goes quickly to the ballroom.*) It's horrible. . . . I can't bear it, I'm going. . . . (*He goes off, but returns right away.*) Everything is finished between us.

LYUBOV ANDREYEVNA (*shouts after him*): Petya, wait! You ridiculous boy! I was joking! Petya!

(*Sound from the vestibule of someone going rapidly to the stairs, then suddenly falling down the stairs with a great din, shouts from ANYA and VARYA, and immediately after, the sound of laughter.*)

LYUBOV ANDREYEVNA: What's going on?

(*ANYA comes running in.*)

ANYA (*laughing*): Petya fell down the stairs. (*She runs out.*)

LYUBOV ANDREYEVNA: What a wild creature this Petya is!

(*The stationmaster plants himself in the middle of the room and begins to recite "The Sinful Woman" by Alexis Tolstoi.[23] They listen to him, but hardly has he gotten out a few verses than from the vestibule come the sounds of a waltz and the reading stops right there. Everybody dances.* TROFIMOV, ANYA, VARYA *and* LYUBOV ANDREYEVNA *return from the vestibule.*)

LYUBOV ANDREYEVNA: Come, Petya . . . come, my pure soul . . . I beg your pardon . . . come and dance with me. . . . *(She dances with* PETYA. ANYA *and* VARYA *dance together. Enter* FIRS; *he puts his cane down near the side door.* YASHA *also appears from the drawing room and looks at the dancing.)*

YASHA: What is it, Grandfather?

FIRS: I don't feel well. In the old days, we had generals, barons, admirals dancing at our balls, now we send for the station-master and the post office employee and even they don't come willingly. I feel quite weak. My poor master, their grandfather, treated all our maladies with sealing wax. I have taken some every day for twenty years now, or even more; perhaps that is why I am still alive.

YASHA: How fatiguing you can get, Grandpa. You ought to hurry up and croak.

FIRS: Go on . . . you clumsy fool!

(He mutters. TROFIMOV *and* LYUBOV ANDREYEVNA *dance in the ballroom and then in the drawing room.)*

LYUBOV ANDREYEVNA: *Merci;* I'm going to sit down a little now. . . . *(She sits down.)* I'm tired.

(Enter ANYA.)

ANYA *(agitated)*: Just now in the kitchen some fellow said that the cherry orchard was sold today.

LYUBOV ANDREYEVNA: Sold to whom?

ANYA: He didn't say to whom. He left. *(She dances with* TROFIMOV; *they go off into the ballroom.)*

YASHA: He's an old man come to tell tales. They don't know him.

FIRS: And Leonid Andreyevich is still not here. All he has on his back is his summer topcoat, he'll catch it. Oh, these young fools!

LYUBOV ANDREYEVNA: I'll die right this instant. Yasha, go and ask to whom it was sold.

YASHA: But he left a while ago, that old fellow. *(He laughs.)*

LYUBOV ANDREYEVNA *(irritated)*: Why are you laughing? What makes you so joyous?

YASHA: That Yepihodov, he's a funny one! A frivolous fellow. Twenty-two Troubles!

LYUBOV ANDREYEVNA: Firs, if the property is sold, where will you go?

FIRS: Where you tell me to go.

LYUBOV ANDREYEVNA: Why are you making such a face? Are you sick; you ought to go lie down. . . .

FIRS: That's right. . . . *(Smiling)* I shall go lie down, and without me, who'll be serving, who'll give the orders. There's only me here for all the house.

YASHA *(to* LYUBOV ANDREYEVNA*)*: Lyubov Andreyevna! I'd like to ask you something, if you would be so good as to hear me out. . . . Would you take me with you, please, if you go back to Paris. It is positively impossible for me to stay here. *(He casts a glance around him and begins to speak in a low voice.)* I don't need to tell you, you can see it, this country is uneducated, the people have no morals, and besides, it's boring, in the kitchen the food is terrible and that Firs wandering about everywhere and muttering the most outlandish things. Take me with you. I beg of you!

(Enter PISHCHIK.*)*

PISHCHIK: Will you grant me . . . a little waltz, my beautiful one. . . . *(*LYUBOV ANDREYEVNA *goes off with him.)* You ravishing beauty, all the same I'll take one hundred and eighty rubles from you. . . . I'll take them. . . . *(They begin to dance.)* One hundred and eighty rubles . . . *(They pass into the ballroom.)*

YASHA *(hums low)*: "Nobody knows the troubles I've seen. . . ."

(At the back of the ballroom we see a person in a top hat with square checked pants who waves his arms agitatedly and jumps around; shouts of "Bravo, Charlotta Ivanovna!")

DUNYASHA *(stopping to put on some powder)*: The young lady

told me to dance, there are many gentlemen and few ladies, but dancing makes me dizzy and gives me heart palpitations. Firs Nikolaievich, just now the postal employee said something to me that took my breath away!

(The music quiets down.)

FIRS: What did he say to you?

DUNYASHA: "You're like a flower," he said.

YASHA *(yawning)*: Ignorant . . . *(He goes out.)*

DUNYASHA: Like a flower . . . I am such a sensitive girl. I'm mad about loving words.

FIRS: You'll come to a bad end.

(Enter YEPIHODOV.)

YEPIHODOV: Avdotya Fyodorovna, you no longer wish to see me, I might as well be an insect. *(He sighs.)* Oh, what a life!

DUNYASHA: What can I do for you?

YEPIHODOV: Indubitably, you are perhaps right. *(He sighs.)* But, of course, if one looks at it from a certain point of view, then, if you permit me to express myself in this way, and if you will excuse my frankness, you have put me into such a state. I know my destiny, every day some misfortune or other befalls me; I've been used to that for a long time now, but I face up to my destiny with a smile. You have given me your word, and though I . . .

DUNYASHA: I beg of you, we will talk about this later, but now leave me in peace. Now I am dreaming. *(She plays with her fan.)*

YEPIHODOV: Every day I have a misfortune, and if you will permit me to express myself thusly, I only smile, and I even laugh.

(VARYA comes in from the ballroom.)

VARYA: Are you still here, Seymon? You are really a man who has no respect. *(To DUNYASHA)* Will you please get out of here, Dunyasha. *(To YEPIHODOV)* A while ago you played billiards and broke a cue, now you walk around the drawing room like an invited guest.

YEPIHODOV: You cannot tell me where to get off, if I may express myself in this way.

VARYA: I'm not telling you where to get off, I'm just telling you. All you know how to do is to go from place to place; as for work, you never indulge in it. We have a bookkeeper, one wonders whatever for.

YEPIHODOV *(offended)*: Whether I work or I walk about, or I eat or I play billiards, only those may discuss it who are older and wiser.

VARYA: How dare you speak to me in this way! *(Bursting)* How dare you! So I don't understand anything? Then get out of here! This minute!

YEPIHODOV *(getting frightened)*: I ask you to express yourself in a more genteel manner.

VARYA *(beside herself)*: This very minute! Out of here! Out! *(He goes toward the door; she follows him.)* Twenty-two Troubles! Get yourself out of here! Don't let me set eyes on you any more! *(YEPIHODOV goes out; from behind the door, one hears his voice: "I'll report you!")* Ah, you're back, are you? *(She takes up FIRS's cane, near the door.)* Come on . . . come on . . . come on, and you'll see. . . . Ah, you're coming? You're coming back? Here's for you. . . . *(She raises her arm to strike, just at the moment when LOPAHIN enters.)*

LOPAHIN: Thank you very much.

VARYA *(angry and superciliously ironical)*: Excuse me!

LOPAHIN: Go right ahead. Thank you for the nice greeting.

VARYA: You're welcome. *(She goes off, then returns and asks softly)* I didn't hurt you, did I?

LOPAHIN: No, it's nothing. Just an enormous bump.

VOICES COMING FROM THE BALLROOM: Lopahin is here! Yermolai Alexeyevich!

PISIICHIK: A sight for sore eyes . . . in the flesh . . . *(He embraces LOPAHIN.)* You smell slightly of cognac, my dear friend. But we aren't having a dull time here, either.

(Enter LYUBOV ANDREYEVNA.)

LYUBOV ANDREYEVNA: It's you, Yermolai Alexeyevich. Why so late? Where is Leonid?

LOPAHIN: Leonid Andreyevich is with me, he's coming. . . .

LYUBOV ANDREYEVNA (*agitated*): Well? Did the auction take place? Speak up!

LOPAHIN (*embarrassed, fearing to betray his joy*): The auction was over about four o'clock. . . . We missed the train, we had to wait for the nine-thirty one. (*Sighing deeply*) Ouf! I'm a little dizzy. . . .

(*Enter* GAYEV; *he has packages in his right hand. With the left, he wipes his tears.*)

LYUBOV ANDREYEVNA: Well, Lenya? Lenya, tell? (*Impatient, on the verge of tears*) Hurry up, for God's sake. . . .

GAYEV (*not answering, making a gesture of resignation; to* FIRS, *crying*): Take this . . . they're anchovies, Kerchenski herrings.[24] I haven't eaten anything today. . . . What I've been through! (*The door to the billiard room is open; the billiard balls can be heard clicking and the voice of* YASHA: "Seven and eighteen!" GAYEV *changes expression and stops crying.*) I am frightfully tired. Firs, come and get me changed. (*He crosses the ballroom to go to his room.* FIRS *follows him.*)

PISHCHIK: Well, how did the auction go? Tell us, already!

LYUBOV ANDREYEVNA: Was the cherry orchard sold?

LOPAHIN: Yes, it was.

LYUBOV ANDREYEVNA: Who bought it?

LOPAHIN: I did.

(*Pause.* LYUBOV ANDREYEVNA *is crushed; she would fall down were it not for a table and an armchair next to her.* VARYA *detaches the keys from her belt and throws them down on the ground in the middle of the drawing room and goes out.*)

LOPAHIN: I bought it! Wait a moment, be so kind, everything is mixed up in my head . . . I can't get a word out. . . . (*He laughs.*) When we got to the auction, Deriganov was already there. Leonid Andreyevich had only fifteen thousand rubles and Deriganov bid thirty more than the debt right away. When I saw that, I got right in there and I bid forty. And he bid forty-five. Then I bid fifty-five. And so he kept raising by fives and I by tens . . . and that's how we got to the end of it. I bid ninety thousand plus the debt and I got it. The cherry orchard is now mine! Mine! *(He laughs wildly.)* God in Heaven, the cherry orchard is mine! Tell me that I'm drunk, that I have lost my mind, that it's all my imagination. . . . *(He stamps his feet.)* Don't make fun of me! If my father and grandfather were to come out of their graves, and could see what is happening, how their Yermolai, this Yermolai, who was beaten, illiterate and went barefoot in the winter . . . how this same Yermolai bought this estate, the most beautiful in the world . . . I bought the estate in which my father and grandfather were slaves, where they didn't even allow them into the kitchen. I must be dreaming. I am having visions, it's only imagination. . . . All this is only a figment of my imagination, shrouded in mystery. . . . *(He picks up the keys, smiles gently.)* She threw down the keys to show that she was no longer mistress here. . . . *(He jangles the keys.)* Ah, well, it's all the same. *(They hear the orchestra tuning up.)* Ha! Musicians, play, I wish to hear you! Come here, all of you, and see how Yermolai Lopahin is going to take the ax to the cherry orchard, how the trees will crash to the ground! We shall construct villas here and our grandchildren and great-grandchildren will see a new life here. . . . Music! Play!

(The orchestra plays. LYUBOV ANDREYEVNA *has fallen into a chair and cries bitterly.)*

LOPAHIN *(reproachfully)*: Why, why didn't you listen to me; my poor, dear friend, you can't turn back now. *(Tearfully)* Ah, if we had all of that already behind us, if our unhappy, mixed-up lives could in some way be transformed.

PISHCHIK *(takes him by the arm; in a low voice)*: She is crying. Come into the ballroom, leave her alone. . . . Come. . . . *(He passes his arm under* LOPAHIN's *and leads him off to the ballroom.)*

LOPAHIN: Well, what! A little more feeling, please! Let it be the way I want it! *(With irony)* Here's the new landowner, the proprietor of the cherry orchard! *(He knocks up against a little round table by chance and almost knocks over a candelabra.)* I can pay for everything!

(He goes out with PISHCHIK. *There is no longer anyone*

in the ballroom, nor in the drawing room, except for LYUBOV ANDREYEVNA, *who, huddled in a chair, cries bitter tears. The music plays softly.* ANYA *and* TROFIMOV *enter quickly.* ANYA *goes to her mother and kneels before her.* TROFIMOV *remains at the entrance to the ballroom.)*

ANYA: Mama! Mama, are you crying? My dear, sweet, good Mama, my marvelous Mama, I love you. I bless you. The cherry orchard is sold, it's not here any more, it's true, but don't cry Mama, you still have your life ahead of you, your heart remains good and pure. . . . Come with me, come, my dear, let's get away! . . . We shall plant a new orchard, more splendid than this one; when you shall see it, you'll understand, and a sweet and profound joy will descend into your heart like an evening sun and you will smile, Mama! Come my darling! Let's go!

CURTAIN

ACT FOUR

The setting of the first act. Neither curtains, nor pictures, only some furniture piled up in a corner, as if for sale. One senses the void. Near the entranceway and at the back of the stage there are valises, bundles, etc.

By the left door, which is open, we hear the voices of VARYA and ANYA. LOPAHIN stands waiting. YASHA carries a platter with champagne glasses. In the vestibule, YEPIHODOV works hard to tie a rope around a case. A vague hubbub comes from the rear of the stage: peasants have assembled to say their good-byes. The voice of GAYEV: "Thank you, my dear friends, I thank you."

YASHA: The simple people come to make their good-byes. In my opinion, Yermolai Alexeyevich, they're not bad people, they just have no comprehension.

(The noise lessens. Coming from the vestibule, LYUBOV ANDREYEVNA and GAYEV arrive; she is pale but does not cry, her face is trembling; she cannot speak.)

GAYEV: You gave them your purse, Lyuba. It's really impossible! Impossible!
LYUBOV ANDREYEVNA: I couldn't help it! I just couldn't.

(They both go out.)

LOPAHIN (*in the direction of the door, after them*): Will you be so kind, please! A little glass before parting. I didn't think of getting any in town; at the station there was only one bottle. Come! (*Pause*) What's the matter? You don't want any? (*He goes away from the door.*) If I had known, I wouldn't have bought any. Well, I won't have any, either. (YASHA *puts the platter down on a chair with caution.*) Take a glass, at least you, Yasha.

YASHA: To the health of the travelers! Good luck to those who are staying behind! (*He drinks.*) That never was champagne, I can guarantee it.

LOPAHIN: The bottle is worth eight rubles. (*Pause*) It's as cold as the devil here.

YASHA: There was no heat today; anyhow, we're leaving. (*He laughs.*)

LOPAHIN: What's got into you?

YASHA: I'm so happy. Such pleasure.

LOPAHIN: We're in the month of October, but it's as mild and sunny as in summer. Good for building. (*He looks at the time and says in the direction of the door*) People, keep in mind, there are only forty-seven minutes before train time! We must leave for the station in twenty minutes. Hurry.

(TROFIMOV, *wearing an overcoat, comes in from outside.*)

TROFIMOV: I think it's time to go. The carriage is waiting. Where the devil did I put my rubbers? They've disappeared. (*From the door*) Anya, I have no rubbers! I didn't find them!

LOPAHIN: And I must go to Kharkov. I'm taking the same train as you. I'll stay in Kharkov all winter. I've been hanging around with you all, I'm exhausted from doing nothing. I cannot live without working, I don't know what to do with my arms; it's funny, they just hang there, as if they didn't belong to me.

TROFIMOV: We shall be leaving in a moment, and you can take up your useful work again.

LOPAHIN: Well, then, have a glass.

TROFIMOV: I don't want one.

LOPAHIN: So, it's Moscow for you?

TROFIMOV: Yes, I'll accompany them to town and tomorrow I leave for Moscow.

LOPAHIN: Good . . . Well, anyway, the professors aren't giving any lectures while they're waiting for you to get there.

TROFIMOV: Mind your own business.

LOPAHIN: For how many years have you been at the university?

TROFIMOV: Think up something new; this joke is becoming old and stupid. (*He looks for his rubbers.*) You know, we may never see each other again, so allow me to give you a piece of advice before we separate: stop waving your arms! Get rid of that habit, that waving. And another thing: this building of summerhouses, and your plans of the summer people one day being turned into private owners—that adds up to the same thing as waving your arms about. . . . But, all things considered, I still like you. You have fine and gentle fingers like an artist. You're a fine and gentle person. . . .

LOPAHIN (*puts his arms around him*): Farewell, little one. Thank you for everything. If you need it, take some money from me for the trip.

TROFIMOV: Whatever for? I don't need any.

LOPAHIN: But you don't have any!

TROFIMOV: Yes, I do. I thank you. I got some for a translation. It's here in my pocket. (*Anxious*) But I can't find my rubbers.

VARYA (*from the other room*): Take your dirty things! (*She throws a pair of rubbers onstage.*)

TROFIMOV: But why are you so angry, Varya? Hmm . . . They're not my rubbers!

LOPAHIN: In the springtime I sowed nearly three acres of poppies, that brought me forty thousand rubles profit clear. When my poppies were in flower, what a lovely picture that was! That's what I'm telling you, it brought me forty thousand rubles, so I'd like to offer you the help because I can do it. Why have you got your nose up in the air? I'm a peasant, I'm blunt.

TROFIMOV: Your father was a muzhik and mine was a druggist, and so what? What does that prove? (LOPAHIN *takes out his wallet.*) Enough of that, that's enough. . . . You could offer me two hundred thousand rubles and I wouldn't take them. I am a free man, and everything that is lofty and precious for you all, rich or poor, has no more power over me than thistledown floating in the air. I can do without you, I can ignore you, I am strong and proud. Humanity is marching toward a higher truth, toward the greatest happiness that it is possible to imagine on earth. I am in the first rank.

LOPAHIN: And will you get there?

TROFIMOV: I shall. *(Pause)* I shall get there on my own, or I shall show others how to get there.

(From afar one hears an ax striking against a tree trunk.)

LOPAHIN: Well, farewell, my boy. Here we are, both of us looking down our noses at each other, and all this time life goes on. When I work for a long time without stopping, it is easier for me to think and I seem to know why I exist. There are lots of people in Russia who exist, my boy, without knowing why. Oh, well, so what, that's not the be all and end all. They say Leonid Andreyevich has taken a job at the bank for six thousand a year. . . . Only, he won't stay there, he's so lazy.

ANYA *(in the doorway)*: Mama asks you not to cut down the trees before she goes.

TROFIMOV: Really, could they be that tactless. . . . *(He goes out by the vestibule.)*

LOPAHIN: Sure, sure . . . they're too much, really! *(He follows him.)*

ANYA: Did they take Firs to the hospital?

YASHA: I told them to, this morning. It must have been done, I guess.

ANYA *(to* YEPIHODOV, *who goes through the ballroom)*: Semyon Panteleich, will you please find out if they really took Firs to the hospital.

YASHA *(offended)*: I told Yegor to do it this morning. Why ask the same thing a dozen times?

YEPIHODOV: That aged Firs, in my final opinion, is too far gone, he can't be fixed up any more. All that's left to him is to join his ancestors. I can only envy him. *(He puts down a valise on a hatbox, which he crushes.)* Well, obviously that was meant to be. *(He goes out.)*

YASHA *(mocking)*: Twenty-two Troubles . . .

VARYA *(behind the door)*: Did they take Firs to the hospital?

ANYA: Yes.

VARYA: Then why didn't they take the letter for the doctor?

ANYA: We'll have to send it on. . . . *(She goes out.)*

VARYA *(from the next room)*: Where is Yasha? Tell him that his mother is here, she wants to say good-bye to him.

YASHA *(with a gesture of his hand)*: They put you out of patience.

> (DUNYASHA *pretends she is busy around the valises; now that she is alone with* YASHA, *she approaches him.)*

DUNYASHA: You might at least give me a little glance, Yasha. . . . You're going. . . . You're abandoning me. . . . *(She throws herself at his neck, weeping.)*

YASHA: Why weep? *(He drinks champagne.)* In six days I'll be in Paris again. Tomorrow we are taking the express and then we'll be off and you won't see us any more. I can't really believe it. *Vive la France!* Here it's not for me, it is impossible for me to live here, nothing to do about that. I've had my fill of this ignorance, that's enough of that. *(He drinks champagne.)* Why weep? Behave yourself, then there won't be any reason to cry.

DUNYASHA *(puts powder on her face in front of a little pocket mirror)*: Write me about Paris. You know I've loved you, Yasha, I've loved you so much! I am such a tender thing, Yasha!

YASHA: They're coming.

> (He putters around the valises, humming softly. Enter LYUBOV ANDREYEVNA, GAYEV, ANYA *and* CHARLOTTA IVANOVNA.)

GAYEV: We must go. We have very little time left. *(Looking at* YASHA) Who smells so strongly of herring?

LYUBOV ANDREYEVNA: In about ten minutes we'll have to get into the carriage. . . . *(She glances around her.)* Farewell, dear house, old grandmother. The winter will pass, the spring will come, and you will be no longer, they will demolish you. What these walls have seen! *(She embraces her daughter passionately.)* My treasure, you look radiant, your eyes are throwing fire, like two diamonds. You're content? Very much so?

ANYA: Very! It's a new life that's beginning, Mama!

GAYEV *(gaily)*: Anyhow, everything's fine now. Before the

sale of the cherry orchard, we were all upset, we suffered, and now that the thing is settled irrevocably, everybody has calmed down, we have even regained our good humor. . . . Here I am a bank employee, I am at this moment a financier. . . . Red to the side pocket, and you, Lyuba, somehow you look better, that's for sure.

LYUBOV ANDREYEVNA: Yes. My nerves are better, it's true. *(They bring her her hat and her coat.)* I sleep well. Take my things, Yasha. It's time. *(To* ANYA*)* My little girl, we shall see one another soon. . . . I am going to Paris, I shall live there with the money that your Yaroslavl aunt sent to buy the estate—long live Auntie!—but that money won't last long.

ANYA: You'll return, Mama, very, very soon . . . isn't that so? I shall prepare my exams, I shall pass them, and then I shall work, I will help you. And we shall read together, all sorts of books . . . isn't that so? Mama? *(She kisses her mother's hands.)* During the long autumn evenings, we shall read, we shall read books, and a new and marvelous world will open before us. . . . *(She dreams.)* Come back, Mama. . . .

LYUBOV ANDREYEVNA: I shall return, my treasure.

(She takes her daughter in her arms. Enter LOPAHIN. CHARLOTTA *hums softly.)*

GAYEV: Happy Charlotta, she's singing!

CHARLOTTA *(takes up a bundle that looks like a baby in swaddling clothes)*: Sleep, my little one, sleep tight. . . . *(One hears the cries of an infant: "Wa! Wa!)* Shhh, you poor little thing. *(She throws the bundle down.)* Please, you must find me a job. I cannot go on this way.

LOPAHIN: We shall find one for you, Charlotta Ivanovna, don't be upset.

GAYEV: Everybody is abandoning us. Varya is going away. . . . All of a sudden, nobody needs us any more.

CHARLOTTA: I have no place to live in town. Well, I must go. . . . *(She hums.)* What does it all matter. . . .

(Enter PISHCHIK.*)*

LOPAHIN: Will wonders never cease! . . .

PISHCHIK (*out of breath*): Oh, let me catch my breath. . . .
I'm exhausted. . . . Honorable people . . . Give me some
water. . . .

GAYEV: You're going to ask for some money, I suppose?
Your humble servant. I'll keep out of trouble. . . . (*He goes
out.*)

PISHCHIK: It's been a little while since I've come to see you,
lovely lady. (*To* LOPAHIN) Ah, you're there, you . . . happy
to see you . . . a man of superior intelligence. . . . Here, take
this. . . . (*He holds out money to* LOPAHIN.) Four hundred
rubles . . . I still owe you eight hundred and forty. . . .

LOPAHIN (*shrugging his shoulders, perplexed*): Maybe I'm
dreaming? Where did you get it?

PISHCHIK: Wait . . . I'm so hot. . . . A most extraordinary
event . . . Some Englishmen came along and found some
sort of white clay on my land. . . . (*To* LYUBOV ANDREYEV-
NA) And here are the four hundred that I owed you . . .
beautiful and adorable lady. . . . (*He gives her money.*) The
rest, later. (*He drinks some water.*) Just now, a young man
was saying in the train that I don't know which great
philosopher recommended jumping off the roof. . . . "Jump!"
said he. "That's the crux of it." (*Astonished*) Imagine that!
Water!

LOPAHIN: Who are all these Englishmen?

PISHCHIK: I leased out the land with the clay on it for twenty-
four years. . . . And now, excuse me, I'm in a great
hurry. . . . I must run along somewhere else. . . . I have
to go over to Zonoikov's, Kardamanov's . . . I owe everybody. (*He drinks.*) I give you my greetings. I'll stop by
Thursday.

LYUBOV ANDREYEVNA: We're in the midst of moving to town,
and tomorrow I'm going abroad.

PISHCHIK: What? (*Disturbed*) Why to town? That's why all
this furniture . . . and the valises . . . Well, it's all the
same. . . . (*Through tears*) Such smart people . . . those
Britishers. . . . No matter . . . be happy. . . . God will help
you. . . . In this world, everything comes to an end. . . .
(*He kisses* LYUBOV ANDREYEVNA's *hand.*) And if ever you
should hear tell that my time in this world has come to an
end, remember this . . . horse and say, "There was once
in the world a certain Simeonov-Pishchik, may the Kingdom
of Heaven be his. . . ." Marvelous weather we're having . . .

yes. . . . (*He goes out in a state of complete confusion, but returns immediately and says from the doorway*) Dashenka sends you her best! (*He goes out.*)

LYUBOV ANDREYEVNA: Now we can go. I take with me two worries. The first is Firs, sick as he is. (*She looks at her watch.*) We still have five minutes.

ANYA: Mama, they took Firs to the hospital. Yasha saw to it this morning.

LYUBOV ANDREYEVNA: My second worry is Varya. She is used to getting up early and working, and when she has nothing to do, she is like a fish out of water. She has gotten thinner, paler, and she's crying all the time, poor thing. . . . (*Pause*) You know quite well, Yermolai Alexeyevich, that I dreamed . . . of marrying her to you; besides, everything led us to believe that you would marry her. (*She says something in a low voice to* ANYA; *the latter makes a signal to* CHARLOTTA *and both go out.*) She loves you, you seem to find her to your taste, and I don't know, I don't know why you seem to wish to avoid one another. I don't understand!

LOPAHIN: I admit I don't understand it very well myself. All this is strange. . . . If it isn't too late, I'm ready right now. . . . Let's be done with it right away and once for all. *Basta!* I have a feeling that without you, I'd never propose to her.

LYUBOV ANDREYEVNA: That's fine. It'll be done in a moment. I'll go call her.

LOPAHIN: The champagne is already poured. (*He looks at the glasses.*) They're empty, somebody already drank it. (YASHA *coughs.*) And that's what's called really lapping it up. . . .

LYUBOV ANDREYEVNA (*animated*): That's perfect, we shall leave you. . . . Yasha, *allez!* I'll go call her. . . . (*Through the door*) Varya, stop everything and come here. Come on! (*She goes out with* YASHA.)

LOPAHIN (*looks at the time*): Yes . . .

> (*Pause. Behind the door, a stifled laugh, murmuring; finally* VARYA *appears.*)

VARYA (*examining the luggage for a long time*): That's strange, seems I don't know where I put it. . . .

LOPAHIN: What are you looking for?

VARYA: I myself put it in a valise, and I don't remember.

(Pause.)

LOPAHIN: Well, where you going now, Varvara Mikhailovna?

VARYA: Me? To the Ragulins' . . . I arranged with them to look after their house . . . as a sort of governess, I suppose.

LOPAHIN: In Yashnevo? About fifty miles from here. *(Pause)* Here in this house, life has come to an end.

VARYA *(examining the baggage)*: Where could it be? . . . Or else it might be in this trunk. . . . Yes, life in this house has ended . . . and will not start up again. . . .

LOPAHIN: I'm leaving now for Kharkov . . . by the same train. I have a lot of work to do. I'm leaving Yepihodov here . . . I've hired him.

VARYA: Well!

LOPAHIN: Last year, at this time, it was already snowing, if you remember, and this year it's nice and sunny. If it weren't for the cold . . . three degrees below.

VARYA: I didn't notice. *(Pause)* Besides, our thermometer is broken. . . .

(Pause. A voice comes from outside the door: "Yermolai Alexeyevich!")

LOPAHIN *(as if he had been waiting for this call for a long time)*: I'm coming!

(He goes out rapidly. VARYA, seated on the ground, her head on a bundle of clothes, sobs noiselessly. The door opens, LYUBOV ANDREYEVNA enters prudently.)

LYUBOV ANDREYEVNA: Well? *(Pause)* We must go.

VARYA *(doesn't cry any more; she wipes her eyes)*: Yes, it's time, little Mama. From today on I'll be at the Ragulins', if we don't miss the train.

LYUBOV ANDREYEVNA *(through the door)*: Anya, get dressed!

(Enter ANYA, then GAYEV, CHARLOTTA IVANOVNA. GAYEV wears a huge overcoat and a sort of wool cap.[25] The servants arrive, the coachmen, too. YEPIHODOV busies himself with the luggage.)

LYUBOV ANDREYEVNA: Now we can be on our way.

ANYA *(joyous)*: On our way!

GAYEV: My dear, dear friends, my dear friends! Leaving this house forever, I could not keep silent. Before saying the last farewell, I could not restrain the expression of the feelings that now fill all of my being. . . .

ANYA *(begging)*: Uncle!

VARYA: No, Uncle dear, don't!

GAYEV *(gloomy)*: Double bank the red into the side pocket . . . I shall keep silent. . . .

(Enter TROFIMOV, *then* LOPAHIN.*)*

TROFIMOV: Well, people, it's time to go.

LOPAHIN: Yepihodov, my overcoat!

LYUBOV ANDREYEVNA: I am going to sit down for one more minute. It seems to me that I have never seen the walls of this house, and the ceilings, and I look at them covetously, with such a tender love. . . .

GAYEV: I remember when I was six years old, it was on Trinity Sunday,[26] I was seated by this window and I was looking at Father, who was going off to church. . . .

LYUBOV ANDREYEVNA: Has all the baggage been taken?

LOPAHIN: I think all of it has. *(To* YEPIHODOV, *putting on his overcoat)* I count on you, Yepihodov, see that everything is in order.

YEPIHODOV *(breathlessly)*: Rest assured, Yermolai Alexeyevich!

LOPAHIN: What's the matter with your voice?

YEPIHODOV: I just drank some water. I swallowed something the wrong way.

YASHA *(with scorn)*: Such ignorance . . .

LYUBOV ANDREYEVNA: Once we leave, there'll be no living soul here. . . .

LOPAHIN: Until spring.

VARYA *(pulls her umbrella from one of the bundles with a sharp movement, as if she was going to beat someone;* LOPAHIN *feigns fright)*: Really, really, I didn't mean it.

TROFIMOV: Come, people, it's time to get into the carriage. . . . It's late! The train is arriving soon!

VARYA: Petya, here are your rubbers, next to the valise. *(In tears)* How dirty and old they are. . . .

TROFIMOV (*puts on his rubbers*): Come on, people!

GAYEV (*very embarrassed, afraid of breaking into sobs*): The train . . . the station . . . Cross to the side, then cushion off the ball into the corner pocket. . . .

LYUBOV ANDREYEVNA: Come on!

LOPAHIN: Everybody here? Nobody remaining behind? (*He locks the door on the left side.*) They've piled up some things in there. I'll lock it up. Come on!

ANYA: Farewell, house! Farewell, the old life!

TROFIMOV: Greetings to the new life!

(*He goes out with* ANYA. VARYA *looks around her and goes out slowly.* YASHA *and* CHARLOTTA, *with her little dog, also go out.*)

LOPAHIN: We'll see one another in the spring. Let's go, people. . . . Bye-bye! (*He goes out.*)

(LYUBOV ANDREYEVNA *and* GAYEV *remain alone. They seem to have been waiting for this moment. They throw themselves in each other's arms and sob, holding back, for fear they may be heard.*)

GAYEV (*in despair*): My sister, my sister . . .

LYUBOV ANDREYEVNA: Oh, my dear, dear, lovely, beautiful orchard! My life, my youth, my happiness, farewell! . . . Farewell! . . .

THE VOICE OF ANYA (*gaily appealing*): Mama! . . .

LYUBOV ANDREYEVNA: A last look at the walls, the windows . . . Mama loved to come and go in this room. . . .

GAYEV: My sister, my sister!

THE VOICE OF ANYA: Mama!

THE VOICE OF TROFIMOV: Yoo-hoo! . . .

LYUBOV ANDREYEVNA: We're coming! . . .

(*They go out. The stage is empty. One hears the doors being locked, the carriages starting up. Silence takes over, cut by the dull thud on the wood, solitary and sad. Footsteps are heard. By the door at the right,* FIRS *appears. He is dressed as usual, with a jacket, a white vest and slippers. He is ill.*)

FIRS (*approaching the door, tries the handle*): Locked. They have gone. . . . (*He sits down on the divan.*) They have forgotten me. . . . That makes no difference. . . . I will sit here for a moment. . . . Leonid Andreich surely left without his fur-lined cloak, went out without his overcoat on. . . . (*Troubled sighs*) I didn't come and oversee things. . . . These youngsters! . . . (*He mutters something incomprehensible.*) Life has gone by, as if I'd never lived. (*He stretches out.*) I shall stretch out for a moment. . . . You have no more strength left, there is nothing left, nothing. . . . Oh, you . . . you clumsy fool! . . .

(*He remains lying down, motionless. One hears from afar, as if coming from the heavens, the sound of a breaking string, a sound that dies out sadly. The silence takes over, and one hears only the faraway thud of the ax on the wood, deep in the orchard.*)

CURTAIN

AFTERWORD

There is a very fine line between comedy and tragedy, and few authors ever walked that fine line more subtly than Anton Chekhov. *The Cherry Orchard* is considered by most admirers of Chekhov's work to be his most felicitous and perhaps most typical work. We know that Chekhov intended it to be a comedy and that he insisted against all odds that it was not a tragedy. "Why," he would ask his wife, "in the advertisements and in the newspaper publicity, is my play obstinately called a drama?" He felt that his interpreters in the Moscow Art Theater had manifestly misunderstood his intentions. To this very day the play is usually presented as a *"comédie larmoyante,"* a slice of life that brings us to the verge of tears. Chekhov's characters are "lovable," but their frailties are, after all, exploited relentlessly. Actually, Chekhov's viewpoint about his characters was razor sharp. He sees them with the lucidity of an Ionesco, aware of their slightest absurdities in speech, and places them in the most farcical of situations. Farce, as we know, is a subtle mélange of comedy with tragic overtones. The peculiar acceleration of rhythm that is the hallmark of farce cannot quite be accomplished unless comedy is threatened by tragic freedom. But all of this risks being a parade of subtle definitions, for one man's comedy can very well be another's tragedy and all the vice versas possible.

The Cherry Orchard presents what might be called the quintessential Chekhovian situation: dispossession. It was already a major theme of Chekhov's earliest play, *Platonov* (known as *Don Juan in the Russian Manner* and *A Country Scandal* in different adaptations), and was probably a literary metamorphosis of the very real fear of dispossession that happened to the Chekhov family when their father went bankrupt early in Anton Chekhov's life. In one way or another, all of Chekhov's characters have a sense of deep loss, whether

277

it be personal or proprietal. All of the characters in *The Cherry Orchard* participate in a dying way of life, almost congenitally unable to unearth themselves from the ennui and sloth of their existence, though lucid enough to sense that their way of life is coming to an end. Since the subject is such a seriously valid one and was, in one sense, a prediction of the impending Russian Revolution, it is easy to see why no one would believe Chekhov when he thought that *The Cherry Orchard* should produce laughter rather than tears.

Stanislavski's own reaction to the play paved the way for the world's misunderstanding of Chekhovian irony. He wrote to Chekhov to disagree with him as to the tone of the play (October 20, 1903):

> In my opinion, *The Cherry Orchard* is your best play. I have become even more attached to it than to your dear *Sea Gull*. It is not a comedy, not a farce as you say it is—it is a tragedy, however it may lead towards a better life—which you suggest in the last act. It produces an immense impression, obtained by half-tones, tender tones of a water color. It possesses more poetry and lyricism, it is more scenic; all the roles, even the one of the "passerby," are brilliantly conceived. If one were to ask me which one I liked the best, I would be embarrassed, they are all so attractive to me. I think it is too subtle for the public. It doesn't understand fine things right away. Alas, how much we would need to keep reading and listening to the play! Despite everything, its success will be immense, for the play takes hold of you. Everything in it holds together so perfectly that not one word could be rejected. I may be prejudiced, but I find no fault in it. Except this one: it must have great actors in it, with much finesse, to reveal all of its beauties. We couldn't possibly do it. At a first reading, I was troubled by the following thing: the play seized me immediately, I began to live it instantly; now that was not true for *The Sea Gull* or for *The Three Sisters*. I was used to the first readings of your plays leaving me with more vague impressions. That is why I was afraid to be less taken

with it on a second reading. Well! I cried like a
woman, I wanted to and I couldn't stop. I hear you
saying: "Allow me to tell you, it's a farce. . . ." No,
for a simple man, it's a tragedy. . . .

Stanislavski's intelligent but rather overbearing decision to
opt for tragedy here is not entirely wrongheaded. *The Cherry
Orchard* is the story of the end of a way of life and comedy
can be made of tragic materials. In fact, comedy cannot really
exist without tragedy. The sale of the orchard, the departure
of Lyubov Andreyevna from her home, the leaving behind
of the faithful retainer, Firs—all these events have tragic
implications. Whereas it is repeatedly suggested that a new
life is about to begin, we are more than well aware that few
if any of the characters of the play will participate in it. They
will continue in their hit-and-miss way of life. For a person
with feelings, *The Cherry Orchard* is tragic in conception. But
let us see how Chekhov undertook to paint his canvas, what
he chose as the great salient moments of his work, how he
depicted his characters and what traits he gave them, the
juxtaposition of scenes and the moments he chose to depict.
We shall see that the tragic situation has been fleshed out in
a comic tone. It is perhaps just as much of an error to see
only the comic aspects of Chekhov's work, but it is useless to
interpret a work of art only in terms of its subject matter.
For an oversensitive person, life is tragic, all of it. Chekhov
was attuned to subtler ironies.

First, the characterizations: Lyubov Andreyevna is an
appealing woman. She was once beautiful. She has strong emotions. What we learn of her is reflected in flashback recollec-
tions as bits and pieces of her life are told. She is essentially
a loose woman who has devoted herself to a wastrel of a
fellow most adept at robbing her of her money and possessions. He sends her telegrams, which she usually tears up,
though she loves him uncontrollably. At the end of the play
she goes back to the same pattern: he will undoubtedly continue to make her suffer. She is a woman of singular lack of
control. She will give her last gold piece to a stranger while
her family goes begging. She is sentimental about her cherry
orchard but she will do nothing to save it. She is vain, selfish
and spoiled. The money she gets from her great-aunt to buy
the cherry orchard she will keep to continue her extravagant

life in Paris. Her brother, Gayev, is a waspish, punctilious bachelor who talks too much and is given to apostrophizing bookcases and talking in restaurants to waiters about literary movements they could never comprehend. He stuffs himself with hard candy and when he is nervous, he makes believe he is thinking of brilliant billiard shots. He is proud of his cherry orchard in a vague familial way but is just as spoiled and childish as Lyubov Andreyevna. They quarrel and bicker like two little children. Yet they love one another deeply and at the end of the play they are like two little children who have lost their playpens and feel like crying together. They remain irrevocably tied to the emotions of their childhood. One could have great compassion for them were they not shown again and again to be so ludicrously petty.

In contrast to them, Lopahin, the merchant, represents the triumph of the crass nouveau riche. Lopahin was once their servant and he continues this role symbolically until the moment when he buys the orchard. He devotes the entire play to trying to get them to take steps to save it, plays the voice of doom to no avail. When, most ironically, it is he who acquires the orchard, he swaggers and behaves like a bully. But he is also the most honest of all the characters in the play. There is a true nobility in his character and he shows generosity where he might be cruel, but he is also aware of his peasant background and blundering nature. He can never erase the crudity, and acquire the natural, superficial finesse of a Lyubov or a Gayev.

Trofimov, the eternal student, the prophet of the new age, is a takeoff on the shabbily dressed self-styled intellectual, old before his time, spouting homilies about the coming of a better world. He may be a noble character but his rubbers are dirty, he is an inept lover and believes he is above love: his lyricism is poverty-stricken.

All of the secondary characters are comic figures. Anya is spoiled, selfish, solipsistic, easily swayed by Trofimov's vision of a life of work, for which she is temperamentally unsuited. Varya is a compulsive, fearful, tearful, fussing creature, superstitious, hard-working, basically unperceptive and choleric. Her perpetual capacity for petulance engenders some of the best comic moments of the plays. Simeonov-Pishchik, the neighbor who is always trying to borrow money because he is further and further crippled by debt, is hale and hearty and believes himself descended from Caligula's horse.

Charlotta Ivanovna is the one anomaly of the play. Chekhov originally intended her to be one of the most important characters and the role was tailored to the talents of his wife, Olga Knipper Chekhova. But as the play evolved she was relegated to a more minor position and some of her dialogue was cut. Hers is the role most suited to the play's theme of dispossession. For it is she who has the obscure background, who feels most dispossessed and cut off in her life. Were it not for her capacity for magic tricks and her petulance, her Germanic oddities, she would be a mysteriously dramatic figure, and at moments in the play she seems to be very much of another place. Yepihodov, "Twenty-two Troubles," is a baleful fellow, awkward and self-pitying, who strums guitars while insisting they are mandolins and constantly meditates suicide or a desperate act. One need only compare him with the eccentric Solyony of *The Three Sisters* to see how the same basic character may be treated in either comic or tragic fashion. Yepihodov fancies he is in love with Dunyasha, the maid, who is a caricature of the young naïve creature who assumes the fantasies of rich young ladies, thinks she is sensitive and imagines that everybody is in love with her. She is forever swooning over her possibilities but she meets her match in the archsnob Yasha, Lyubov's new valet, who is more slob than snob and attracted like iron filings to the magnet of Paris, caviar, champagne and the high life. Last, but certainly not least, is the delightfully crotchety eighty-seven-year-old retainer, Firs, who is left behind at the end of the play to die because everybody has put him out of mind in the haste of leaving. He considers Lyubov and Gayev to be little children who must be managed and catered to—and for the most part his vision of them is accurate. The twelve characters of *The Cherry Orchard* are provided with more than their share of foolish foibles. And so the characterization, as we see, is very much of a comic complexion.

The events of the play: Unlike the other plays of Chekhov, in which there are big scenes and climaxes, *The Cherry Orchard* is a series of kaleidoscopic vignettes. Cameo scenes mingle with each other in rapid succession and, in sharp contrast to Chekhov's other plays, it is not till the end of an act that one feels that the scene is complete. Act One is the moody homecoming of Lyubov Andreyevna and Anya. It is fraught with poetry of varying tastes: almost everyone becomes lyrical about the homecoming. Lopahin is as nervous as a little boy. Yasha discovers Dunyasha and flirts outrageously. Anya falls asleep on Varya as she bewails her unpleasant surroundings. Gayev makes a speech to the bookcase and generally rhapsodizes about the difficulty of living. Trofimov makes Lyubov cry and awakens Anya. Charlotta's dog eats hazel nuts. Firs chides everybody and is happily in his element. The homecoming of Act One is a bustle of happy possibilities.

Act Two is a *fête champêtre*. Lyubov, Gayev and Lopahin have been to town, eaten too much, talked too much, drunk too much, and each is out of sorts. Gayev hates Yasha and they insult each other. Lyubov gives her money to a passerby, who frightens Varya. Trofimov talks on about a new life to come. Lopahin warns them all that the cherry orchard is to be sold at auction. Anya's platonic affair with Trofimov becomes serious. Varya jealously tries to spy on them at every opportunity. The outdoor scene is a comedy of small errors.

Act Three represents the awaited, climactic scene. Lyubov waits for the results of the auction. It is the wrong night for inviting guests and the famous local Jewish orchestra. But there they are and Charlotta does magic tricks to amuse the guests. Simeonov-Pishchik, as always, tries to borrow money from the guests. The party is a mockery of the old days, when true elegance prevailed. Now even the post office clerk grumbles when he is invited. Trofimov claims he is above love and Lyubov makes fun of him. He falls down a flight of stairs and Lyubov placates him by dancing with him. Yepihodov pines with love for Dunyasha and she pursues Yasha with her favors. Yepihodov breaks a billiard cue and angers Varya to the point where she wishes to strike him with Firs's cane. Lopahin walks in at that moment and receives the blow. The running gag of the entire play has been the impending marriage of Varya and Lopahin. Everyone talks of it and both parties are mystified. Neither is the least bit fond of the other and they tease each other mercilessly. Now Lopahin has bought the orchard, he exults, knocks over tables and claims he will pay for the damages. Lyubov's despair is counterpoint to Lopahin's exaltation. She cries to the background of a sentimental waltz. Lopahin pities her but he can no longer help her. Anya pities her and prattles on about a better life. The ludicrous climax of Act Three is one of the great Chekhovian moments and shows us clearly how close tragedy and comedy can come. The suffering of Lyubov and Gayev is so inevitable, the triumph of Lopahin so much a matter of history (*The Cherry Orchard*, like *The Marriage of Figaro*, prefigures a great social upheaval in terms of the deftest farce). The end of the act is heartbreaking, and yet full of comic poetic justice. Gayev can only think he hasn't eaten since morning. He brings back some herring. The little irrelevancies of life bring tragedy down to a mundane level.

The last act of *The Cherry Orchard* is a slow leave-taking, lugubrious and full of lulls. It is also full of deft comic situations. Dunyasha begs Yasha to be nice to her, for she is such a tender creature. Trofimov looks for his rubbers and Varya keeps finding the wrong pair and throwing them at him. Lyubov and Gayev keep saying farewell and talking too much. Simeonov-Pishchik arrives with money for everyone; by some mad irony, valuable clay has been found on his land. He barely notices that everyone is leaving. Yasha assures everyone that Firs has been taken to the hospital. Firs's last words, as he is walled in, echo the sentiment that his life has truly not been lived (worthy of a Samuel Beckett moment). Varya and Lopahin are finally thrust together for their big moment. Varya talks on about irrelevancies and Lopahin is infinitely relieved to be able to go off without proposing. The entire last act is a comedy of errors, mumbling and grumbling, as a way of life comes ingloriously to its end. Tragedy is fraught with comic situations and ludicrous moments.

In *The Sea Gull*, Chekhov had difficulty manipulating the farce with the tragic overtones. Some of his comic scenes were too heavy for their tragic content. Suicide never seems quite funny when it is accomplished. The characters were also a bit too romantic to remain caricatures. In *Uncle Vanya*, the tone is uniformly dark and the last act is a long elegy of farewell that contains no comic relief. *The Three Sisters* is an authentic drama and the characters of Masha, Irina and Olga are definitely not comic creations. In all of Chekhov's major plays before *The Cherry Orchard*, suicide or murder is an integral element of the plays' plotting. In *The Cherry Orchard* the pistol shot has been exorcized. Yepihodov may threaten to commit suicide but the threat is an empty one. Grisha, Lyubov's son, has died long since, and Firs is spiritually dead long

before the end of the play. He has lived his life. Chekhov chose
to emphasize traits in each of his characters that become
characteristic and funny: Lyubov's inability to keep money;
Gayev's fondness for candy and billiards; Varya's crybaby
nature; Anya's utter belief; Lopahin's humble pride; Trofimov's
belief in platonic love; Yepihodov's unflagging self-pity; Firs's
crotchets; Yasha's snobbery and Dunyasha's ladylike airs;
even Charlotta's Germanic precision. The play unfolds like a
badly timed vaudeville skit. Gayev talks to a bookcase,
Varya means to hit Yepihodov and swipes Lopahin instead.
Chekhov's finely timed, offbeat ironies are subtly cruel, the
kind of cruelty that is often called compassion because it is
all-knowing in its lucidity. In his work, the fine line between
comic technique and tragic awareness is barely perceptible and
the reader as well as the spectator—and certainly the interpreters—must walk that fine line and understand one in terms
of the other.

NOTES

First performance: January 17, 1904, Moscow Art Theater.

First published in two editions, St. Petersburg, 1904: one by Chekhov's publisher, Marks, and the other by the Znaniye Company.

1. The Russian word for "peasant" is so rich in sound that it plays a useful part in the translation—it is one of those onomatopoeic words that are better left untranslated. The word "peasant" has had too many pejorative connotations in English, and so the original word is highly preferable.

2. Kvass is a Russian beer made from barley, malt and rye.

3. Menton is a winter resort on the Mediterranean, near Nice and Monaco.

4. Kiev is the capital of the Ukraine, on the Dnieper River.

5. Pishchik's costume probably consisted of a *poddyovka*, a long-waisted coat that comes down over the knees, and *charovari*, wide trousers worn tucked inside the boots and falling over them.

6. Chekhov admitted that he had forgotten how to play billiards and that his billiard indications were a bit confusing. The Russian billiards game uses a yellow ball, for instance, and so the translations are more an indication of our game of billiards than the Russian version of the game. Here we have billiards, snooker and billiard pool; the terms used here try to remain with the game of billiards. The important thing is to see beyond the expression to its real meaning, which, in each

case, is an attempt on Gayev's part to steer clear of the embarrassment of the moment. It is a magnificent subterfuge, very similar to his feeding on hard candies, a form of gratification with the value of a placebo.

7. A penetrating perfume derived from an East Indian plant.

8. The dessiatine actually equals 2.7 acres.

9. Yaroslavl is a river port and railway junction north of Moscow.

10. Gayev means that he came to adulthood in the eighties and shares the ideologies of the period, a time of unrest after the assassination of Czar Alexander II. Gayev is also referring to his social consciousness and his feeling for the lot of the common man. Gayev wishes to be thought of as a man of the people, despite his aristocratic feelings.

11. A death-defying acrobatic jump.

12. An excerpt from a ballad of the period. The song sums up Yepihodov's yearnings so aptly.

13. Henry Thomas Buckle (1821–1862), an English historian who was an autodidact, mastered eighteen foreign languages and amassed an enormous library to help him in the writing of a *History of Civilization in England*. He used a scientific method in writing history.

14. "Decadent" is a word used to describe the Symbolist literary and art movement in Russia in the last decades of the nineteenth century. Lyubov's remark has nothing to do with her literary understanding, only with her instinctive knowledge that such topics could never be in the ken of the waiters at the restaurant.

15. Some other ballad of the time, most probably: what is important is the word "money," Lopahin's great preoccupation. It is money that will change his entire destiny.

16. The serfs were emancipated in February, 1861, during the reign of Czar Alexander II.

17. The passerby chants excerpts from poems by Nadson and Nekrassov. In the highly effective Moscow Art Theater production of recent date, the passerby's role becomes an unforgettable cameo when he sings from Bizet's *Carmen* (the Toreador song) before he leaves. Naturally, the poems and the refrains mean nothing to a contemporary foreign audience. Their social-conscious commentary is, however, easy

to discern and Chekhov thus simply provides material that is useful for a telling stage moment. The passerby is used symbolically here as a foreign element that briefly touches Lyubov Andreyevna's life—a heralding of the moment when such people will surpass her.

18. *Oxmeliya* is a pun on the name of Shakespeare's heroine. It incorporates the Russian word *xmel,* which means "intoxication," and also the hops that cause it. Lopahin's mean jokes to Varya simply exteriorize his healthy dislike of her. Varya would, of course, like to be in a nunnery. The jest is even richer when we remember that "nunnery" also meant, in Shakespeare's time, a house of ill fame. That was the cream of Hamlet's jest. Lopahin would hardly know that—although he is punning on the idea of getting drunk. It all comes down to his desire to make Varya mad.

19. It was customary for cultured people to use French whenever possible. There is also a ludicrous element in having Pishchik call out the dance steps. "The gentlemen, on their knees and thank their ladies." Chekhov was ever aware of ridiculous moments. It is also rich in characterization: Pishchik was once, perhaps, before Dashenka and his money troubles, a dashing fellow.

20. The impious Caligula (A.D. 12–41) made his favorite horse a member of the college of priests and a consul.

21. The *lezghinka* is a Caucasian dance tune.

22. Charlotta's speeches are peppered with a little German here and there to help create the brittle Germanic quality that Chekhov sought. In this case, it shows her natural disdain for men. The expression—"A good man, but a bad musician" —is somewhat of a *non sequitur,* although Charlotta probably does know that Pishchik is, despite being a good fellow at heart, not very cultured.

23. "The Sinful Woman" is a poem by Count Alexey Konstantinovich Tolstoi (1817–1875). The beginning of the poem is a happy, bustling event and is an ironic commentary, therefore, on the false gaiety of Lyubov's ball.

24. The Kerchenski herring is processed in Kerch, a Black Sea port also known for its caviar. Gayev's mention of the herrings is one more indication (with the billiards and the candies) of his childish preoccupation with eating and playing, his endless subterfuges to get away from the meaning of a

moment. He is, however, very much aware of his loss, despite his outward concern with the creature comforts.

25. The *bachlik* is a hooded cap to protect one from the cold.

26. The Sunday after Pentecost, a festival in honor of the Holy Trinity.

OUTSTANDING COLLECTIONS
 OF SHORT STORIES
from WASHINGTON SQUARE PRESS

FRENCH STORIES AND TALES. Sixteen works by such noted authors as Stendhal, Balzac, de Maupassant and Gide.　　　　　　　W·0533/60¢

GERMAN STORIES AND TALES. Mann's "Death in Venice," Kafka's "The Metamorphosis," as well as works by Hesse, Broch and fourteen others.
W·0535/60¢

SPANISH STORIES AND TALES. Twenty-three works by Spanish and Spanish-American writers, including Cervantes, Unamuno, Borges, Mallea and Alarcón.
W·0536/60¢

IRISH STORIES AND TALES. Thirty-two selections representing the best of modern Irish writing by Yeats, Shaw, Joyce, Wilde and many others.　W·0534/60¢

15 GREAT RUSSIAN SHORT STORIES. Works of the nineteenth- and twentieth-century master Russian storytellers, including Chekhov, Dostoevsky, Tolstoy and Gorky.　　　　　　　　　　　　　　　W·0925/75¢

FAMOUS CHINESE SHORT STORIES. Twenty of the finest Chinese short stories in fresh and inspired translations by Lin Yutang.　　W·0532/60¢

A POCKET BOOK OF SHORT STORIES. Twenty-two classic stories by the world's greatest storytellers, including de Maupassant, Mann, Maugham, Bunin, Hemingway and Twain.　　　　　　　　　　　W·0255/45¢

A POCKET BOOK OF MODERN AMERICAN SHORT STORIES. A unique collection of American fiction from the twenties and thirties, including works by Faulkner, Hemingway, Thurber, Steinbeck, Caldwell and Saroyan.　W·0530/60¢

MID-CENTURY. Twenty outstanding American stories written since World War II by such authors as E. B. White, James Michener, Jean Stafford and Louis Auchincloss.　　　　　　　　　　　　　W·0529/60¢

GREAT TALES OF FANTASY AND IMAGINATION. Twenty-one eerie tales including Stevenson's "The Bottle Imp" and other favorites.　W·0704/60¢

GREAT GHOST STORIES. Thirteen tales for the witching hour by such masters as Poe, Kipling and Alexander Woollcott.　　　　　W·0592/60¢

If your bookseller does not have these titles you may order them by sending retail price, plus 10¢ per book for mailing and handling to MAIL SERVICE DEPARTMENT, Washington Square Press, Inc., 1 West 39th St., New York, N.Y. 10018. Please send check or money order—*do not send cash.*　　WSP 6-67

The FOLGER LIBRARY General Reader's
SHAKESPEARE

Distinguished editions of the plays and poems edited by Louis B. Wright, Director, and Virginia A. LaMar, Executive Secretary, Folger Shakespeare Library, Washington, D.C.

The text is printed on right hand pages only, with notes on the facing pages keyed by line number for easy reference.

Each edition contains an introduction, biographical information, a discussion of the Shakespearean theatre, summaries of each scene, and illustrations from the Folger collection.

Shakespeare for Everyman

By Louis B. Wright. An illuminating introduction to Shakespeare for the general reader. Annotated bibliography, index, extensive illustrations from the Folger collection. W • 1081/90¢

ꆆ WASHINGTON SQUARE PRESS, INC.

If you are unable to obtain these books from your regular dealer, you may order them by sending the retail price, plus 10¢ per book for postage and handling, to: Mail Service Department, WASHINGTON SQUARE PRESS, INC., 1 West 39th Street, New York, N.Y. 10018. Please enclose check or money order—*do not send cash.*

The Folger Shakespeare Library Editions

THE FOLGER LIBRARY SHAKESPEARE

All of Shakespeare's comedies, tragedies, histories, and the collected sonnets, each in a single volume featuring authoritative explanatory notes keyed by line number facing each page of text, extensive background material on Shakespeare, his work and his theatre, a key to famous lines, as well as illustrations from the Folger Collection.

SHAKESPEARE FOR EVERYMAN

An exciting and informative introduction to Shakespeare and the qualities upon which his reputation is based, including extensive material on the Elizabethan stage, anti-Shakespeare cults, guidance in selecting materials for further study and bibliographies, written by Louis B. Wright, Director of the Folger Shakespeare Library, 1948-1968.

THE FOLGER SHAKESPEARE RECORDINGS
A New Series

Now available, the complete text of *Romeo and Juliet,* including narrated stage directions, sound effects, and musical score on four long-playing records. Recorded for the first time by an all-American cast under the supervision of Louis B. Wright and Virginia A. LaMar.

A complete brochure of these materials is available free upon request from Washington Square Press, Inc., Educational Department, 630 Fifth Avenue, New York, N.Y. 10020.

WSP 2/68

An invaluable reference library of
WSP *illuminating study guides to enrich your*
understanding and appreciation of the
great works of fiction

Each volume includes reviews of fifty novels
containing: —*plot outlines*
—*character analyses*
—*critical evaluations*
—*author's biographies*
—*notes on selected works by the same author*

PLUS: an Introduction on "How To Read a Novel" and an
index of titles, authors, and main characters.

A STUDENT'S GUIDE TO 50 AMERICAN NOVELS   W • 0901/75¢
Edited by Abraham Lass

Guides to such classics as *Billy Budd, The Scarlet Letter, Arrow-smith, The Bridge of San Luis Rey, Light in August, The Human Comedy, The Naked and the Dead, Invisible Man,* and *The Catcher in the Rye.*

A STUDENT'S GUIDE TO 50 BRITISH NOVELS   W • 0902/75¢
Edited by Abraham Lass

A collection of summaries ranging from *Pilgrim's Progress* to *The Lord of the Flies* and including such works as *Gulliver's Travels, The Pickwick Papers, Vanity Fair, The Return of the Native, Lord Jim, Of Human Bondage, Brave New World,* and *1984.*

A STUDENT'S GUIDE TO 50 EUROPEAN NOVELS   W • 0900/75¢
Edited by Abraham Lass and Brooks Wright

A remarkably comprehensive collation including classics such as *Don Quixote* and *Candide,* contemporary masterpieces such as *The Stranger* and *Doctor Zhivago,* and encompassing the most famous works of Russian, French, Italian, German, and Spanish fiction.

WSP
WASHINGTON SQUARE PRESS, INC.